Successful Writing

FIFTH EDITION

Successful Writing

Writing

FIFTH EDITION

Maxine Hairston

THE UNIVERSITY OF TEXAS AT AUSTIN

Michael Keene

THE UNIVERSITY OF TENNESSEE AT KNOXVILLE

W. W. Norton & Company

NEW YORK · LONDON

Manufacturing by Courier Companies.
Book design by Martin Lubin.
Production manager: Diane O'Connor.

Photo of Rosa Parks (p. 236): Reuters NewMedia Inc./Corbis.

Library of Congress Cataloging-in-Publication Data

Hairston, Maxine.
    Successful writing / Maxine C. Hairston, Michael Keene.—5th ed.
        p. cm.
    Includes index.

ISBN 0-393-97818-4

1. English language—Rhetoric. 2. Report writing. I. Keene, Michael L. II. Title.

PE1408 .H297 2003
808'.042—dc21

2002032978

W. W. Norton & Company, Inc., 500 Fifth Avenue, New York, N.Y. 10110
www.wwnorton.com

W. W. Norton & Company Ltd., Castle House, 75/76 Wells Street,
London W1T 3QT

1 2 3 4 5 6 7 8 9 0

Brief Contents

Contents

6   Writing Clearly   59

● ●

7 Holding Your Reader 72

8 Crafting Paragraphs 93

9 Revising   113

10 Editing   122

14 Giving Oral Presentations 217

Model Documents 231

Mastering the Conventions of Documentation   271

● ●

And so this edition of *Successful Writing* has been expanded to offer students the help they need for these various writing situations.

As you will see, there are a number of new features in this edition. But perhaps the most important addition is a new co-author, Michael Keene, a former student and colleague, and today a friend of many years, who will describe what's new in the book.

Maxine Hairston and I have shared a long and happy friendship over the years, starting with her teaching me how to teach writing. ("What's your approach to teaching writing?" Maxine the new freshman composition director asked Mike the new graduate student. "Approach?" said Mike, bewildered.) But in the thirty or so years we've known each other, we've never written together. So it's a treat and a thrill for me to join her in this new edition of *Successful Writing*. While Maxine's task has been mostly to update existing chapters, mine has been to add several new ones. In particular, the Fifth Edition of *Successful Writing* offers the following **new and noteworthy features:**

> ❍ *A new chapter on electronic communication*, emphasizing the ways writing for online readers needs to be adjusted to the electronic medium, with particular attention to the do's and don'ts of email.
>
> ❍ *A new chapter on oral presentations*, offering eight steps to planning and delivering the kind of informal five- or ten-minute talk common in many classroom and professional settings today.
>
> ❍ *A new chapter on designing documents and Web pages*, emphasizing both the *process* and the finished product—and a wonderful new design for the book itself, one that reflects the principles of audience appeal that we promote throughout the book.
>
> ❍ *Much-expanded coverage of MLA and APA documentation.*
>
> ❍ *A collection of model documents* showing good examples of the many kinds of writing students now need to do, from letters to reports to résumés to a full MLA-style research paper.
>
> ❍ *A Q&A feature in each chapter* that answers many of the questions students most often ask.

○ *Greatly expanded coverage of the research-and-writing process,* with particular attention to the many new ways research is being done via computers, including the important step of judging the reliability of information found on the Internet.

We have tried to be guided by three principles of textbook writing: Is it clear? Is it useful? Is it true? We hope you'll find this new edition of *Successful Writing* meets those tough standards.

Maxine Hairston, Austin, Texas
Michael Keene, Knoxville, Tennessee

ACKNOWLEDGMENTS

We would like to thank the many people at Norton who have contrbuted to this edition: English editor Marilyn Moller for her thoughtful guidance, Debra Morton Hoyt for the charming cover design, Marian Johnson for overseeing the copyediting, Richard K. Mickey for the actual copyediting, Martin Lubin for the new interior design, and production manager Diane O'Connor for making sure the book was produced well and on time. Michael Keene would like to thank Mary Jo Reiff (at the University of Tennessee, Knoxville) and Katherine Adams (at Loyola University, New Orleans) for their insight into classroom experiences with previous editions and their advice concerning this one.
We would also like to thank all the reviewers who have contributed to shaping this book over its more than twenty years of publication:

Douglas Atkins (University of Kansas)
Martha A. Bartter (The Ohio State University, Marion)
Mary Bly (University of California at Davis)
P. Michael Brotherton (Labethe Community College)
Linda Cades (University of Maryland)
Edward P. J. Corbett (The Ohio State University)
Toby Fulwiler (University of Vermont)

Greg Cowan (Texas A & M)

Richard Gebhart (Findlay College)

Gary Sue Goodman (University of California at Davis)

William Harmon (University of North Carolina)

JoAnn Harrill (Virginia Polytechnic Institute and State University)

Betty L. Hart (University of Southern Indiana)

E. D. Hirsch Jr. (University of Virginia)

Paula Johnson (University of Wyoming)

Andrea Lunsford (Stanford University)

Donald P. McNeilly (University of Maryland)

Susan Miller (University of Utah)

Amy Richards (Wayne State University)

Robert Rudolf (University of Toledo)

Philip A. Snyder (Brigham Young University)

Mary Trachsel (University of Iowa, Des Moines)

Joseph Trimmer (Ball State University)

Steven J. Vander Weele (Calvin College)

John Walter (University of Texas)

John Webster (University of Washington)

Successful Writing

FIFTH EDITION

Writing in College

1

○ *If you're a good writer, you're always more likely to get what you want.*

People who have good writing skills enjoy an advantage in almost any situation. They generally make better grades in school or college than people who are poor writers; they're able to communicate their ideas effectively in school and in business; and when they lodge complaints or make requests, they usually get results. Most people also find that as their writing skills improve, their self-confidence grows, and they feel better able to tackle problems and challenges.

So investing the time and energy to improve your writing will pay off not only while you're a student writing essays, creating a Web site, or putting together an oral presentation, but also in later years when you may write grant proposals, business documents, or political speeches. The writing strategies you learn now will serve you well for the rest of your life.

STRATEGIES FOR WRITING IN COLLEGE COURSES

Although some kinds of college writing assignments are so specialized that they could require instruction in technical writing, for most assignments you'll do well if you begin by following these three guidelines:

❶ Analyze your writing situation.
❷ Limit your writing topic.
❸ Lay out a plan of organization.

Before you start your first draft, take time to analyze your writing situation. Consider the following questions:

> ◑ What is your purpose? What do you want to accomplish with this piece of writing?
>
> ◑ Who is your audience? Why would they want to read this piece?
>
> ◑ What constraints are you working under? How long should the piece be, and how long do you have to write it?

If you take the time to write out the answers to these questions before you begin your project, you'll benefit in several ways. First, from the very start you'll be thinking about who is going to read your writing. Second, you'll be more aware of the limitations you're working under and start planning accordingly. Third, you'll focus your mind on your task and start to generate ideas.

Here's an example of how you might analyze your writing situation if you were planning a 2,500-word paper for a history course on Elizabethan England:

WRITING SITUATION ANALYSIS

Working title. Why Were There No Women Shakespeares?

Purpose. To show why no well-known women writers emerged in Elizabethan England; to demonstrate that cultural and social conditions would have made it almost impossible for a woman to make her mark as a writer in that era.

Audience. The instructor and other students in the history class. Assume that they're interested in understanding the forces that shaped women's lives in the time of Elizabeth I and that they've heard questions such as *Why were there no great women writers or scholars in earlier centuries?* Assume also that they already know a good deal about the Elizabethan era.

Constraints. Paper can be no more than ten double-spaced pages; first draft due in two weeks. Required to cite four sources, only two of which can come from the Internet. Will require at least two trips to the library.

Many writers get into trouble because they choose topics that are too broad to treat adequately in a limited space. For instance, if you were asked to write a 1,500-word piece (six double-spaced pages) in an ancient history course and selected a sweeping topic such as "The Beginnings of Democracy in Ancient Greece," you'd quickly run into difficulties. You would have so many subtopics to cover that you wouldn't have room to supply the anecdotes and details you'd need to make the piece interesting and informative. So it's important to limit your scope and write more about less. One professor suggests, "Always choose the smallest possible topic out of which you can squeeze the requisite number of words." Pretty good advice.

Deciding how broad a topic you can reasonably handle in a paper of a specific length is tricky and will remain so even when you've become a very experienced writer. Some rough guidelines may help:

1,000–1,500 words (four to six pages, double-spaced): A short paper, probably one of several you'd be writing for a course. Some topics that might be adequately developed in such a paper:

> A biographical sketch of Ellen Malcolm, founder of Emily's List, a political action committee that supports pro-choice women candidates for office
>
> The meaning of the green light at the end of the dock in the last paragraph of *The Great Gatsby*
>
> What to keep in mind when applying for a credit card

2,500–3,000 words (ten to twelve pages, double-spaced): A piece that covers a limited topic in some detail, giving background information and examples. You wouldn't want to tackle "Women Artists," but you could write on the topic "Rosa Bonheur, Nineteenth-Century Woman Artist." Some other possibilities:

> The Heifer Project: a program that gives farm animals to poor families in underdeveloped countries
>
> How the discovery of the Chauvet caves in southern France caused art historians to revise theories about prehistoric art

How city taxpayers are subsidizing the giant sports stadiums being built in major cities

4,500–5,000 words (eighteen to twenty pages, double-spaced): Such a piece allows you to go into substantial detail about a complex issue. It will usually require extensive research, and may constitute a major factor in grading for a course. Here are some topics that could be adequately treated in such a paper:

How the women's suffrage movement started in the United States

How the gaming industry has changed the face of gambling

The life and work of Artemisia Gentileschi, a woman master painter in seventeenth-century Italy

POTENTIAL PITFALLS IN CHOOSING TOPICS

"Hot issues" such as abortion, the death penalty, or gun control: Readers are so biased that they're not open to argument. It's hard to say anything new.

Current events: It's difficult to locate material in the library. The Internet may yield too much material, much of it dubious.

Religious issues on which people have strong views: It's difficult to discuss such topics in critique groups.

● **LAYING OUT A PLAN OF ORGANIZATION**

Not everyone works well from outlines, but you should start by drafting a strong introduction that forecasts your central idea and making notes about the main points you'll cover in your writing. Then organize your notes into some kind of coherent order and choose a pattern of presentation: possibilities are comparison and contrast, assertion and support, cause and effect, or chronological order. Any pattern can be modified as you work, but it's a good idea to have some plan to help you get started.

You may well want to start with the useful strategy of drafting a thesis sentence, a single, comprehensive statement that captures the essential content of your writing and tells your readers what to expect. Many instructors require writers to include a thesis sentence in their first paragraph.

Academic writing is not all alike. Writers work in many different disciplines, and the conventions for style, documentation, and evidence vary from one field to another. So we can't set clear-cut guidelines for writing college papers or presentations. Nevertheless, it's possible to formulate general principles for academic writing, because we know that instructors do tend to reward certain characteristics in writing that is submitted to them. Here are seven precepts that apply to writing in college:

① *If the assignment permits you to choose your topic, write on a subject that interests you even if it will require a fair amount of work.* It's nearly always a mistake to choose a topic just because it looks easy. Too often writers bog down because they hate their topic.

② *Don't overstate your case.* If you make sweeping claims and big generalizations, you'll quickly damage your credibility. Avoid terms like *always* and *never* and *everybody knows*; instead choose phrases like *this suggests, it may be,* and *it seems likely.*

③ *Support your claims.* Professors are skeptical readers who expect writers to back their claims with evidence and reasons. They like to ask "What's your evidence?" and "How do you know this?"

④ *Argue logically and avoid highly emotional language.* Depend on the weight of facts and rational argument to make your case. Avoid sarcasm and extreme examples.

⑤ *Choose a title that accurately reflects your content.* Your title introduces you and your ideas, so make sure it's clear and forceful.

⑥ *Cite your sources, either formally or informally.* Although the assignment may not require formal documentation, let readers know where you got your information and what authorities you're citing.

⑦ *Make your work look good.* Leave plenty of white space around your text, double-space, and avoid long paragraphs and dense-looking pages. Proofread carefully. See Chapter 11, on document design, for more tips on looking good in print.

Q *What is a "logical" argument? How can I tell if an argument I write is logical?*

A A logical argument is one in which a writer or speaker makes a claim and supports that claim with evidence from reliable sources. A writer who makes such an argument does so in much the same way a lawyer prepares a case to present in court, stating a claim and backing it up with data, statistics, examples, and the testimony of witnesses or experts. The impassioned speeches lawyers make to juries may not always make logical arguments, but the cases lawyers argue before a judge do—if they are to be successful. Judges expect facts and solid evidence.

For example, a judge would want to hear the arguments each side might make in a suit brought by an environmental group to stop a contractor from building 400 condominium homes in an undeveloped area at the edge of a city. That judge would not be impressed by the environmentalists' claim that the trees and creeks on the building site were so pretty that they shouldn't be disturbed. The group would need to produce studies by a reputable engineering firm that would show the impact that 400 homes would have on the limited water resources of the area. The judge would also want a professional opinion about how the runoff from paving streets for the new development would affect the quality of underground water. Nor would any judge believe contractors' assurances that they were "green builders" and wouldn't cause any environmental problems. They would need to show evidence to back up that claim. Both sides would also need to show they had considered the important counterarguments that might challenge their claims.

You don't have to sound completely objective when you present a logical argument—few of us are wholly objective when writing about issues we care about—but you do need to make a reasonable, calm assertion and back it with good evidence. To find out more about what constitutes good evidence in college writing, see the section "Reasoning from Evidence" in Chapter 5.

Q *When I get a writing assignment, I like to start writing right away and work until I get it done. Why do I need to take the time to analyze my audience and purpose? Won't that just slow me down?*

A It might seem time-consuming to stop to figure out who you're writing to and why, but if you think about it, in real-world writing situations you're always conscious of your audience and your purpose. If you were writing a scholarship application, you'd be asking yourself what the people giving the scholarship want to know about you and how you could make a good impression. If you were writing a report to present to the city council on the need for a bicycle trail between downtown and your campus, you'd be thinking about what kind of information the council would expect and how you could present that information effectively.

So it's excellent practice to start thinking about audience and purpose when you're preparing writing assignments for class. In fact, you may well write a more focused draft in a shorter time if you invest in a preliminary audience analysis. For example, if your instructor asks you to write a 500-word review of the documentary movie *Hoop Dreams* in a class on sports literature, a review you would later present to the class, start by analyzing what your audience knows. If you assume that your classmates have seen the movie, you won't have to summarize its plot and you can refer to specific scenes or actors without detailed explanation. You will also know that your classmates will expect you to relate your discussion of the movie to issues you're studying in class. With that much background, you can start off purposefully. If you begin to write without knowing where you're going, on the other hand, you may actually waste considerable time and effort.

FOR PRACTICE

1 Pick one of the several topics for writing described in this chapter. Assuming you were to begin writing that paper for this class, analyze the writing situation (as illustrated in the list on p. 2) for that topic. Be sure to consider the length of the paper you're planning, and to note down any possible pitfalls.

2 Find a paper you have written for some other class. Write a paragraph describing that paper, and then consider the seven criteria for academic writing in the list in this chapter, asking yourself whether and how well your paper met those criteria. Write a couple of sentences describing how your paper stacked up against each criterion.

● ● ● **FOR WRITING** ●

1 Using the list of criteria for academic writing in this chapter, analyze a paper you've written for some other class, and then revise that paper to better meet those criteria.

2 For an audience consisting primarily of the other students in your class, and secondarily of your class's instructor, write a short, informal essay (about 500 words should do) on the subject "My History as a Writer." What kinds of things have you written in the past? What kind of responses did you receive, and how were they evaluated? What kinds of writing come relatively easy for you, and what kinds are more difficult? Do you do any "personal" writing (letters, a diary or journal, etc.), and if so what kinds? If you could choose just one or two things to work on in your writing this term, what might they be—and why?

Part of your purpose is for the other students and your instructor to get to know you a little better as a writer. You may also begin to think about your own writing, and what you might want to improve.

What Makes Writing Successful?

2

> ◑ *When you write, think more about communicating than about following rules.*

Y ou can count on good writing to have three qualities:

It says something of consequence
to a specific audience
for a specific purpose.

While really excellent writing also has other qualities, these three are the basics.

Thus it's evident that good writing can take many shapes. You can find it in *Parade* magazine as well as in the *New York Times*; in *Car and Driver* as well as in *Esquire*; on a Web site as well as in a set of clear instructions for assembling a bird feeder. Its central quality, whether its purpose is to inform, persuade, or entertain, is this: *It communicates the writer's ideas effectively to the audience for whom it is intended.*

The qualifier *for whom it is intended* is particularly important. When you write, consider who is going to read your work and ask yourself how skilled your readers are and why they are reading your particular piece. Remember also that what works with one group of readers may fail miserably with another group. We'll talk more about audience in subsequent chapters.

In spite of the ways in which writers work to adapt their tone, style, and vocabulary to different audiences, it's still possible to identify certain qualities that characterize effective expository writing—that is, nonfiction, factual writing. We call such writing "working writing" or "writing to get the job done." It meets at least the following criteria:

- It says something of consequence.
- It's clear.
- It's well organized.
- It's economical.
- It's grammatically acceptable.
- It has no spelling errors.

If your writing meets these standards, it may not be dazzling or graceful, but your readers will understand it. That's worth a great deal.

If you aspire to move beyond this level of competence, you'll need to stretch beyond the basics and work at bringing two other characteristics into your writing: vigor, and an authentic voice. More about these qualities later in this chapter.

● GOOD WRITING SAYS SOMETHING OF CONSEQUENCE

For writing to be effective, its intended readers should find something in it that they enjoy or want or need to know—something interesting, informative, or even surprising. So when a writer just strings together a series of generalities or repeats obvious arguments, the result isn't good writing, no matter how smoothly or correctly it's put together.

Understandably, you may feel that trying to say something a reader enjoys or wants or needs to know could be a challenge when that reader is an instructor or a professor. How are you supposed to know what an instructor wants or needs to know or what she might find surprising? Of course, you don't know, but you should be able to make some good guesses. First, she wants solid information that pertains to the assignment; she also wants clear assertions, supported with details or examples. And she will be pleased and surprised if you have taken the time to dig out some unusual details about your subject—for example, that Elizabeth I often referred to herself as a "prince," or that condoms in the United States were first marketed by a German immigrant sausage maker who made them from surplus animal intestines.

You can test for significant content in something you've written by answering the following questions:

> Have you made clear assertions with adequate detail?
> Have you done research to gather some pertinent examples?
> Have you shown what you learned while working on the project?

If you can answer yes to these questions, you're probably saying something of consequence that someone wants or needs to know, whether you're writing for an instructor or a more general audience.

● GOOD WRITING IS CLEAR

Your writing is clear if your intended readers can grasp your meaning when they read carefully. The phrase *intended readers* is a major qualification, of course. It's important for you to identify those readers and consider whether you're using specialized terms that they won't understand or assuming too much about their background knowledge. If you are, you'll need to either add explanations or bring your writing down to a more general level. In Chapter 4, on analyzing the writing situation, we'll suggest ways to identify your readers and reach them in your writing.

Professional writers whose livelihood depends on being able to write clearly on a broad range of topics for a variety of readers are experts at analyzing their audiences. They also employ many different strategies to get their meaning across. Those strategies, which can range from telling stories to arranging information in lists, aren't difficult to master, and we'll be giving you many of them in Chapter 7, on holding your reader, and Chapter 6, on writing clearly.

In recent years writers have acquired new tools for making their writing clearer and more accessible—such tools as different type faces and sizes, borders and boxes, graphs, charts, and color highlighting. These tools come from the field of document design and from the new capabilities the computer offers. With such tools you can make your writing look good, more appealing to potential readers. The added features may be especially useful in writing that will be read on-screen. We'll tell you more about them in Chapter 11, on document design.

● GOOD WRITING IS WELL ORGANIZED

In all good writing one can sense a controlling pattern, a kind of master plan that holds the parts together. One idea easily leads to another as the writer lays down a path, points readers in the direction he wants them to go, and moves them along with frequent signals in the form of transitions. The controlling pattern might be one of the organizational patterns described in Chapter 5, on drafting: definition, cause and effect, comparison, assertion and support, process, or narration. A thesis sentence in the first paragraph is also a strong organizational device that lets readers know what to expect and helps them anticipate the major points the writer is going to make.

Here is a tightly organized paragraph from the well-regarded—and well-paid—writer David Halberstam; he begins with a strong, eye-catching assertion and then develops it with rich, specific detail:

> There was nothing conventional about [Margaret] Sanger's life. As a mother she was, at best, erratic and distant—when her son Grant was ten he wrote from boarding school, asking what to do about Thanksgiving, since all the other boys were going home. He should, she answered, come home to Greenwich Village and Daisy, the maid, would cook him a fine dinner. She had little time for such intrusions as children and holiday dinners. She was an American Samurai and she had spent her life on a wartime footing. Her principal enemies were the Catholic church and clergy, because in her struggle to inform women about birth control, they did much to prevent her from reaching the urban poor, who were often Catholic.
>
> DAVID HALBERSTAM, *THE FIFTIES*

Here is a brief paragraph by a historian of the Civil War that is unified by comparison and contrast:

> So [Ulysses S.] Grant and [Robert E.] Lee were in complete contrast, representing two diametrically opposed elements in American life. Grant was the modern man emerging; beyond him, ready to come on stage, was the great age of steel and machinery, of crowded cities and a restless, burgeoning vitality. Lee might have ridden down from the old age of chivalry,

lance in hand, silken banner fluttering over his head. Each man was the perfect champion of his cause, drawing both his strengths and his weaknesses from the people he led.

BRUCE CATTON, "GRANT AND LEE: A STUDY IN CONTRASTS"

Whatever controlling pattern professional writers use, they keep their prose stitched together with frequent transitional terms, little signals like *first, second, finally, then,* and *consequently.* They use other signals that tell readers when to expect a qualification, terms like *however, nevertheless, in spite of,* and so on. You'll find more on these important devices in Chapter 7, on holding your reader.

● GOOD WRITING IS ECONOMICAL

Economical doesn't necessarily mean sparse. It does mean eliminating words that don't do anything—terms like *really, sort of, in the case of, actually,* and *one might point out.* Because good writers don't want to waste their readers' time, they try to cut such excess words from their writing. Their goal is to get rid of what William Zinsser, author of *On Writing Well,* calls "clutter." Notice that Zinsser enlivens his description of the inattentive reader with concrete details that show a familiar scene:

> The reader is someone with an attention span of about 30 seconds—a person assailed by other forces competing for attention. At one time these forces weren't so numerous: newspapers, radio, spouse, home, children. Today they include a "home entertainment center" (TV, VCR, tapes, CDs), pets, a fitness program, a yard and all the gadgets that have been bought to keep it spruce, and that most potent of all competitors, sleep. The person snoozing in a chair with a magazine or a book is a person who was being given too much unnecessary trouble by the writer.

> WILLIAM ZINSSER, *ON WRITING WELL*

You will read about unnecessary repetition and other kinds of clutter in Chapter 10, on editing.

● GOOD WRITING IS GRAMMATICALLY ACCEPTABLE

We use the words "grammatically acceptable" to describe the style of English that most educated people in the United States use and expect other educated people to use. It's known as standard English; it is the kind of English you encounter in books, newspapers, business documents, and commercial and academic Web sites. Most of the time, such language conforms to those rules of grammar you learned in elementary and high school.

But only most of the time. If you have an alert ear for English usage, you'll notice that many successful and well-educated people don't always write or speak absolutely correct English. They may confuse *lie* and *lay*, or *among* and *between*, or forget that absolute words like *perfect* and *unique* shouldn't have adverbs before them. But such mistakes are minor, so common in everyday conversation that they're acceptable. They don't set off negative signals in readers' minds.

The grammatical errors that do send negative signals to readers are glaring ones like "Me and her went to school together," or "He brung his wife with him." Such conspicuous lapses will almost always damage a writer's image. So the bottom line is that you simply don't want to make such errors; they cost too much. Chapter 10, on editing, should help you identify some of the more common problems.

● GOOD WRITING HAS NO SPELLING ERRORS

Spelling matters. Granted that English spelling is irrational, inconsistent, and difficult to master, you still need to edit your "public" writing—writing for which people will judge you—to be sure you've spelled everything properly. A surprising number of people are outraged when they encounter misspelled words, and they jump to the conclusion that the author is uneducated or ignorant. Of course, such a judgment isn't fair—many intelligent and well-educated people are poor spellers.

But you're not likely to encounter misspelled words in the published writing of those intelligent people, because they'll do whatever is necessary to correct the errors in their work before exposing it to outside readers. They know that many readers, particularly business people or other professionals, react to poor spelling so negatively that they assume the writer is careless and indifferent to opinion. And, they reason, someone who is so careless about spelling is likely to be equally careless about other important details. That's not an impression you want to leave.

What about writing online, you may ask. Hasn't the casual, easy-to-use writing tool of email changed attitudes about spelling? In some cases, it probably has. Most of us now write back and forth to friends and family more frequently than we've written in years, and we're pretty casual about capitalization and punctuation when we do. Relaxing your standards in such circumstances seldom does any damage. It's important to remember, though, that the informality—read, sloppiness—of email exchanges doesn't come from the medium. It comes from the writing situation. You're writing to people with whom you *feel* informal—it's like wearing shorts and a tank top to a picnic.

But when you're using email for business correspondence, your situation is likely to be formal—more like the atmosphere at a business luncheon. In those circumstances, it's just as important to check the spelling in your email as it is to clean your fingernails before you meet a business prospect. The same is true when you're creating a professional Web site. Don't jeopardize the impression you want your site to make by being careless about spelling and punctuation.

In Chapter 10, on editing, you'll find several ways suggested to check on and improve your spelling. Unfortunately, you won't find any shortcuts there, but if you consistently apply the strategies you read about, you can overcome most of your spelling problems.

● ● **EXTRA TOUCHES**

● **VIGOR**

You sometimes hear an author's writing described as "strong" or "vigorous," terms that are easier to illustrate than to define. Usually they mean that a writer shows the readers what is happening through active verbs and clear images, that he or she uses specific examples and striking metaphors to get ideas across, that the writing is concrete, direct, and efficient. It moves along like a person walking vigorously and confidently toward a goal.

Vigor is a quality that you can almost count on finding in the writing of first-rate journalists and essayists like Garry Wills, Thomas Friedman, Ellen Goodman, or Anna Quindlen, and in books by essayists like Nikki Giovanni and Henry Louis Gates Jr.

The following passage from Nikki Giovanni vibrates with simplicity and strength; its rhythms are quick, and its images and personal references bring the writer right into the reader's presence:

[. . .] I am a sixties person. It's true that I didn't do tie-dyed T-shirts or drugs, and I never went to jail. I argued a lot in the coffeehouses and tried at one point to be a social drinker. It didn't work. I can't hold liquor at all. But I was nonetheless a sixties person and continue to be today because I actually believe in the people. That was never just rhetoric to me, although it has often been my undoing. Believing in the people is dangerous, because the people will break your heart. Just when you know in your heart that white people are not worth a tinker's damn and the future depends on us, some Black person will come along with some nihilistic crap that makes you rethink the whole thing.

NIKKI GIOVANNI, "CAMPUS RACISM 101"

Vigorous writing commands attention.

● AUTHENTIC VOICE

When you read first-rate writing, you feel the *presence* of the writer. The writer's character and sense of self permeate the writing and project authenticity. This writer, you think, knows what he's talking about and means what he says; you feel that only this particular writer could have written that particular piece—it is stamped with his personality. You are drawn into this writer's world and engage with it. Here's an example from Doris Kearns Goodwin's chronicle of her childhood enchantment with the Brooklyn Dodgers:

I listened with both my parents to the final game [before the World Series] which took place on a Sunday afternoon at Shibe Park in Philadelphia. The Dodgers scored five runs in the third, but by the bottom of the ninth, the Phillies had bounced back to tie the game at seven apiece. I couldn't sit still. My mouth felt so dry that it hurt, but I was afraid to leave the room. "Now you're learning what it means to be a Dodger fan," my father said.

DORIS KEARNS GOODWIN, WAIT UNTIL NEXT YEAR

You don't have to be passionate about your subject to project an authentic voice, although it helps. But you can still establish your own voice by referring to personal experience, using colorful examples, and trying to make your writing concrete, straightforward, and personal rather than abstract and impersonal.

Q *My high school English teachers said I should never use* I *in my academic writing. Should I stick by that rule when I'm writing in college?*

A That depends on your writing situation. Check out the audience and purpose for the project you're working on. Does it strike you as quite formal—for instance, are you writing an analysis for a government class of the rhetoric of Franklin D. Roosevelt's Fireside Chats during his presidency? In this case, you would probably have little reason to use *I*. It might also sound too casual for such straightforward, informational writing on a serious topic.

But if you were writing a response to assigned readings in an American studies course on the civil rights movement, a piece that would be posted on the electronic blackboard your instructor has set up for the class, *I* might be quite appropriate. For example, you might write, "I was surprised to learn that Rosa Parks's refusal to go to the back of the bus was not spontaneous, but part of a protest planned by the local NAACP, a protest that led to the successful Birmingham bus boycott." Here the informality of the electronic blackboard, plus the fact that the assignment is to "write a response," makes use of *I* reasonable. Or if you were writing about the novels of Barbara Kingsolver for a course on selected modern American women writers, a sentence like this might be appropriate: "I found the two women protagonists of *Prodigal Summer* fit the female model that Kingsolver established so effectively in her earlier novels: the autonomous, self-reliant woman, engaged with but not part of her community." Here the fact that these are *your* findings—as opposed to something you read somewhere else—supports your making a more personal statement.

So consider your audience when you decide whether to use *I* in your college writing. If the atmosphere in your class feels casual and your instructor seems to encourage informality, try using *I*, but do so carefully.

FOR PRACTICE

① Read carefully the following three passages from professional writers. Then, either working in a group with two or three others in your class or writing on your own, comment on each of the passages. What qualities of good writing do you find in each of them? What specific phrases or sentences do you find especially effective? How would you characterize each paragraph in just a few words?

> The "work" the [chain] gangs do is valueless. The rock breaking is pure photo opportunity. The highway crews allegedly clear weeds and debris, but this is impossible to do on any useful scale with five men chained eight feet apart, each stumbling when the next one does. The real reason for stretching legions of chained, white-suited men for a mile or so along the highway is to let motorists gorge on a visible symbol of punishment and humiliation. Hanging, too, was once a public entertainment. No one would be surprised if some ambitious politician suggests making it so again.
>
> BRENT STAPLES, "THE CHAIN GANG SHOW"

> When I was a boy I could not tell a man what I felt, if I believed what I felt was unmanly. We went back to the trench, down into it, and I picked up the shovel I had left there at noon, and shoveled all the loose earth between me and the man in front of me, and then put the shovel beside the trench, lifted the pick, raised it over my shoulder, and swung it down into the dirt. I was dizzy and weak and hot; I worked for forty minutes or so; then, above me, I heard my father's voice, speaking my name. I looked up at him; he was here to take me home, to forgive my failure, and in my great relief I could not know that I would not be able to forgive it. I was going home. But he said: "Let's go buy you a hat."
>
> ANDRE DUBUS, "DIGGING"

> How do we tell the truth in a small town? Is it possible to write it? Certainly, great literature might come out of the lives of ordinary people on the farms and ranches and little towns of the Plains, but are the people who farm, the people who work in these towns, writing it? The truth, the whole truth, tends to be complex, its contentments and joys wrestled out of doubt, pain, change. How to tell the truth in a small town, where, if a discouraging word is heard, it is not for public consumption?
>
> KATHLEEN NORRIS, "CAN YOU TELL THE TRUTH IN A SMALL TOWN?"

2 How comparatively readable are the following two examples from students' papers? What specific comments or suggestions might you make to the authors?

> Today in the world there are more than 200 breeds of dogs and these can further be divided into six groups. Dogs perform a variety of services to the community. They have the intelligence and also the ability to bond with humans. It enables them to help us in different tasks. One such group is the "working dogs," which do many of these tasks. Dogs are helpful to many individuals in our society and are becoming more than just a household pet.

In bicycle racing, it takes much more than physical exertion to place well consistently. At the pro level, all racers have excellent fitness. Those who most often succeed go beyond that level. They must know when to exert themselves. They must know when not to. They must know how to cruise to minimize effort. And they must know how to relax during times of less than full effort. The whole game revolves around who has been best able to conserve his energy, using it only in controlled bursts to keep in contention or take advantage of a competitor's weakness.

3 Reread the two passages in the preceding exercise. How strong a voice do you think each writer projects? Do you find the voice authentic? Does the writer seem to be talking about something he or she knows and cares about? If so, how is that impression conveyed? If not, what goes wrong?

FOR WRITING

Write an informative or persuasive essay on some topic that you find interesting and on which you have already done some reading or which you have already discussed with someone—perhaps an issue you are studying in another class, such as censorship in art, the high cost of political campaigns, or obesity in children. Approximate length should be four to six double-spaced pages (1,000 to 1,500 words). Select a publication in which you, were you a professional writer, might get such an essay published, and write its name under the title of your essay. Some possibilities could be *Parade* magazine, *Newsweek*, or *Health Today*. Here are some ideas:

1 Discuss the issues that are raised in censorship battles of the kind that occur in a school district when a group of parents try to have a book banned. For example, groups of parents in recent years have wanted Margaret Atwood's book *The Handmaid's Tale* removed from their high school libraries because they felt this work was unsuitable for students in advanced placement courses. (Atwood's book is a science fiction novel about a strict religious community of the not too distant future in which women have lost their civil rights. Severe environmental pollution has led to widespread female infertility, and so the government has designated certain young women to be mated with elders of the community in order to ensure the survival of the ruling class.) Other parents contended that the book should be kept, that it was well written and dealt with substantial ethical issues. Remember to focus on the censorship issue and not take sides in the argument.

2 Drawing on your own high school experience, identify two characteristics of a high school that you think help to create a good environment for learning and healthy emotional development. As an alternative, identify two characteristics of a high school that you believe create an unhealthy environment that hampers learning and character development. In either case, describe the characteristics in some detail and give specific examples. Some possible places to publish: *Reader's Digest* or *Change* (a magazine for educators).

How Do Writers Write?

3

○ *You don't need special talent to become a good writer.*

People to whom writing doesn't come easily may assume that good writers have special gifts, that for them writing comes naturally and without much effort. Like most myths, this one has a grain of truth in it, but only a grain. The best writers are likely to be gifted as well as diligent, but most writers who write frequently and well have no magic talent. They write well because they are disciplined, because they work hard at their craft, and because they have developed a set of practices that enable them to turn out good work consistently.

It may be useful to look at the ways many professional writers— those people who make a living from writing—go about it. Here's what our research shows:

Professional writers . . .

○ Don't wait for inspiration. They start writing whether they feel like it or not.

○ Work on a schedule, in a regular place, using the same tools.

○ Have trouble getting started occasionally, but they expect such delays and don't panic.

○ Gather material constantly. They file clippings, observe what's going on around them, and take notes.

○ Work best under a deadline; if necessary, they even set their own deadlines.

- Seldom know exactly what they will write; they expect to discover new ideas and insights as they work.
- Plan before they write, but they keep plans flexible, subject to change as they work.
- Work with an audience in mind.
- Work slowly; many say they consider four to six double-spaced pages a good day's work.
- Expect to do two or three drafts of anything they write.
- Often procrastinate, but they usually know how long they can put off writing and still avoid disaster.

DIFFERENT WAYS OF WRITING

Many things affect how writers work, but one important variable is the kind of writing they're doing. Here we'll consider two kinds of writing: *explanatory* writing and *exploratory* writing. Explanatory writing is writing that conveys information; exploratory writing is writing that deals with ideas.

● EXPLANATORY WRITING

Professional writers who set out to explain something—perhaps how to organize a fund-raising project or how to distinguish between reliable and unreliable sources on the Internet—usually have a good idea of what they are going to write before they start. They may not know all the details and will often discover more material as they work, but their general content is set. Most start out with a plan—a page of notes or perhaps even a full outline. Such plans help them organize their material and keep track of it as they write. Professional writers frequently start out with an assertion, then support it with evidence. They may draw comparisons to make a point, use an anecdote to clarify an idea, or give an illustrative example. Much of the writing that you'll do in college will be explanatory; so is most business writing.

For instance, you'd be engaged in explanatory writing if you wrote an essay on Jean-Jacques Rousseau's ideas on the education of women or showed how a network of canals helped communication in colonial America. A business report on the impact of radio advertising would also be explanatory writing. This kind of writing takes work. You have to invest time and effort to present factual material clearly and accurately and in a way that holds readers' interest. Much of your work—gathering information and organizing it effectively—comes before you ever put down a word. You also have to think who your readers will be before you start and decide on the language and writing style that will work best with them.

When you finish a substantial first draft for a piece of explanatory writing, go over it and ask yourself these three questions: (1) Is it clear? (2) Is it true? (3) Is it useful? If you can say "I think so" to all three questions, you're off to a good start.

● EXPLORATORY WRITING

Professional writers usually begin an exploratory writing project with an idea or a question and some sense of their general purpose. For example, in writing an essay on Homer's *Iliad* you might reflect, "At the beginning of the *Iliad*, Achilles and Agamemnon boast and bait each other in a way that makes me think of adolescent gang leaders challenging each other. I'd like to explore the possible parallels." From that germ of an idea, you could start digging for material, taking notes, drawing comparisons, and working out a thesis.

Because writers don't know at the outset exactly what they are going to say in exploratory writing, it's often hard to make a detailed plan or outline ahead of time. They can, however, make copious notes and work out a tentative thesis. For the suggested essay on the *Iliad*, the thesis might read, "In Homer's *Iliad* the conflict between the Greek chiefs Agamemnon and Achilles stems from the same issues that cause wars between young gang leaders in today's cities: competition over girls, taunts about cowardice, quarrels over booty, and fear that someone is being 'dissed.'" Such a sentence could serve as an anchor for a first draft, but it could change or even disappear as the paper developed.

An exploratory piece is no harder to write than an explanatory piece, but it is harder to plan because it resists a systematic approach. Often it takes longer and requires more drafts. Nevertheless, many writers enjoy the process of discovering ideas through the act of writing. It can be exciting to see suddenly how two ideas connect or to recognize parallels between a current celebrity scandal and a novel you're studying. Many college writing projects are exploratory, particularly in the liberal arts; so are many magazine articles and personal essays. For instance, your writing would be exploratory if you wrote a profile of a political activist on your campus or a reflective essay on the inequities of college entrance exams.

Start your exploratory project by choosing a promising topic; then look at several sources for material, and explore your central idea through brainstorming or talking to people. Choose an audience, but only tentatively—you can't always know in advance whom you're writing for—and find your focus. When you finish a substantial draft of an exploratory piece, review it and ask yourself three questions: (1) Is it clear? (2) Is it thoughtful? (3) Is it interesting? If you can say "I think so" to all three you probably have an effective start.

● WRITING THAT EXPLAINS AND EXPLORES

Not all writing fits into one category or another. Sometimes you may want to present information and explore ideas in the same paper. For instance, you might document a statistical shift in population, then explore the cultural impact of that shift. So don't hesitate to mix the two kinds of writing if it makes the case you're presenting stronger.

Why bother to think what kind of writing you're doing? For at least two reasons. First, it's helpful to realize there isn't just one writing process. There are different writing processes, and some work better than others for different writing situations. Second, you'll be a better writer if you develop the habit of analyzing your own writing situation ahead of time. Then you can consciously choose the process that is most likely to work for a particular task. (See Chapter 4 for more on assessing your writing situation.)

Don't assume that one kind of writing is better than another. It's not. The imaginative, thoughtful writing about theories and issues that we label *exploratory* is important because it is writers' way of generating thoughtful discussion and communicating their ideas. Writers who excel at it help to stimulate the ongoing dialogue about values and change that plays a central role in our society. The informative, factual writing that we label *explanatory* is important because readers depend on it to find out about events and developments in the world. It keeps the machinery of society going, and those writers who are good at it are invaluable. Get comfortable with both.

People who write professionally go through several predictable stages: preparation and planning, drafting, incubation, revision, and editing. We discuss the early stages in this chapter and deal with revision and editing in later chapters. An outline of the stages would look something like this:

> ○ *Preparation and planning:* Identify your topic. Then read and do research; find examples; take notes; brainstorm or consult with others to generate ideas. Finally, consider ways to organize your material, and rough out an outline.
> ○ *Drafting:* Write a first draft, even if it's mostly exploratory.
> ○ *Incubating:* Take time out and let your ideas percolate in your subconscious for a while.
> ○ *Revising:* Read your draft carefully, consider changes, get feedback, and rewrite, perhaps more than once.
> ○ *Editing and proofreading:* Edit for style, word choice, and grammar. Proofread and run a spell checker to catch typos.

Such a list makes the writing process look clear-cut and straightforward, but in practice, the process is often messy, inexact, and unpredictable as writers move back and forth between stages, replanning and revising as they go. Nevertheless, most writers write in a similar sequence of stages, and it can be useful to work systematically through each stage.

● PREPARATION AND PLANNING

You can divide the preparation and planning stage of writing into two parts: a preliminary, stocking-the-bank stage, and a more direct, hands-on stage. The preliminary part includes drawing on all the information and ideas you've been storing up and thinking about for years, and also gathering new information for your project. The direct part is the focused, get-to-work stage.

You can work at stocking your idea bank in a number of ways:

○ Carry a notebook and jot down ideas, questions, and observations.

○ For the project at hand, read a major newspaper and some general-interest magazines. Clip articles you find especially interesting.

○ For the long term, keep a file of newspaper and magazine clippings about a variety of topics.

○ Watch for announcements of lectures and public appearances by noted politicians, educators, and writers and other prominent individuals. Attend when you can.

○ Ask questions. Draw people out about what they do and what they're interested in.

○ Surf the Internet to find out about a topic that interests you. Type keywords into a search engine like Google or HotBot and see where it takes you.

○ Read book reviews regularly and keep a list of books that interest you. Start a library even if you don't read everything immediately.

In other words, develop a personal radar that sweeps your environment constantly and picks up signals on a broad range of topics.

GETTING DOWN TO WORK

To get down to work, first identify your topic:

○ *Brainstorm.* Jot down all the ideas that occur to you about your writing topic.

○ *Narrow your topic.* Pick out one aspect of the topic to develop.

○ *Freewrite.* Write quickly about the topic without sorting out points or worrying about organization.

○ *Run a computer search.* Check online library catalogs to see what books are available. Type keywords into a search engine to find relevant Web sites.

○ *Talk to people about your topic.* Ask questions.

Next, bring your project into sharper focus:

- ❍ Tentatively identify your audience and purpose.
- ❍ Do more formal, in-depth research.
- ❍ Make a list or scratch outline organizing main points.
- ❍ Choose a tentative title.
- ❍ Write a tentative thesis sentence.

ONE STUDENT'S EXAMPLE

We'll be following the progress of one student's writing project throughout this book. In this section we're going to take a look at the preparatory stages Eleanor Hennessy worked through for her paper. Her assignment was to write a paper of about 5,000 words on the career of a woman artist from an earlier century. She chose to write about Artemisia Gentileschi.

IDENTIFYING THE TOPIC

Brainstorming. Women in 17th-c. Italy had almost no rights. Anything they produced belonged to fathers or husbands. Society fanatic about women's chastity. Any hint of sexual lapses could ruin a woman. Women assumed to be intellectually inferior by natural law. Most women painters came from families of painters. Sometimes their work attributed to a man. Gentileschi was an apprentice in her father's shop. Knew Caravaggio. Defied convention by traveling to paint. G. raped by her teacher when she was 17. Her reputation was ruined but she refused to hide. Some of her most famous paintings seem to illustrate her anger about that attack.

Narrowing the topic. Focus on Gentileschi's remarkable achievement in overcoming the damaging fallout from a public rape trial to go on to become one of the best-regarded painters of her era.

Freewriting. Qualities of talent and fortitude that enabled Gentileschi to go against the grain of her society when constraints on women were so severe. Show how strength she gained from ordeal of her rape and trial was reflected in her paintings. Her success as a businesswoman in getting commissions for portraits. Connections at court. Prejudice against women painters in the art world. Specific obstacles like cost of paint and canvas, ban on working with nude models.

Running a computer search. Type in Gentileschi's name to see what's available. Look at Web sites from fine arts and women's studies. Check online library catalog for useful books or articles.

Talking to people about the topic. Mention Gentileschi to friends and ask for ideas. Talk to art historian friend. Tell family about research.

FOCUSING THE TOPIC

Tentatively identifying audience and purpose. Possible audience: other students in art history course or women's studies course. Tentative purpose: to describe how G., a talented painter, defied conventions in her time and earned recognition.

Doing in-depth research. Look at Web sites on Gentileschi; choose most valuable material and print it out. Check out biography by Garrard. Look at chapter on G. in Greer's *Obstacle Race*.

MAKING A SCRATCH OUTLINE

I Social environment in 17th-c. Italy that repressed women
Women not educated
Obsession with women's chastity

II World of art hostile to women
Assumed women weren't creative
Difficult to get training

III G's special background that helped her become an artist
Father was a painter
Lived in Rome
Grew up around artists

IV Important events in G.'s life that affected her career
Raped by teacher at 17
Humiliating public trial
Married another artist and moved to Florence

V Anger at men a theme in many paintings
"Susanna and the Elders"
"Judith Slaying Holofernes"

Tentative title: Artemisia Gentileschi: Courageous Woman Painter in 17th-Century Italy

Tentative thesis sentence: The 17th-century painter A.G. overcame bias in the art world and a humiliating public rape trial to achieve recognition as an outstanding artist.

● DRAFTING

It's important to form good writing habits early. Mostly such habits involve being organized and consistent:

> ◐ Pick a place to write that's comfortable, readily available, and fairly quiet. It may be a desk at home or a corner in the library where you can plug in a laptop. The important thing is to get used to writing in a specific place so that when you go there, your subconscious says, "Time to write."
>
> ◐ Choose a time that suits your schedule and gives you a couple of hours of uninterrupted work. Indulge any little habits that help you concentrate—background music, Gummi Bears, Diet Cokes.
>
> ◐ Become proficient with one computer operating system and one word processing program, and try to stay with them. The frustrations that come from switching back and forth between systems and programs can upset your train of thought and hamper your writing.

A caution here. Sometimes when you're under pressure, you can't afford the luxury of having everything the way you want it. The authors of this book have both written speeches on airplanes and stayed up late to meet deadlines, and you too may sometimes have to throw your routines aside and do the best you can. Routine can be enormously helpful, but less-than-ideal conditions shouldn't become an excuse for not writing.

OVERCOMING WRITER'S BLOCK

Even experienced writers sometimes have trouble getting started. Because most of us sense that beginnings are important, we sometimes take them too seriously, feeling that they have to be good. Not necessarily. Remember, when you begin a project you're only writing a draft—whatever you put down can be revised later. So if you stall because no opening sentence seems good enough, just lower your standards and put down something—anything—that will get you moving. What you should *not* do is wait for inspiration. As the economist and author John Kenneth Galbraith has put it,

> All writers know that on some golden mornings they are touched by the wand—are on intimate terms with poetry and cosmic truth. I have experienced those moments myself. Their lesson is simple: It's a total illusion. And the danger in the illusion is that you will wait for those moments. Such is the horror of having to face the typewriter that you will spend all your time waiting. I am persuaded that most writers, like most shoemakers, are about as good one day as the next [. . .], hangovers aside. The difference is the result of euphoria, alcohol, or imagination. The meaning is that one had better go to his or her typewriter every morning and stay there regardless of the seeming result. It will be much the same.
>
> JOHN KENNETH GALBRAITH, "WRITING, TYPING, AND ECONOMICS"

If you're working on a long project, you may hit a temporary block when you start up again after a day has passed. When that happens, try reading back over what you wrote the day before. Backtracking will usually get you moving again.

FINDING YOUR PACE

Writers work at different paces, and you need to find the rhythms that suit you best. Some writers compose their first draft rapidly, getting ideas down quickly and seldom hesitating about word choice. We call these writers *sprinters*. Most sprinters think of their first draft as a discovery draft and plan to revise heavily on the next draft. (One of the authors of this book is a sprinter.)

Other writers write first drafts much more slowly, stopping frequently to reread and think about what they've written. They change words, delete, and move sentences around, and spend considerable time staring at their screen. They may also pace, snack, stop to do little chores, and worry. We call these writers *plodders*. While the plodder doesn't usually regard the first draft as final, he or she feels that when it is done the hardest part of the job is probably over. (The other author is a plodder.)

Then there are the perfectionists. These writers have to get everything right the first time—to think out each sentence as they write it and change words as they work. They cannot go on to another paragraph until they are completely satisfied with the one they've just written. A good term for writers like this is *bleeders*. They suffer more than other writers, and it takes them forever to produce a piece of writing.

Try to start out as a sprinter. Sprinting gets you started, and you create a text you can start working on. But if you're not the sprinter type, don't worry about it. Many productive writers are plodders, and some of us just have to work out our ideas as we go. In the long run, plodders may not take any more time than sprinters to turn out a good finished product.

But don't allow yourself to be a bleeder. Bleeders are the most likely to develop writer's block and to miss their deadlines. The agony is rarely worth it.

POSTPONING CORRECTIONS

Whether you are a sprinter or a plodder, put off making corrections in spelling and mechanics until the end. When you are actually writing, you shouldn't be fretting about where to put commas and whether *harass* has one *r* or two. You can fix such details later. Writers who worry about mechanics too soon stifle their creativity and divert energy needed for developing their ideas. Better to write first and edit later.

When you've finished your draft, put it aside—overnight if you can—to allow your mind to clear and give you a fresh outlook on what you've written. This is the time for incubation, a period to let your unconscious mull over what you've done before you start to revise.

● INCUBATING

We're strong believers in intervals of downtime when you write, particularly if you're stuck at some point. Such intervals allow your brain to function out of sight for a while. We don't really know what happens during these time-outs, but for most writers they seem to help. When a solution surfaces, the conscious mind can say "Aha!" and move ahead.

Short periods of incubation may happen several times during a writing project—perhaps when you take time out to run or to do the laundry. Count on them for those times when you stall. For a long project, have faith that your brain will work while you're sleeping. Plan, prepare, and draft, then relax when you need to and trust your subconscious to come through for you.

Two cautions. (1) Be ready to seize the moment when a solution surfaces. Get to your computer immediately or grab a pen to make notes. (2) Don't wait too long for lightning to strike. If your deadline approaches and your subconscious is still snoozing, go back to your writing. Chances are good that whatever has been bubbling under the surface will emerge.

Q *Although my writing teacher keeps reminding us to remember our audience and sometimes even specifies that audience, isn't the real audience for the writing I do in college the instructor who gives me a grade? What's the point of pretending I'm writing for a different audience?*

A Your writing instructor wants you to develop the habit of asking yourself these essential questions: Who am I writing for? What information does that reader need? What questions does that reader have that I need to keep in mind? Thus your instructor creates a hypothetical writing situation to help you learn to think in terms of audience, and will evaluate your work partly on how well you adapt your writing to your readers.

There's no such thing as "good writing" in the abstract. You're always writing for someone and with some purpose, and whoever evaluates your writing will judge it on how well it accomplishes that purpose. So try not to think that you're writing just for a grade; you're writing to demonstrate something, to make an impression on someone, to tell someone something, or to persuade someone. If you can achieve that broader view of your writing—as being focused on *purpose* and *audience*—you'll be a more successful writer both in and out of college.

FOR PRACTICE

1 Working with a group of three or four other writers, choose one of the following topics, and brainstorm for an explanatory paper: (1) home schooling, (2) singles clubs, (3) credit cards for students. Ask the common journalistic questions to generate material:

Who? What people participate?

What? What is involved in the activity?

Why? Why do people participate?

When? When does this activity take place?

Where? Where does this activity occur?

How? How is the activity carried out?

2 Working in a group with three or four others, choose one of the listed topics and brainstorm to generate a store of material that could be useful for drafting an exploratory piece. Draw on personal experience, television documentaries or talk shows, magazine articles or books, or insights you've gotten from one of your courses. Ask a recorder from the group to take notes.

Television and other media have recently given increased attention to extreme sports.

Critics claim that broad access to the Internet has fostered intellectual isolation, as users seek out like-minded individuals and participate in chat groups to reinforce each other's biases.

In 2001, over half the first-year students in schools of law and medicine were women. How might this statistic impact those professions?

By 2005, the United States will need 2 million additional teachers in the public schools. What steps might state and national governments take to address this problem?

3 Write a summary of about 100 words—or create a detailed outline—giving the main ideas you would focus on in a short piece on one of these topics:

Finding a part-time job that is a good fit for you

The best discount stores for students

Choosing your laptop

Meeting people through classified ads

The pros and cons of belonging to several chat groups

FOR WRITING •

1 For your college paper or the Web site of an organization in which you're active, write a short *explanatory* piece—no more than 300 words—about one of the following events:

A barbecue to celebrate the opening of a citywide day care center for children of teachers in the local public schools.

Homecoming weekend on your college campus, which will feature tours of new buildings on campus and showcase the college jazz band and the new swimming complex. A major purpose of the weekend this year is to attract alumni in the hope of getting them to donate to a newly established scholarship fund for low-income students.

Organizational meeting of a forum for beginning writers in which they can exchange short stories and plays and critique each other's work.

2 For a weekly alternative newspaper in your community, one that features essays on local cultural, political, or social concerns, write a short *exploratory* piece—no more than 500 words—about one of the following issues:

A proposal before the city council to impose an 11:00 p.m. weeknight curfew on youngsters under eighteen in a two-block area near your college where local bands play during the summer.

A petition from an animal rights group to establish a no-kill policy at the city-financed animal shelter that accepts homeless cats and dogs and puts them up for adoption. At present, because of its limited facilities, the shelter has to destroy any animal that has been there more than ten days. An alternative new policy would need to specify what is to be done with these animals.

The proposed demolition of an art nouveau movie theater that has been the venue for foreign films, art films, and film festivals in your community since the 1950s. Representatives of the chain that has bought the theater say they will keep it open if they can find a way to keep it profitable.

What Is Your Writing Situation?

4

> *Always start with your readers—who are they, and what do they expect from you?*

Whenever you start on any writing task, it's a good idea to take a few minutes to think about your writing situation. Ask yourself three questions:

- Who is your *audience*?
- What is your *purpose*?
- What is your *persona*?

AUDIENCE

The most important question in any writing situation is, *What readers am I writing for, and what do they expect from me?* Your answer to that question will affect every choice you make—choices about language, about style, about tone, about organization, about supporting examples. Sometimes your choices will be intuitive—you know almost without thinking that when you're writing for one of your college instructors, you'll use straight-forward, unemotional language and a serious tone. If you were writing an editorial for your college paper, you'd make different choices. Then you'd choose more colorful language and perhaps try for an ironic tone.

In less clear-cut writing situations, however, answering a set of basic questions can help you anticipate your readers' needs and expectations. Here are some we think can be useful:

QUESTIONS ABOUT AUDIENCE

- Who are your readers?
- Why will they be reading what you write?
- What kind of evidence will interest them?
- How much do they already know about the topic?
- What additional information will they need or welcome?
- What questions will they want answered?

If you write out the answers to these questions, you'll begin to get a feeling for the readers you want to reach.

Let's look at an analysis of the audience for the model project from Chapter 3 on the artist Artemisia Gentileschi:

AUDIENCE ANALYSIS

Who are the readers? Instructor and fellow students.

Why will they be reading this piece? To learn about a major woman artist from an earlier century.

What kind of evidence will interest them? Historical information about the artist's life and her contributions.

How much do they know about the topic? Students know little about this particular artist or about obstacles women faced in her time.

What additional information will they need or welcome? What was special about Gentileschi's career? What specialized information about her art, techniques, subjects, etc., will interest readers?

What questions will they want answered? What specific problems did Gentileschi have? How did she overcome them to become famous?

● ● ● **PURPOSE**

When you begin a writing project, think specifically about why you are writing. As a student, of course, your first answer might be that you're writing to fill an assignment. Fair enough, but you still need to ask yourself what you are specifically trying to accomplish with this project. Here's a set of basic questions that can be helpful:

QUESTIONS ABOUT PURPOSE

○ Do you want primarily to inform, entertain, or persuade your readers?

○ What major points do you want to make?

○ What change, if any, do you want to bring about?

○ How do you want your readers to respond?

Writing out answers to these questions not only can help you decide what you want to accomplish with your writing, but will also help you generate material. Even if your purpose changes somewhat as you draft, you need to have a clear idea about what you want to say in order to begin.

Here's how an analysis of the writer's purpose for the project on Gentileschi might look:

PURPOSE ANALYSIS

Do you want primarily to inform, entertain, or persuade? My primary purpose here is to inform.

What major points do you want to make? I want readers to understand the obstacles Gentileschi overcame to achieve recognition.

How do you want your readers to respond? I'd like them to think about some of the circumstances that affect artists' work and the handicaps under which women painters had to work.

What change do you want to bring about? I have no particular change in mind.

PERSONA

Every time you write, you assume a *persona* (pronounced per-*sone*-a). Like an actor, you create a role, and you play it for your readers. You can take the role of the passionate advocate of some cause, an informed authority on some topic, a compassionate observer of social injustice—many roles are possible. Think about the personas that radio and TV personalities project—Jay Leno as satiric observer, Dr. Laura as scolding parent,

Jim Lehrer as experienced and wise reporter. As a writer, you also leave an impression. Here are some of the elements that affect it.

● **YOUR LANGUAGE CHOICES**

When you choose everyday, familiar language, address your readers as "you," use contractions frequently, or use the first person "I," you're creating a friendly, easygoing persona who feels relaxed with readers and close to them. Such a persona would suit you when you were composing a newsletter or creating a personal Web site. You wouldn't choose it when you were submitting a research project to a professor. Then, you'd want to present the image of a serious-minded, careful, and respectful student, and you would avoid slang or language that's too casual. Probably you wouldn't address your professor as "you."

Your choice of vocabulary also affects your persona. If you use a technical vocabulary for a physics project you're presenting online—and use it correctly—you assume the role of an authority on your topic. If you use the latest slang terms and the first names of current pop stars in a concert review, you take on the persona of someone who's tuned in to the contemporary music scene. And if you use terms like *abs, quads,* and *glutes* when you're describing an athlete whose physique you admire, you come across as someone knowledgeable about exercise and fitness.

● **TONE**

Tone, the feeling or attitude that you project in a piece of writing, also plays a crucial part in the persona that comes through in your writing. We often characterize tone in terms used to describe attitude. This list suggests just some of the possibilities:

sarcastic	flippant	mocking
sentimental	ironic	dogmatic
serious	patronizing	superior
militant	concerned	moralistic

For instance, a movie critic lambasting a heavy action film may sound mocking and superior; articles on the Web site theonion.com often sound flippant and sarcastic; a letter of advice from an older sister may seem patronizing. Readers react strongly to the tone in your writing. If it offends them, they're likely to discount what you're saying or perhaps stop reading altogether. So when you're reading a draft of your work, ask yourself, "What attitude am I projecting here? Is this the tone I want?" If it's not, consider how you can improve it.

● **AUTHENTICITY**

A third important element of an effective persona is the authenticity and good character of the writer. Readers react positively to writers who give an impression of competence, integrity, and authority, writers like the columnists William Raspberry or Ellen Goodman who write about serious issues in a straightforward and authoritative way. Such writers have earned their reputations and the trust of their readers over a period of years, but beginning writers can create their own authentic character in a number of ways. Here are some strategies you might adopt:

- When appropriate, research and document your findings.
- Quote authoritative sources to support your assertions.
- Respect your readers.
- Acknowledge other points of view.
- Avoid extreme claims.
- Sound confident.

Here's how an analysis of the writer's persona might look for the model paper that was introduced in Chapter 3:

PERSONA ANALYSIS

What kind of persona do you want your language choices to reflect? I want to give the impression of a serious writer who wants to inform her readers about a talented woman from an earlier century.

What tone do you want to project? I want to come across as enthusiastic and admiring, impressed by Gentileschi's accomplishments and the force of her character.

How can you communicate your authenticity? I'll make reasonable, not extravagant claims about Gentileschi's work and use supporting evidence to show I've done my research and am well informed about my topic.

Q *Most English teachers I've had consider a sentence fragment a serious grammatical error. But I often see fragments in advertisements and sometimes in stories or news articles. Why are students penalized for doing what professional writers do all the time?*

A In some writing situations, a writer might use an intentional fragment to achieve a special effect. That is, the writer knows that although a word or phrase he's using doesn't have all the parts of a complete sentence, it does convey a complete idea forcefully, as in the following example from *Newsweek*: "The virtues that some Asian statesmen call 'Asian values' are, after all, the virtues of a precapitalist, preconsumerist culture. Thrift, hard work, respect for family. They used to be called the Protestant ethic."

In advertising we often find several short phrases strung together to increase the tempo or to create a staccato effect: "It's the perfect cell phone. No failure, no waiting, no limits."

So there are times when a phrase or clause without all the essential elements of a sentence may be appropriate. It depends on your writing situation. If that situation is informal and you want to create a breezy, hip tone, you might use a fragment intentionally. You might also use an occasional fragment in a journalistic piece. But in most writing situations you'll encounter in college or business, you should avoid sentence fragments. They're seldom appropriate when you're writing a report, doing an evaluation, or performing an analysis. In such situations, your readers expect straightforward standard English, and you'll do better not to jar them with incomplete sentences.

FOR PRACTICE

❶ Here is a sample of a writing situation you might face, followed by an audience analysis you might arrive at:

The writing situation: You're in charge of drafting the copy for a Web page to be sponsored by a volunteer group you belong to, Tutors for Teens. You're seeking college students to help eighth- and ninth-grade students improve their math skills.

Audience analysis: College students with good math skills who would like to be involved in a community project and who feel comfortable with thirteen- and fourteen-year-olds. They would need to be reliable and conscientious, willing to commit two hours a week for a full semester.

Write a similar audience analysis in the following writing situations:

A brochure for middle school students inviting them to attend a one-day early career awareness fair on your college campus. The goal of the fair is to convince these ten- to twelve-year-old youngsters to take science and math courses so they can enroll in college preparatory classes when they get to high school.

A letter to your state senator urging her to support a bill that subsidizes child care for single mothers who are returning to school to get a high school diploma.

A short personal essay to accompany your application for a tuition grant for the coming semester from the college alumni club in your city.

2 Here is a sample showing how you might analyze your purpose in another writing situation:

The writing situation: A movie review for the campus newspaper, due the day after the movie opens at local theaters.

Purpose analysis: To let readers know what kind of movie it is—violent action, sophisticated comedy, family entertainment, war spectacle—and whether it's a good representative of its genre. Give a brief view of the plot, name the actors, and evaluate the film for acting, dialogue, originality, and general interest.

Write a similar analysis of the writer's purpose in the following writing situations:

A company brochure announcing a health and exercise program for company employees, summarizing the benefits for employees of signing up to participate in the program

A Web site for the local children's museum that describes its exhibits and educational programs and invites families to buy memberships

An email message to be sent to all residents in a particular dorm on campus asking them to limit the number of electrical machines and appliances they bring back to school for the fall term so that the building will meet local fire code standards

3 Here is an example showing how you might analyze the persona you wanted to create in a writing situation:

Writing situation: A driver is writing to appeal a six-month suspension of her driver's license that was imposed because she has received five speeding tickets.

Persona: The writer wants to project the persona of a sober, industrious young woman who has learned her lesson and who must be able to continue driving because of her job.

Analyze the persona a writer might want to create in these writing situations:

A *petition* to the college administration asking it to increase the salaries of campus custodial workers to 150 percent of the minimum wage

A *news story* for the campus newspaper announcing the opening of a Writing Center that will be open six days a week to all students who want help with their writing projects

An *opinion piece* for your hometown newspaper asserting that binge drinking is not a problem at your college

● ● ● ● **FOR WRITING** ●

Draft an argument on one side of the dispute over whether public schools should be encouraged to accept free television sets for showing educational programs if those programs also include up to ten minutes' advertising each hour. Choose one of the following audiences, and before you start your argument write a one-paragraph analysis of your readers:

The parent-teacher association of the middle school that you attended

The Rotary Club (a club made up of business and professional people in the community) of your city

The students of a middle school, the twelve- to fourteen-year-olds who would be the viewers of the proposed television programs

Drafting 5

> ○ *When you write down your ideas, you generate more ideas.*

Even the most seasoned writers will tell you that sometimes the hardest part of a writing project is getting down that first sentence. However, remember that when you're writing a draft you don't have to take the beginning of your piece too seriously. But you do need some kind of launching pad from which to start. Just put down something and start writing—the rest will begin to come. In fact, you'll often find that writing down ideas helps to generate more ideas. Later, as your piece takes on a little more shape, you can review your opening to see whether what worked to get *you* going may need some modification in order to get your *readers* going.

GETTING STARTED

But how *do* you begin a piece? This chapter illustrates some of the common strategies that authors who write regularly rely on to get their work moving. They're not complicated, and once you're familiar with them, you'll begin to notice how often magazine and newspaper writers use them as openers. Here are five that work well:

- ○ An illustrative example
- ○ A quotation
- ○ An anecdote

    ● A scene-setting description

    ● A thesis paragraph

● STARTING WITH AN ILLUSTRATIVE EXAMPLE

If when you start working on your draft you have a good idea of what your thesis is going to be, you might start by looking for a relevant example that will catch your readers' interest. In the following, see how Craig Stanford uses an example to introduce an essay about the threat posed to mountain gorillas by the territorial wars in the Congo. The opening graphically introduces the reader to Stanford's topic; it anchors his essay and gives him a point to push off from:

> High among the Virunga volcanoes, along the eastern edge of the Democratic Republic of Congo, there lives a group of gorillas with little interest in international politics. Day by day and week by week they wander through meadows of bracken fern, eating bamboo and nettles, mating in polygynous groups and fastidiously grooming one another. Although there are only around six hundred mountain gorillas left in the world, [. . .] the gorillas themselves seem unconcerned about that fact. Their most aggressive, most territorial act toward people is to bite a farmer on the behind now and again.
>
> CRAIG B. STANFORD, "GORILLA WARFARE"

Here's another example, from a biography of the painter Andrew Wyeth; it opens a chapter on the intense relationship between him and his wife, Betsy:

> Nothing has ever *truly* mattered to Wyeth except his work—not family, friends, money, sex, pain, or pride. On the very few occasions when he has sought an intimate relationship, he has intuitively known that it would support and advance his painting. Wyeth once explained, "I've never been interested in women that say, 'Andy, I think you're darling.' I think that's a bunch of shit, and I don't want it. I think it's saccharine. Nonsense. Weakening. They want you to take care of them. I find it terribly aggravating. Betsy doesn't have to give a shit about me. I want her to love my work, not me. That's the important thing. I'm a very queer man."
>
> RICHARD MERYMAN, *ANDREW WYETH: A SECRET LIFE*

● Starting with a Quotation

A quotation that relates to your topic can make a good opening for a piece of writing. See, for example, how a student used a quotation in an article about one athlete's disenchantment with playing college football:

> The English wit Oscar Wilde once said, "There are two tragedies in life: one is not getting what you want; the other is getting it." That irony resonates with George Hillary now that he has finished his first year playing football for Jefferson College, a year in which he tore a rotator cuff in his shoulder, clashed disastrously with the line coach, and went on scholastic probation.

Here's an example from a large-circulation magazine, *Texas Monthly*. In this case the writer uses the brief quotation to introduce an article about how wrong professional critics can sometimes be:

> "A limited series, with a limited future." So wrote one *Variety* critic after viewing the 1978 pilot episode of *Dallas*, the CBS show that would become the second-longest running dramatic series ever (only *Gunsmoke* lasted longer). For thirteen seasons audiences around the world were captivated by the trials and tribulations of the most dysfunctional family ever to grace the TV screen. *Dallas* was a giant in television history; it set viewing records and was the prototype of prime-time soap operas, inspiring at least one spin-off (*Knott's Landing*) and a host of imitators (*Dynasty, Falcon Crest*).
>
> Courtney Bond, "Dallas"

We should add a caution about using a quotation to kick off your draft. Unless you have a particularly apt quotation at your fingertips or know exactly where to go to find what you need, use some other strategy for getting started. You can waste a great deal of time looking for just the right quote.

● Starting with an Anecdote

Starting off a piece of writing with a colorful anecdote about a person can work well to catch readers' interest, because we all like stories. The biographer David McCullough uses an anecdote about Harry Truman's mother to begin an article about several highly successful men for whom a strong relationship with their mothers was extremely important. This simple story about President Truman's calling his mother to tell her about the surrender of Germany at the end of World War II dramatizes McCullough's point:

> Early in the evening of August 14, 1945, in the living room of her yellow clapboard house in Grandview, Missouri, a small, spry woman of 93, talking to a guest, excused herself to take a long-distance call in another room. "Hello, hello," the guest heard her begin. "Yes, I'm all right. Yes, I've been listening to the radio. [. . .] I heard the Englishman speak. [. . .] I'm glad they accepted the surrender terms. Now you come to see me if you can. All right. Good-bye."
>
> DAVID MCCULLOUGH, "MAMA'S BOYS"

Sometimes you may remember an incident from your own life that might make a good opening anecdote. Here the novelist and essayist Barbara Kingsolver does just that in the first paragraph of her essay about how much friendlier people in Spain are toward children than are people in the United States; by telling about a potentially offensive incident to which many women can immediately relate, Kingsolver catches her readers' attention and draws them into the body of her essay:

> As I walked out the street entrance to my newly rented apartment, a guy in maroon high tops and a skateboard haircut approached making kissing noises and saying, "Hi, gorgeous." Three weeks earlier, I would have assessed the degree of malice and made ready to run or tell him to bug off, depending. But now, instead, I smiled, and so did my four-year-old daughter, because after dozens of similar encounters I understood he didn't mean me but her.
> This was not the United States.
>
> BARBARA KINGSOLVER, "SOMEBODY'S BABY"

● STARTING WITH A DESCRIPTION

Many authors like to start out with a vivid description that sets the mood and creates a picture for their readers. If you're aware that a particular place or scene plays an important part in the piece you're going to write, you can create your own description. Here's how the South African leader, Nelson Mandela, describes the harsh environment of the gold mines where black African miners toiled under terrible conditions; such a stark picture prepares the reader for Mandela's account of the exploitation of black labor under the apartheid regime in his country:

There is nothing magical about a gold mine. Barren and pock-marked, all dirt and no trees, fenced in all sides, a gold mine resembles a war-torn battlefield. The noise was harsh and ubiquitous: the rasp of shaft-lifts, the jangling power drills, the distant rumble of dynamite, the barked orders. Everywhere I looked I saw black men in dusty overalls looking tired and bent. They lived on the grounds in bleak, single-sex barracks that contained hundreds of concrete bunks separated from each other by only a few inches.

NELSON MANDELA, *LONG ROAD TO FREEDOM*

Here's another vivid description that the journalist Brent Staples uses to begin a new section of his autobiography, *Parallel Time:*

A journal of Chicago is a journal of weather. Winter lasts forever there. Dirty gray ice hangs on in the gutters through Easter. June suckers you outside in shirtsleeves, then shifts its winds, bringing January to rake your bones. Warm weather smells of an ambush until August. Then the lake heats up, the breeze stops, and it's too hot to breathe.

BRENT STAPLES, "MR. BELLOW'S PLANET"

● STARTING WITH A SUMMARY PARAGRAPH

If you know the main points you want to make, you may want to start with a paragraph that sets out those main points briefly and acts as a takeoff point for your essay. Such a draft paragraph can give you momentum. Here's an example of such an opening paragraph from a noted sociologist; this kind of opener serves as a thesis paragraph to help you focus your writing as you work:

The social problems of urban life in the United States are, in large measure, the problems of racial inequality. The rates of crime, drug addiction, out-of-wedlock births, female-headed families, and welfare dependency have risen dramatically in the last several years, and they reflect a noticeably uneven distribution by race. [. . .] Liberal social scientists have nonetheless been reluctant to face this fact. Often analysts make no reference to race at all when discussing issues such as crime and teenage pregnancy, except to emphasize the deleterious effects of racial discrimination or of the institutionalized inequality of American life.

WILLIAM JULIUS WILSON, *THE TRULY DISADVANTAGED*

When you're considering how to organize your draft, it can be useful to review some common patterns; one of them might work well for you:

- Reasoning from evidence
- Assertion and support
- Definition
- Cause and effect
- Comparison and contrast
- Classification
- Narration

● **REASONING FROM EVIDENCE**

Reasoning from evidence resembles the scientific method. You gather evidence, examine it, and draw conclusions. Here's a fairly typical example in which a writer cites statistics and then theorizes about what they mean:

> Japan's population is aging more rapidly than any on the planet—by 2015 one in four Japanese will be elderly. The birthrate has sunk to 1.34 per woman, well below replacement levels. (The birthrate in the United States, by contrast, is 2.08.) Last year Japan dropped from the eighth-largest nation in the world to the ninth. The smallest class in recorded history just entered elementary school. Demographers predict that within two decades the shrinking labor force will make pension taxes and health care costs untenable, not to mention that there will not be enough workers to provide basic services for the elderly. There are whispers that to avoid ruin, Japan may have to do the unthinkable: encourage mass immigration, changing the very notion of what it means to be Japanese.
>
> PEGGY ORENSTEIN, "PARASITES IN PRÊT-À-PORTER"

You can use this pattern in two ways: you can give the evidence first and then generalize from it, as the preceding passage does; or you can state your main point first and then present the evidence, as the following example does:

> As absorbed as society seems to be with alcohol, most people know shockingly little about alcoholism. Here's a disease that affects between 5 and 10 percent of the population; causes half of all violent deaths from

accidents, suicides, and homicides; triggers fatal diseases ranging from cancer to cirrhosis; and costs Americans about $180 billion a year. Yet smart, educated people don't even accept that it's a disease or that it may be our most egregiously undertreated epidemic.

JIM ATKINSON, "SOBER"

Keep three cautions in mind when you're arguing from evidence:

◐ Give enough evidence to warrant your conclusion. If you make a claim on the basis of only a few examples, you will damage your credibility.

◐ Be sure your sample is representative and takes data from a range of evidence. You don't want to look as if you're stacking the deck.

◐ Be sure your facts are accurate, and cite your sources to show where you got them.

Remember also to highlight statistical evidence in a graph or chart when possible and to use lists to present several points. For suggestions, see Chapter 11, on document design.

● ASSERTION AND SUPPORT

Under the organizational pattern of assertion and support, you state your main claim and then give specific evidence to support it. For example:

Nothing so marked out the "new science" of the seventeenth century as its proponents' repeated claims that it *was* new. Corpuscular and mechanical philosophers, on many occasions, vigorously insisted that their innovations represented radical departures from traditionally constituted bodies of natural knowledge. Text after text stipulated the novelty of its intellectual contents. In physics Galileo offered his *Discourses and Demonstrations concerning Two New Sciences*; in astronomy there was Kepler's *New Astronomy*; in chemistry and experimental philosophy Boyle published a long series of tracts called *New Experiments about the Void*. Bacon's *New Organum* was labeled as a novel method meant to replace the traditional organon, [. . .] and his *New Atlantis* was an innovative blueprint for the formal social organization of scientific and technical research.

STEVEN SHAPIN, *THE SCIENTIFIC REVOLUTION*

Shapin makes his assertion, that "nothing so marked out the 'new science' of the seventeenth century as its proponents' claims that it was new," and then expands on it with five specific examples taken from books by famous scientists. Such arguments, typical of those that lawyers present in court, are a kind of informal logic; they don't use formal syllogistic reasoning, but they appeal to common sense and common knowledge.

When you use an assertion and support pattern for your writing, keep these points in mind:

○ Make a strong opening assertion, but don't overstate your case.

○ Choose the kind of supporting evidence that you know will work well with your readers. For example, Shapin's paragraph cites books that readers interested in the scientific revolution would recognize. If he were writing for readers with little knowledge of science, he might give different kinds of examples.

● DEFINITION

When you define something, you analyze it and try to show its essential traits. Here are some of the strategies writers typically use:

○ Attributing characteristics

○ Analyzing components

○ Giving examples

○ Stating function

○ Defining negatively; that is, showing what something is not

Definition is an especially useful pattern of organization when you want to establish a standard by which to make a judgment. First you state the qualities that characterize the thing you want to define; then you show how that thing does or doesn't have those qualities. For example, if you wanted to define a good day care center, you might list qualities such as a low child-attendant ratio, a director with training in child development, and so on; then you would apply those criteria to a specific day care center to evaluate it.

Here's a definition paragraph taken from a book that defines a new socioeconomic class, a new type of educated elite; the author has fun here defining the new educated classes by how they buy and then giving examples that illustrate his point:

> Members of the educated class are distinguished not only by what they buy but by how they buy. It's commonly observed, for example, that almost nobody in an upscale coffee house orders just a cup of coffee. Instead, one of us will order a double espresso, half decaf–half caffeinated, with mocha and room for milk. Another will order a vente almond Frappucino made from the Angolan blend with raw sugar and a hint of cinnamon. We don't just ask for a beer. We order one of the 16,000 microbrews, picking our way through winter ales, Belgian lagers, and blended wheats. Thanks to our influence, all the things that used to come in just a few varieties now come in at least a dozen.
>
> DAVID BROOKS, *BOBOS IN PARADISE*

Here's a piece of writing that defines by characteristics; it's a feature story about a California teenager who believes that she's defined by her shoes:

> Jamillon Tucker knows being a teenager is all about the shoes. Get the right kicks, and respect will follow. So when she walks the halls of John F. Kennedy High School in a tough part of Richmond, California, the 15-year-old freshman can't help staring at the shoes on parade. There goes a pair of red and white Nike Shox. Here come some rainbow-colored Air Max. And check out those shiny gray Air Jordan XI Retros. Their proud owner, a kid with cornrow braids à la NBA superstar Allen Iverson, leaves the laces untied and walks in a flat-footed waddle to keep the leather from creasing. "It's all about fashion and status," Tucker says with a laugh. These days, she, too, is turning lots of heads—or, as the kids say, "breakin' hella necks." Using money she made working after school, she just bought a pair of black and red Nike Air Prestos, stylish slip-on running shoes that match her black jeans and red Nike shirt. "They're tight," Tucker says, referring not to the fit, but to the fashion.
>
> BROOK LARMER, "TWO GIRLS AND A SHOE"

● CAUSE AND EFFECT

A cause-and-effect pattern is one of the first options you might consider for organizing your writing. As a fundamental thought pattern, it can be used in a number of ways. Explanations (why something happened) and arguments (why something will cause something to happen) are two typical uses. Here's a cause-and-effect explanation that shows how Nevada's beginnings as a mining state influenced the environment there today:

> [Nevada's] evolution as a family-values-free zone can be explained, historians say, by its origins as a mining state, populated largely by single men. Toward the end of the nineteenth century, there were three men for every woman, and a significant number of those women were using the gender disparity to their economic advantage. Nevada, unlike its neighbor Oregon, was not settled by small farmers agitating for moral reform; instead, it remained a saloon society, dominated by cowboys and hustlers. Its inhabitants realized a long time ago that handsome profits could be made by inviting the rest of America into those saloons.
>
> REBECCA MEAD, "LETTER FROM NEVADA"

Here's a cause-and-effect paragraph arguing that a certain invention, the screw, had far-reaching effects:

> It's not an exaggeration to say that accurately threaded screws changed the world. Without screws, entire fields of science would have languished, navigation would have remained primitive, and naval warfare as well as routine maritime commerce in the 18th and 19th centuries would not have been possible. Without screws there would have been no machine tools, hence no industrial products and no Industrial Revolution. Think of that the next time you pick up a screwdriver to open a can of paint.
>
> WITOLD RYBCZYNSKI, "ONE GOOD TURN"

● COMPARISON AND CONTRAST

Writers frequently develop an essay or an argument by showing similarities and differences between two or more people, things, or events. The pattern often works well to unify a piece of writing and emphasize important points. For example, in the following opening paragraph a science writer uses comparison and contrast to begin an essay about the public relations campaign that affected tuna fishing:

> The yellowfin tuna is not celebrated for its intelligence. It's celebrated for its flavor. The spotted dolphin, on the other hand, is famously brainy and

no one will tell us how it tastes. The killing of dolphins is a national outrage; the killing of tuna is a given. There are some good reasons and some bad reasons, I think, which haven't been closely examined or even sorted apart.

DAVID QUAMMEN, "WHO SWIMS WITH THE TUNA?"

Here's another comparison, written in a straightforward but colorful style, that alternates contrasting statements about two contrasting men:

They were the odd couple of American politics: Kennedy the charming aristocrat, debonair, self-confident and beloved; Nixon the perpetual outsider, calculating, self-conscious and maligned. One would be remembered as the martyred king of Camelot; the other as "tricky Dick," the dark prince who resigned the presidency in shame. The two men began together in Congress as friends, and later became bitter rivals for the highest office in the land. They would go down in history, in Nixon's own words, as "a pair of unmatched bookends."

MICHIKO KAKUTANI, "COMPETITION THAT MADE KENNEDY AND NIXON FOES"

ANALOGY

An analogy is a form of comparison that seeks to explain the unknown by comparing it to something that is familiar to the reader. Analogies can take the form of metaphors (the heart *is* a pump) or similes (a hummingbird is *like* a tiny helicopter) or can be more elaborate comparisons. The prizewinning science writer Natalie Angier counts on using analogies to help her readers understand the complex creatures she writes about. She says, "I'll do anything to come up with similes and metaphors. I do it for myself to make the abstract concrete, and I do it in writing to keep the plot going." Here's one of her analogies:

They are the P. T. Barnums of the flower kingdom, dedicated to the premise that there is a sucker born every minute: a sucker, that is, with wings, a thorax, and an unquenchable thirst for nectar and love. They are the orchids, flowers so flashy of hue and fleshy of petal that they seem thoroughly decadent. And when it comes to their wiles for deceiving and sexually seducing insect pollinators, their decadence would make Oscar Wilde wilt.

NATALIE ANGIER, "THE GRAND STRATEGY OF ORCHIDS"

And look at this clever analogy in which the writer draws an extended comparison to suggest that a Nielsen report about television ratings shook the big TV networks as drastically as Galileo's theories shook his world:

> Like Galileo's observation that the earth revolves around the sun, the A. C. Nielsen Company's report of an unexpectedly sharp drop in the national television audience last winter has altered the accepted view of reality. And like the telescope Galileo used, a new instrument—the "people meter"—provided the new information. The big three networks are fighting the conclusion and trying to force the messenger to recant. But like those who believed the sun circles the earth, they seem fated to find themselves on the wrong side of the revolution.
>
> RANDALL ROTHENBERG, "BLACK HOLE IN TELEVISION"

The ability to write such vivid and engaging analogies comes in part from talent, of course, but it's an ability that's worth your while to develop regardless of your talent. Writers who want to engage their readers are always looking for the striking comparison, the right image that will clarify the unknown by linking it to the familiar.

● CLASSIFICATION

When we classify information, we organize it according to some system. When you're writing, you can create such a system in order to organize what you have to say and set a pattern for developing your ideas. For example, you could organize painters according to time period—Renaissance, nineteenth century, modern, and so on. You can organize writers by genre—novelists, essayists, technical writers, science writers, etc. Any such system lets you break down your material into component parts and then explain the typical characteristics of those parts.

You can set up categories according to cost, class, usefulness, politics, status—almost any yardstick you like. In the following paragraph, the author classifies the different kinds of horses in nineteenth-century England by their uses:

> Horses were specialized in what they could do. The hack was the ordinary, everyday horse you used for just clip-clopping along. In addition, there was the sleek, nervous racehorse. Also the hunter—a horse bred specifically for fox hunting. [. . .] For fat people, there were cobs—short, sturdy draft horses suitable for carrying or pulling heavy loads. For riding,

stallions were usually too frisky, geldings best, and mares were in between, but women and children favored ponies. Ponies were smaller and
easier to handle than horses, and, if women did drive horses, they usually
drove a one-horse carriage. [. . .] On horseback, ladies rode side saddle,
alternating sides each day so as not to develop an over enhanced buttock
on one side.

DANIEL POOL, *WHAT JANE AUSTEN ATE AND CHARLES DICKENS KNEW*

● NARRATION

Although we think of narration as simply storytelling, it can be an effective way to organize an essay or introduce an argument. Many writers start
off with a story that leads into their main theme. Here is an example that
opens a book about the power of emotions:

> Ponder the last moments of Gary and Mary Jane Chauncey, a couple com-
> pletely devoted to their eleven-year-old daughter Andrea, who was con-
> fined to a wheelchair by cerebral palsy. The Chauncey family were
> passengers on an Amtrak train that crashed into a river after a barge hit
> and weakened a railroad bridge in Louisiana's bayou country. Thinking
> first of their daughter, the couple tried their best to save Andrea as water
> rushed into the sinking train; somehow they managed to push Andrea
> through a window to rescuers. Then, as the car sank beneath the water,
> they perished.

DANIEL GOLEMAN, *EMOTIONAL INTELLIGENCE*

Here's another effective narrative that a writer uses to anchor an essay
about how she writes:

> Every once in a while after a reading, someone in the audience will come
> up to me. "Have I got a story for you!" They will go on to tell me the story
> of an aunt or sister or next-door-neighbor, some moment of mystery, some
> serendipitous occurrence, some truly incredible story. "You should write it
> down," I always tell them. They look at me as if they've just offered me
> their family crown jewels and I've refused them. "I'm no writer," they tell
> me. "You're the writer."

JULIA ALVAREZ, "GROUNDS FOR FICTION"

When you build a paper around narrative, remember that good narrators
use vivid language to *show* their readers what is happening, to make the
reader see something.

When you're drafting a piece of writing, it often helps to review the common patterns of organization so you can select one that might work particularly well for your purpose and your audience. For example, if you're constructing an argument for a hard-to-convince audience, a cause-and-effect pattern might work well. So could a reasoning-from-evidence pattern or assertion and support. All of these methods are based on logic and thus appeal to a certain kind of reader. At other times, you might want to create a more personal or psychological slant in your writing. Then consider narration or comparison.

But we also know that many experienced writers seldom stop to think how they're going to organize their writing. They could probably identify the pattern they're using, but they choose a way to organize instinctively, and often they combine two or more patterns in one project. So don't feel you need to choose a pattern to write by when you start drafting. Just know what the patterns are and use them creatively as you work. But when you're having trouble getting started, it sometimes helps to ask yourself, "Can I find a story to start off with?" or "What claim am I going to make and how can I support it?"

● ● ● KNOWING WHEN YOU HAVE AN ADEQUATE DRAFT

So how do you know when you have an adequate first draft, one you can submit to your instructor or your peer group with a good conscience? We propose the following criteria:

> ◗ Your draft is a good faith effort, one that shows you've taken the assignment seriously and shown respect for your readers. Those readers—your instructor and peers—can't be expected to invest their time responding to a draft in which you've invested very little.
>
> ◗ It's reasonably complete, with a central idea that's fairly well developed. Just an outline or a first paragraph followed by a summary isn't enough.
>
> ◗ It's legible and easy to read. Whether you're submitting it online or in a printed copy, make sure it's double-spaced and readable. Be sure that paper copies are dark enough to read, and leave some margins for response.

Q

I work hard as I draft a paper and usually feel good when I finish it. Do I always need to write a second draft if I like the way I wrote my paper in the first place?

A

Even if your first draft looks good to you, you'll always benefit from getting other writers to read it over and give you their reactions before you turn it in for a final grade or for publication. Those second readers serve as an audience who can give you some perspective on your work—point out some particularly strong features, make suggestions for strengthening certain points, or identify places where the reader needs more information. They can be especially helpful when they point out things they just don't understand. When a reader tells you that, there's no point in trying to explain what you mean. Just recognize that you haven't made yourself clear, and plan to rewrite the passage in question.

Although it can be uncomfortable to have other people critiquing your writing, such critiques are an important part of the writing process. They help you to develop as a writer by becoming aware of your audience and learning to adapt to it. And as you get used to the system of writing multiple drafts, you'll find that in the first draft you can concentrate on finding, developing, and organizing your ideas without worrying about matters such as word choice or punctuation, knowing that you'll get some help from your friends on the second round. And a second draft gives you the chance to polish and refine what you've written. Even people who write frequently don't always do their best work on a first draft.

FOR PRACTICE

1 Working with other students in a small group, consider what illustrative example or anecdote a writer might use as an opening for an essay on one of the following topics:

The advantages of starting one's college education at a community college

The widespread marketing of credit cards to college students

A proposal to make eighteen the legal age for buying or possessing alcohol, the same as it is for voting or registering for national service

2 Review the sections on arguing from evidence and on assertion and support as patterns of organization. Then, working in a small group, write down the claim

or assertion you would make in writing an essay on one of the following topics, and jot down ideas for the kind of supporting evidence you could use:

The National College Athletic Association should (should not) set guidelines for college athletic departments requiring that the head football or basketball coach for a university or college not be paid more than the president of that institution.

The National Booksellers' Association should (should not) establish a rating system for novels similar to the rating system used for movies, recommending that stickers be put on the dust covers of books ranking them as G (General), PG (Parental Guidance), PG-13 (Parental Guidance under 13), and U (Unsuited for readers under 16).

A high school principal did (did not) make a wise decision when she imposed a two-week suspension on a senior student who during a schoolwide assembly publicly criticized the commercial sponsor of the assembly after that sponsor distributed merchandise coupons to students who attended.

● ● ● **FOR WRITING** ●

Draft a cause-and-effect argument to support or oppose one of the following propositions:

Your city council has a proposal before it to adopt a no-loitering ordinance that would prevent people from sitting on a sidewalk or other public thoroughfare. (One effect would be to penalize homeless people who sit on sidewalks or lean against buildings, walls, or signs.)

The board of trustees of your church has asked members for their response to a proposal to install soft drink and candy vending machines in the corridors of the church building and use the revenue from those machines to improve the facilities in the religious education wing.

Writing Clearly

6

○ *Your first job as a writer is to make yourself clear.*

When asked what they value most in writing, nearly all readers say, "I want it to be clear." Good writing has other qualities too, but clarity comes first, way ahead of whatever might be second. Your first responsibility as a writer is to make yourself clear. It's tempting to think that clear writing must come easily to professional writers, but that's hardly ever the case. Professional writers write clearly because they work at it. Like people who stay fit through discipline and exercise, effective writers produce clear, forceful writing because they work at their writing and have developed a set of strategies that make it readable and engaging. In this chapter we give you an overview of five such strategies:

○ Illustrating general statements with specific examples
○ Making your readers see something
○ Putting people in your writing
○ Choosing concrete words
○ Adding metaphors for clarity

ILLUSTRATING GENERAL STATEMENTS WITH SPECIFIC EXAMPLES

When you want readers to grasp your ideas quickly, use personal and specific examples to illustrate your general statements. Writers all have to generalize at times; if they didn't they could never get beyond the examples. But notice how often magazine or newspaper writers begin an article with specific examples that lead up to a broader statement they want to make. In the following account of the aftermath of the September 11 attacks, the impact of the larger statement about grandparents' taking on new families comes from the specific opening example:

> Geneva Dunbar's days are a blur of snowsuits, snacks, and subtraction problems. From early morning, when she readies three children for school, to nightfall, when she tucks them into bed, she is like any bone-weary, two-hands-aren't-enough mother.
>
> The difference is that Mrs. Dunbar, 51, has already raised her family [. . .] but when her daughter died in the terrorist attack on the World Trade Center, Mrs. Dunbar found herself part of a vast army of grandparents suddenly thrust into a second round of child-rearing.
>
> JANE GROSS, "GRANDMA HELPS FILL THE VOID LEFT BY SEPTEMBER 11"

Watch how Anna Quindlen illustrates her generalization about the success of the national school lunch program in this opening paragraph:

> The school lunch program [. . .] has been by most measures an enormous success. For lots of poor families, it's become a way to count on getting at least one decent meal into their children. America's Second Harvest, the biggest nonprofit supply source for the food banks, talks of parents who go hungry themselves so their kids can eat, who put off paying utility and phone bills, who insist that their children attend remedial summer-school programs simply so they can get a meal. The parents themselves are loath to talk: of all the humiliations attached to being poor in a prosperous nation, not being able to feed your kids is at the top of the list.
>
> ANNA QUINDLEN, "SCHOOL'S OUT FOR SUMMER"

Here's an example from the paper about Artemisia Gentileschi:

> The sheer size of the canvases required for the history paintings so highly valued in the Renaissance posed problems for women [painters]. They were expensive, and most women had no independent source of income. Moreover, an artist trying to work on such a large scale needed an apprentice. Almost no woman apprentices existed, and male apprentices didn't want to work for a woman. If a woman painter did succeed in engaging a male apprentice, inevitably there were prurient rumors about a

sexual relationship between them. Painters of historical subjects, either biblical or from myth, needed models; not only were they expensive, but women painters weren't allowed to draw from nude models.

You strengthen your writing when you use specific examples:

❶ Specifics add the weight of facts to your writing and anchor it to the real world. If you write about the effect of the nonprofit organization The Heifer Project on rural communities in Central and South America, you'll have more impact if you tell specific stories about families in those regions who received heifers (or goats or rabbits) from the project.

❷ Specific details catch your readers' attention and give them stories they can visualize. If you were doing a project about the effect of poor child care on the careers of professional women in your community, you could make the deficiencies of the U.S. system vivid by comparing child care in your city with the national child care system in France and describing some features of the French system.

❸ When you reinforce general claims with specific facts and details, you earn the confidence of your readers. Those of us who are concerned about social issues such as racial injustice, inadequate health insurance coverage, or violence in the public schools can generalize about such problems to little effect. But when we reinforce those statements with specific accounts and true-life stories, and we suggest concrete solutions, we become credible witnesses.

Of course when you start giving your readers specifics and details, you're taking a risk. If you were to generalize that public school teachers are underpaid, many of your readers would agree, but if you proposed starting salaries of $50,000, some readers would protest that such salaries are unthinkable. Readers might agree in general that young people should be educated about healthy sexual practices, but some would be outraged if you were to suggest that high school students should learn about contraception. Nevertheless, if you want to gain your readers' trust and respect, you need to take the risk of giving them specifics and details.

When you can, use words that make your readers see somebody doing something. We live in a visual culture, surrounded by television, videos, movies, DVDs, and pictures on the Internet. We expect visual reinforcement of messages, and you can give your readers that reinforcement by using language to create images. This excerpt from the model paper we're using in this book shows how it can be done; the passage describes a picture in such vivid detail the reader can almost see it:

> Gentileschi portrays herself dramatically in her self-portrait, which she titled *La Pittura*. [. . .] It shows her as a handsome, buxom woman with the edge of a creamy bosom revealed above the top of a lace-trimmed silk gown. She is totally engrossed in her work, lips slightly apart and strands of dark hair curling at her temples. She radiates vitality, and everything in the painting reveals her talent—the warm flesh tones, the expressive eyes, the details of the delicate lace trim, the lights and shadows that highlight the sheen of the fabric, and the delicate gold chain at her neck.

Here is an example from a professional writer; notice how she dramatizes the horror of sailors' lives aboard eighteenth-century ships by giving you images:

> Long voyages waxed longer for lack [of knowledge] about longitude, and the extra time at sea condemned sailors to the dread disease of scurvy. The oceangoing diet of the day, devoid of fresh fruits and vegetables, deprived them of vitamin C, and their bodies' connective tissues deteriorated as a result. Their blood vessels leaked, making the men look bruised all over, even in the absence of injury. When they were injured, their wounds failed to heal. Their legs swelled. [. . .] Their gums bled too, as their teeth loosened. They gasped for breath, struggled against debilitating weakness, and when the blood vessels around their brains ruptured, they died.

> DAVA SOBEL, *LONGITUDE*

● ● ● ● **PUTTING PEOPLE IN YOUR WRITING**

Readers expect certain kinds of writing to be impersonal and abstract—technical reports or critical analyses, for instance. When you're doing that kind of task, you may need to write objectively and keep your tone impersonal. For many other kinds of writing—an opinion column, history or English papers, a personal Web page, or an oral presentation—you can introduce characters, personalities, or historical figures into your writing and write about what they've done or invented or accomplished. This simple strategy of putting people into your writing always makes it clearer and more readable.

Readers react favorably to such writing because we're all interested in people and their stories. When we know who is behind ideas or actions or whom they affect, those ideas and actions become more interesting. For example, we're more likely to take an interest in the discovery of a new drug or a new technology in cell phones if we know who made the discovery and whom it will benefit. Moreover, the author who is writing about people or groups of people is more likely to use strong active verbs to describe what they're doing and get rid of weak verbs like *is* and *are* and feeble verb phrases like *it is the case that* or *there is a possibility that.*

When you mention actual people in your writing, you're likely to use fewer abstract terms—they just don't fit well with active verbs. For example, compare the two versions of this sentence:

Original: A workforce with a high proportion of illiterates is a deterrent to productivity.

Revision: Workers who cannot read and write cut down productivity.

The original sentence has a bland, abstract subject, *a workforce with a high proportion of illiterates,* and an inactive verb, *is. Workers* is the concrete subject of the revised sentence, and *cut down* is the active verb.

We'll have more advice about culling out such abstract terms in the next section.

● MAKING PEOPLE YOUR SENTENCE SUBJECT

When you can, choose people as the subjects of your sentences. By doing so you give your readers a solid anchor early in the sentence and make the sentence easier to follow. For instance, compare these two versions of the same sentence:

Original: The affordability of hotels is a major factor in drawing tourists to Baja.

Revision: Tourists flock to Baja because of its affordable hotels.

The second sentence is easier to read and understand because it uses *tourists* as a subject and combines it with an active verb, *flock*, instead of the uninteresting verb *is*. Now compare the following:

> *Original:* Voluntary employee participation in the plan is requisite for its success.
>
> *Revision:* Employees will have to participate in the plan willingly if it is going to succeed.

The first version sounds like government-issue language; the second is a straightforward statement about people. Another example:

> *Original:* The likelihood that plagiarism will be a problem in college courses has increased greatly because of the Internet.
>
> *Revision:* Because of the Internet, today's college students have more opportunities to plagiarize.

The original sentence here never mentions human beings; the revision makes people the subject of the sentence.

• • • CHOOSING CONCRETE WORDS

• AVOIDING DEADWOOD NOUNS

Avoid using what we, the authors, call "deadwood nouns" whenever you can. That's our term for nominalizations, nouns created by tacking endings onto adjectives and verbs. Here are some typical examples:

capability	immediacy
cognizance	modernity
competitiveness	accountability
viability	inclusiveness
enhancement	utilization
marketability	continuation

When you edit, keep an eye out for such words, those that end in *-ity*, *-tion*, *-ness*, *-ance*, *-ment*, and *-ism*, and get rid of most of them. Sometimes they're absolutely necessary, of course, but not as often as you think. These clunky words have no life, no zip. They're flabby words; and used too often, they'll make your writing dull and hard to read.

● CHOOSING STRONG VERBS FOR CLARITY

Verbs are the lifeblood of writing. Because they affect not only clarity but also the tone and rhythm of what you write, it's worth giving them special attention. Notice how choosing strong verbs can improve a sentence:

> *Original:* In March most movie directors are thinking about the Oscar awards.
>
> *Revision:* In March the Oscar awards dominate movie directors' thoughts.

USING *BE* VERBS SPARINGLY

Although we all have to use the *be* verbs at times—*is, was, are, have been, will be*—they're often weak and can easily get overwhelmed by other words. Notice how much easier it is to understand the second sentence below:

> *Original:* The invention of barbed wire in the 1870s was a major factor in bringing about change in cattle raising.
>
> *Revision:* Barbed wire, invented in the 1870s, radically changed how cattle were raised.

In the original version, the verb *was* gets buried by abstract phrases on both sides; in the revision, the verbs *changed* and *were raised* enliven the sentence.

In this paragraph, notice how Gordon Parks chooses active verbs (italicized here) to create a compelling image of the fabled jazz musician Duke Ellington:

> For me, and many other black people then, his importance as a human being *transcended* his importance as a musician. We had been *assaulted* by Hollywood grinning darky types all of our lives. It was refreshing to be a part of Duke Ellington's audience. Ellington never *grinned*. He *smiled*. Ellington never *shuffled*. He *strode*. It was "Good afternoon, ladies and gentlemen," never "How y'all doin?" We *wanted* to be seen by whites in the audience. We *wanted* them to know that this elegant, handsome, and

awe-inspiring man playing that ever-so-fine music on that golden stage
before that big beautiful black band was black—like us.

GORDON PARKS, "JAZZ"

Sometimes your writing needs only to be clear, not colorful or striking.
But when you want to make your writing strong and interesting to read,
choose verbs that do something.

CHOOSING SHORT, DIRECT VERBS

When you can, substitute simple one-word verbs for strung-out verb
phrases. For example:

WHY WRITE . . .	WHEN YOU COULD WRITE . . .
be cognizant of	recognize
put the emphasis on	emphasize
is reflective of	reflects
make an attempt to	try
have an understanding of	understand
make a comparison	compare
grant permission to	allow

The longer verb phrases, although not wrong, tend to slow down writing
and make it clumsy.

CHOOSING ACTIVE VERBS MOST OF THE TIME

When you want your writing to be clear and direct, choose active verbs
that immediately let your reader know who's doing what and to whom. For
example:

> From childhood, Artemisia *breathed* the ambience of the artist's
> workshop and *absorbed* the traditions of the heroic school of
> painting.

You need passive verbs when you don't know who or what did something
or when you would rather not call attention to the person who acted. For
example, they're necessary in these sentences:

No woman *had ever been admitted* to the Academy before.

Many of Gentileschi's paintings *have been lost.*

But avoid passive verbs that conceal who's responsible for doing something. For example:

One of Gentileschi's paintings of Judith killing Holofernes *was regarded* by some critics as obscene.

Better to put it like this when you know who's doing what:

The Victorian art critic John Ruskin *regarded* Gentileschi's painting of Judith killing Holofernes as obscene.

● USING ADJECTIVES AND ADVERBS SPARINGLY

Your writing will be livelier and clearer if you choose nouns and verbs to carry your meaning instead of relying too much on adjectives and adverbs. Keep these hints in mind:

○ Get rid of unnecessary doublings such as *common* courtesy, *fundamental* difference, *final* destination, *absolutely* essential, and consensus of *opinion*.

○ Edit out extravagant adjectives such as *marvelous, terrific, fabulous,* and *fantastic* and use sparingly those overworked modifiers *really, very,* and *definitely*.

○ Don't overstate your case. Qualify a claim you couldn't prove by using provisional terms such as *probably, for the most part, on the whole,* or *in general*.

● ● ADDING METAPHORS FOR CLARITY

Like analogies, metaphors and similes do wonders to help readers understand difficult or abstract ideas. They explain the unfamiliar with something familiar, or show something commonplace in a new light. Here a writer helps us look at the Internet in a new way:

The Internet in the 1990s is just like the railroads in the 1840s. It is still in its infancy, its growth is exploding, and no one yet knows how to make money at it. It also performs the same economic function: connecting things. And there is no more potent force than connecting buyers and sellers. The gross product of an economy, after all, is nothing more than the sum of all these connections. The more buyers and sellers there are, the greater the wealth generated. That's why the railroad was the seminal invention of the 19th century and the Internet will undoubtedly be of the 21st.

JOHN STEELE GORDON, "THE GOLDEN SPIKE"

Metaphors and similes enrich your writing with vivid comparisons, but they can also serve as a kind of shorthand that helps you explain a point you want to make. Here are three vivid comparisons:

Promoting novels in a sound-bite culture is like selling elephants from a gumball machine.

BARBARA KINGSOLVER

Too much money attracts administrators and experts as sugar attracts ants.

WENDELL BERRY

Sometimes it seems as if everyone wants to compete with the Jewish tragedy, in what an Israeli friend called the Olympics of suffering.

IAN BURUMA

And here's one of our favorites:

Exercise is like money. It's good for almost everything.

Q *Are there people who just* naturally *write well? When I spend five hours on a piece and get a B and someone else in the class spends two hours and gets an A, it makes me wonder whether the ability to write is something some people just have but other people have to work long and hard at.*

A Yes, there probably are people who naturally write better first drafts than other people write. But we don't like them very much. (That's a joke, borrowed from Anne Lamott, a wonderfully clear writer who works very hard at her craft.) Seriously, for the two authors of this book, clarity is something to work at all the time. Sometimes we achieve it earlier and easier in a project, and sometimes it comes later and harder. It *is* true, though, that the more you use the strategies you studied in this chapter to improve your writing, the more they will become ingrained in your writing, so that over time some of that clarity should start showing up earlier in your writing process.

1 Working with two or three other students, discuss ways to revise the following sentences using more concrete and specific language:

> Your accepting our recommendation would mean elimination of homeless elements on our city streets.
>
> A knowledge and understanding of the law is a necessity for those who want an alteration of it.
>
> The result of the election is an indication that the legislator has an environmentally aware constituency.

Working together, write a clear version of each sentence and compare it with versions by other groups.

2 Revise these sentences, adding people or a person as the subject of each:

> The burden of responsibility for Joseph's behavior is on his parents.
>
> A stringent self-evaluation is needed to remedy your problem.
>
> The anxiety of choosing a profession is a major cause of stress.

3 Working with two or three other students, discuss ways in which one could revise these sentences using more vigorous verbs:

> There are several advantages that will be achieved by this ruling.
>
> Vitamins are substances the body requires in small amounts.
>
> There are many things to examine when looking for a used car.

When you are finished, write a stronger version of each sentence.

4 Revise the following sentences to replace passive verbs with active verbs, and get rid of any nominalizations you think are weakening the sentences:

> Uneducated women often feel serious apprehension when they are forced into the job market for the first time.
>
> Information should be made available to consumers before they ask for it.

What should be considered is the capability and suitability of the individual for each job.

It is recommended by administrators that maturity and high school performance be a key element in decision making for admissions.

The requirements were put into effect by a group of uninformed people before the problem had been fully studied.

5 Photocopy a magazine article in which the author uses metaphor well, and bring it to class. Analyze the writer's reason for using allusion and metaphor. To what extent do you find the technique effective?

FOR WRITING

For each of the following assignments, write a detailed analysis of your audience. Specify characteristics of your audience you need to keep in mind as you write, the problems such an audience might present, and what the audience would expect to get from reading your paper. Also analyze your purpose in writing, specifying what you hope to accomplish with the paper. If appropriate, include an accurate and descriptive title for your paper.

1 Observe carefully a street, neighborhood, building, or small area in your city, and write an objective report on it that might be used for a project in an urban sociology class or a course on city government. Use concrete and specific but neutral language; try to convey a visual impression, and avoid using vague adjectives. Think about what kind of information your reader would want to get from the report. Some possible topics for description:

A school building that needs to be modernized

A vacant lot that could be converted into a playground

A block close to campus that is being invaded by X-rated bookstores and porno movie houses

The county courthouse that was built in the last century

2 The generous retirement pay of people who have served twenty years or more in the armed services costs U.S. taxpayers a substantial amount of money. For example, a colonel may retire at forty-two and receive more than $3,000 a month retirement pay while holding down another job; a four-star admiral may retire at the age of sixty with a pension of more than $90,000 a year. These benefits also have the advantage of being tied to the cost of living so that they increase regularly. Defend or oppose these benefits and write an article expressing your views.

Think carefully about the consequences of your argument and support your points. Direct your paper to a specific audience, perhaps a congressional committee that is considering budget cuts or the readers of your local newspaper.

3 Write a short article for young people from ten to fourteen years old explaining the basic concepts of some subject on which you are well informed and in which you are very interested. Assume that your readers are bright youngsters who read well and who enjoy learning something new. Try to explain your ideas or give your information in terms they will understand, using concrete examples and analogies. Keep your focus narrow enough that you can treat the subject in no more than 1,000 words. Here are some suggestions for topics:

A new discovery in geology, astronomy, archeology, or another science

How a young person trains to become a dancer, lawyer, journalist, physician, or college professor

How the weather is forecast

How airplanes fly, ducks swim, or whales breathe

How to budget and spend a clothes allowance

Remember that your audience doesn't have to read your article and will do so only if you hold its interest. It would be a good idea to look at some children's magazines like the *Junior National Geographic,* or at the column for young people in a magazine such as *Sierra*, to get a feel for what kind of writing appeals to youngsters. And remember: *Don't preach.*

Holding Your Reader

7

○ *If there is any way for your readers to get lost, they will.*

R eaders can be a fickle lot, hard to please and easy to lose. And once lost, they're hard to recapture. Thus the first rule for holding your readers is to capture their interest. You can usually do that by teaching them something, since most readers want to stay with a writer as long as they are learning. So it's important, as you work, to ask yourself, "Am I telling my readers what they want and need to know?"

But when you're drafting and revising, it's also helpful to keep in mind some specific strategies for holding your readers. We suggest nine such strategies:

- ○ Choose a good title.
- ○ Write a strong lead.
- ○ Keep your writing tight and unified.
- ○ Keep sentences and paragraphs to a reasonable length.
- ○ Chunk your writing into manageable units.
- ○ Avoid antagonizing your readers.
- ○ Make your writing look good.
- ○ Use figurative and connotative language sparingly.
- ○ Avoid stereotypes and offensive labeling.

CHOOSE A GOOD TITLE

Because readers often decide whether they want to read something solely on the basis of its title, try to draft a title that is clear, accurate, and interesting. A good title does several things:

> First, it predicts content.
>
> Second, it catches the reader's interest.
>
> Third, it reflects the tone or slant of the piece of writing.
>
> Fourth, it contains keywords that will make it easy to access by a computer search.

Notice how the title "Artemisia Gentileschi: Artist against the Grain" meets the criteria for a good title. It tells you the piece is about the artist Artemisia Gentileschi; it piques your interest to learn why she was considered against the grain; it reflects a positive tone to the piece; it contains keywords that would allow a reader to find it quickly in an online search. Do resist giving your projects cute or facetious titles. They may fall flat with your readers, and they can mislead someone who's trying to classify or find your work.

WRITE STRONG LEADS

Notice the importance William Zinsser attaches to opening sentences:

> The most important sentence in any article is the first one. If it doesn't induce the reader to proceed to the second sentence, your article is dead. And if the second sentence doesn't induce him to continue to the third sentence, it's equally dead. Of such a progression of sentences, each tugging the reader forward until he is safely hooked, a writer constructs that fateful unit the "lead."
>
> WILLIAM ZINSSER, *ON WRITING WELL*

Leads can make or break you with your readers. Editors, executives, admissions directors, and many other readers are busy and often impatient people. If your opening doesn't engage their interest in two or three minutes, they'll move on. "But," you may say, "that's not true of professors. They *have* to read what I write." Well, yes, that's what they're paid to do. But if your first paragraph rambles, you're off to a bad start. And if readers can't grasp your main idea by the middle of the second page, they may lose interest in what you're saying. A good lead does these things:

- ⊃ It engages the reader's attention.
- ⊃ It makes a promise about what's to come.
- ⊃ It sets the tone for the piece.
- ⊃ It gives readers a reason to continue reading.

You can accomplish these goals in various ways. Here are two reliable strategies: (1) catch your reader's interest with a provocative statement or question, and (2) make your reader anticipate what is to come.

The writer who seeks to engage the reader may do so with an anecdote, an analogy, reinterpretation of a maxim or cliché, intriguing facts, or a series of informative questions. Here's an example of a lead that wryly interprets a maxim:

> Ever since the first Florentine loaned his first ducat to his first Medici, it has been one of the most shopworn clichés of the financial industry that the best way to rob a bank is to own one. This maxim, like all maxims, is rooted in a basic truth about human nature: to wit, if criminals are given easy access to large sums of money, they will steal, and under such tempting circumstances, even honest men may be corrupted. To forget this is to invite madness and ruin.
>
> **L. J. DAVIS, "CHRONICLE OF A DEBACLE FORETOLD"**

To trigger the reader's interest in her subject, the science writer Natalie Angier opens an article about scorpions with a series of intriguing facts about four ancient civilizations:

> To the ancient Chinese, snakes embodied both good and evil, but scorpions symbolized pure wickedness. To the Persians, scorpions were the devil's minions, sent to destroy all life by attacking the testicles of the sacred bull whose blood should have fertilized the universe. In the Old Testament, the Hebrew King Rehoboam threatened to chastise his people, not with ordinary whips, but with scorpions—dread scourges that sting like a scorpion's tail. The Greeks blamed a scorpion for killing Orion, a lusty giant and celebrated hunter.
>
> **NATALIE ANGIER, "ADMIRERS OF THE SCORPION"**

The following opening paragraph illustrates the strong informative lead:

> Any woman who has devoted herself to raising children has experienced the hollow praise that only thinly conceals smug dismissal. In a culture that measures worth and achievement almost solely in terms of money, the intensive work of raising responsible adults counts for little. One of the most intriguing questions in economic history is how this came to be; how mothers came to be excluded from the ranks of productive citizens. How did the demanding job of rearing a modern child come to be trivialized? When did caring for children become a "labor of love" smothered under a blanket of sentimentality that hides its economic importance?
>
> ANN CRITTENDEN, "HOW MOTHERS' WORK WAS 'DISAPPEARED' "

The paragraph introduces a chapter that traces how attitudes have changed in the past century about the work women do as mothers and housewives. This kind of informative lead works particularly well for serious pieces and class projects because it gives readers an immediate signal about what they're going to learn.

You'll find more suggestions about opening paragraphs in Chapter 8, on crafting paragraphs.

KEEP YOUR WRITING TIGHT AND UNIFIED

Whatever you're writing, you want your readers to be able to move through it smoothly without getting lost or having to backtrack and reread. You can achieve that necessary unity by following one of the organizational patterns discussed in Chapter 5, on drafting, and by using strong transitions throughout. Here are some key transitional devices:

- Directional terms—links and nudges
- Repeated words
- Conjunctions at the beginnings of sentences

LINKS AND NUDGES

Links are words and phrases that hold writing together by signaling connections. *Nudges* are terms that give readers a little push from one point to the next and keep them moving in the right direction. All writers need to have a stock of such terms at their fingertips and to develop a sense of when and where these terms are needed. Here are some of the most common:

LINKS	NUDGES
also	this, that, these, those
although	then
moreover	first
for example	consequently
in addition	therefore
however	next
in spite of	thus
nevertheless	hence
and	since
similarly	as a result
not only	for instance
because	

Here's a paragraph from our model paper on Artemisia Gentileschi with both linking and nudging terms italicized:

> The talented Gentileschi [. . .] was fortunate in being born into a painter's *family* in Rome in 1593. *Her father,* Orazio, was a friend of the painter Caravaggio and well established in the artistic community of Rome; the *family* lived in the artists' quarter of the city surrounded by other painters. *Thus from childhood* Artemisia breathed the ambience of the artist's work-shop and absorbed the traditions of the heroic school of painting of the day that emphasized myth and legends from the Bible and the classical era. *From her early teens* she worked in her *father's* studio, which would have been considered the *family business,* developing her expertise in mix-ing paints and preparing canvases, and benefiting from the opportunity to draw from models that was essential for any serious painter of the day *but* almost impossible for women artists to attain unless they came from a *painter's family.*

The links come from the repeated mention of *family, father,* and Artemisia's age (childhood, teens); the nudging terms are *thus* and *but.*

● REPEATED WORDS

Although you will often want to edit out repetitious language as you revise, occasionally you may choose to unify your writing by deliberately repeating a key word or phrase. Here's an example in which repetition works well:

> For tens of thousands of years on the plains of North America, many forces of nature worked to sustain the grasslands. Of those forces, *fire* was perhaps the most important in the health of the prairie. Before the West was settled, grass *fires* were a natural part of the prairie ecosystem. [. . .] *Fire* helped burn back old-growth plants. On the plains, *fire* helped remove the dead grasses and allowed new plants to emerge from the charred soil. Often, if an area goes for an extended time without the benefit of *fire* or some other disturbance, it becomes a monoculture, in which only one type of plant grows.
>
> RUSSELL GRAVES, *THE PRAIRIE DOG*

Here's another, from the African American poet Nikki Giovanni:

> The *fact of slavery* is no more our fault than the *fact of rape*. People are raped. It is not their choice. *How the victim becomes responsible* for the behavior of the victimized is beyond my understanding. *How the poor are responsible* for their condition is equally baffling. *No one chooses* to live in the streets; *no one* chooses to go to sleep at night hungry; *no one* chooses to be cold, to watch their children have unmet needs. *No one* chooses misery, and our efforts to make this a choice will be the damnation of our souls. Yet such thinking is one of the several troubling legacies we have inherited from [W. E. B.] Du Bois.
>
> NIKKI GIOVANNI, "CAMPUS RACISM 101"

● USING CONJUNCTIONS TO CONNECT SENTENCES OR PARAGRAPHS

You may remember some authority telling you that you shouldn't start a sentence with *and* or *but* because they're conjunctions whose purpose is to join parts of sentences. Well, they are conjunctions, and they do join things, so you wouldn't want to use either one as the very first word of a piece of writing. But they are also strong signal words that can work well for beginning a sentence or a new paragraph when you want to emphasize a connection or show a contrast. They also help hold the parts of your writing together. The next examples, taken from essays reprinted in the

Best American Essays series, show that you can begin sentences or paragraphs with *and* or *but* (we've italicized the conjunctions) without making a grammatical blunder; both words can serve as important hooks to unify your writing:

> [. . .] If we are using our land wrong, then something is wrong with our economy. This is difficult. It becomes more difficult when we recognize that in modern times, every one of us is a member of the economy of everybody else.
>
> *But* if we are concerned about land abuse, we have begun a profound work of economic criticism. Study of the history of land use [. . .] informs us that we have had for a long time an economy that thrives by undermining its own foundations.
>
> WENDELL BERRY, "IN DISTRUST OF MOVEMENTS"

> [. . .] Corey knows how to work a crowd, sometimes too well. Last year in one of the season's crucial games, Corey was all alone under the basket, tried a fancy lay-up and blew it. The coaches rose to their feet, howling in rage. Corey jogged downcourt shrugging, palms turned toward the ceiling. "Relax, guys," he said, nonchalance itself. "It's just *basketball*."
>
> *And* then there is Stephon. He is making his debut as a high-school player today, but he takes the court as he always does—ever confident, leaning forward onto the balls of his feet in happy anticipation, arms jangling at his sides. "Mission day," he announces with a clap. "Time to get busy." Within moments he is making quick work of his competition, stunning the crowded, noisy gym into reverential silence.
>
> DARCY FREY, "THE LAST SHOT"

● ● ● KEEP PARAGRAPHS AND SENTENCES TO A REASONABLE LENGTH

It may be that television and the Internet have made all of us less patient readers than we should be. Whatever the reason, it's a fact that many of us quickly become impatient with lengthy sentences or paragraphs, especially when we're reading online and have to scroll the text up a few lines at a time. That's when we may stop reading, so it's definitely in a writer's best interest to try to keep sentences and paragraphs reasonably short. (See Chapter 8 for more discussion of paragraphing.)

● PARAGRAPHS

You can check on paragraph length in different ways, but the simplest is just to look at what you've written. Does a single paragraph take up almost a whole screen or whole page? If so, it's probably too long, and you need to find places to break it. (See pages 94–96 in Chapter 8 for specific suggestions.) Ask yourself if you are trying to cover too much in one stretch and would do better to focus on one small point at a time. Readers can process only a limited amount of information at a time, and if you crowd too much data into a few paragraphs, they'll lose interest. For example, this paragraph is overstuffed:

> It takes a bold paleface to attempt a comprehensive history of Native American life nowadays—after being forced to swallow five hundred years of insulting and mainly inaccurate Anglo-European generalizations about their character and behavior, the Native Americans are justifiably tetchy. Get it wrong and Russell Means, the activist-turned-actor who has managed to play both the last of the Mohicans (Chingachgook, in Michael Mann's adaptation of James Fenimore Cooper's novel) and the fiercest of the Sioux (Sitting Bull, in my own *Buffalo Girls*) might show up on your doorstep, wearing his big hat; or Vine Deloria, Jr., the unmellowed Sioux polemicist, might launch a lightning bolt or two, possibly from that bastion of nativism, the Op-Ed page of *The New York Times*; or the young rumbler from the Northwest, Sherman Alexie, recently anointed by *Granta* as one of the twenty best young American writers, might pop onto one of the paleface talk shows and complain.
>
> LARRY McMURTRY, "CHOPPING DOWN THE SACRED TREE"

(More about this caution in Chapter 8, on paragraphing, and in the next section, on chunking your writing.)

● SENTENCES

Your sense of your audience should help you decide how long to make your sentences. If you're writing an opinion column for a newsletter or an editorial for the college paper, you can assume that your readers are probably reading hurriedly and won't take time to process long complex or rambling sentences. You also would intuitively write relatively short sentences if you were creating a Web page for a club you belong to or writing a presentation you will be giving orally.

More experienced readers, such as your instructors or people who read a great deal in their profession, can, of course, handle relatively long sentences without any problem. Larry McMurtry, for example, originally published the essay quoted above in the *New York Review of Books,* which appeals to highly educated, expert readers. Even so, we think McMurtry's sentences are too long and complicated. Why tax readers' patience? Whoever your audience is, it's a good rule of thumb to check your sentences for length as you revise and edit. When you see a sentence is running to more than six or seven lines on the page or screen, look to see if you can break it up. Usually you can, and you will probably improve it in the process.

And it is possible to make long sentences readable. Use people or specific nouns as your sentence subjects; focus on showing someone doing something; use active verbs; avoid strung-out noun or verb phrases. You can also make a long sentence readable by writing a sequence of parallel clauses, particularly when each clause is colorful and interesting in itself. For instance:

> Long-distance buses have become the habitat of busted souls who've lost their cars to the finance company or lost their licenses because of driving drunk; of childless, indigent old people; or frightened new immigrants from Laos, Nigeria, or Guatemala, who have too many kids to manage; of people who have just been released from an institution; of legally blind people like me.
>
> EDWARD HOAGLAND, "I CAN SEE"

Of course, writers who create sentences like this expend time and effort to get such striking results. It's not easy, but an elegant sentence can be worth the investment.

● ● ● **CHUNK YOUR WRITING INTO MANAGEABLE UNITS**

You can also make your writing easier to read by *chunking* it: that is, by breaking up long stretches of writing into separate units so they're easier to process. Chunking is the principle behind grouping digits in telephone, Social Security, and credit card numbers—would you ever remember your sister's phone number if it were written 2140117760? But if you break it into smaller units—214-011-7760—it's easier to read and remember.

You're chunking your writing when you break up long sentences into shorter ones and divide long paragraphs into shorter paragraphs, as we discussed in the previous section. You can also break paragraphs into manageable chunks by inserting numbers that mark off units. Here's an example:

> For several reasons, you can't count on scores from standardized tests to predict a student's college performance accurately. (1) Tests don't measure perseverance, a crucial quality for success in college. (2) They don't test a person's study habits or ability to set priorities. (3) Tests don't reflect the value a student's family places on grades and intellectual achievement. (4) Tests don't measure a student's confidence and maturity.

Notice how the numbers break the paragraph into chunks but also retain its unity. They also act as nudges that move the reader along in the right direction.

Another good way to break up a long sentence or paragraph is to display the contents in a list. For example, you would probably lose your readers' attention halfway through this sentence:

> Successful bosses know that factors that make for job satisfaction are complex and include challenge, recognition, autonomy, status in the group, harmony on the job, variety of tasks, intellectual stimulation, and significant work as well as money.

There's just too much information jammed together. But if you break the same information out into a list, readers can absorb it.

> Successful bosses know that employees get job satisfaction from many factors, not just money. They include:

challenge	harmony on the job
recognition	variety of tasks
autonomy	intellectual satisfaction
status in the group	significant work

You can also break your writing into chunks by setting off material in boxes, pasting in graphics or pictures to break up long passages of text, creating charts, or dividing your writing into columns if you're creating a brochure or a newsletter. You'll find more tips about breaking up your writing and displaying information effectively in Chapter 11, on document design.

• • • AVOID ANTAGONIZING YOUR READERS

An important reminder about holding your readers comes from basic psychology: Don't make them angry. You'll surely lose them if you do. Few of us are open-minded enough to read through a piece of writing that attacks our beliefs or makes fun of people or institutions we cherish. But you can often get people to consider your point of view if you use moderate language and keep certain principles in mind:

> ○ *Show respect for your audience.* Assume your readers are intelligent, thoughtful people of goodwill who will respond to a reasoned argument. Emphasize values and goals you may have in common and work from there.

> ○ *Use moderate language.* Avoid extreme adjectives such as *vicious, immoral,* and *intolerable* when you're constructing an argument. Readers who don't already agree with you will get defensive and quit reading; those who do agree may be offended by your diatribes.

> ○ *Write provisionally, not dogmatically.* State your points in tentative and conditional terms that get your ideas across but don't sound aggressive. Try expressing your ideas with phrases like *it's possible that . . . , we might consider . . . , perhaps we should think about . . . ,* or *can I suggest. . . .* Sentences like *Let's see if we can agree* and *I hope you'll take our suggestion into consideration* create an atmosphere of cooperation and courtesy in which your readers can pay attention to your proposals because they're not forced to defend their positions.

Unfortunately, because the hosts of TV and radio talk shows seem to believe that controversy attracts more viewers than a courteous exchange of opinions would, we have few public models of people engaging in dialogue to reach agreement. The reality is, however, that in democracies you get things done through compromise and negotiation. Those are good skills to work on in your writing.

MAKE YOUR WRITING LOOK GOOD

When impatient readers—and there are lots of them—look at a long page of unbroken print, they're apt to think, "I'm not sure I want to read that." You can try to avoid that reaction in several ways. Here are some of the things you can do to make your writing look better in print or online.

○ Put your title and any headings in a bold, easy-to-read type font. (See Chapter 11, on document design, to learn more about using headings and different type fonts.)

○ Leave plenty of white space around titles, illustrations, and blocks of print. Be sure your writing doesn't look crowded and dark.

○ Add graphs and charts to reinforce and dramatize statistics or chunks of data.

○ Use illustrations and graphics when appropriate.

○ Keep paragraphs short, especially if your writing is going to appear in columns or online.

○ Look for ways to break your writing into units; use lists, boxes, headings, and captions as appropriate.

We'll add here that you may want to postpone working on the "body language" of your project until you get to either the small-scale revising or editing stage. Too much early concern about appearance could distract you in the drafting stage.

USE FIGURATIVE AND CONNOTATIVE LANGUAGE SPARINGLY

Except for those who write scientific and technical articles, few writers would claim that they always use neutral language that has no emotional content. Nor would they want to. Anyone who wants to write colorful and engaging prose that involves people will use vigorous language at times and will want to use images and metaphors. Images and metaphors are seldom neutral. Notice their effect in this paragraph by William Zinsser:

> I was the smallest of boys, late to grow, living in a society of girls who shot up like mutants and were five-foot-nine by the age of twelve. Nowhere was the disparity sharper than at the dances I was made to attend throughout my youth. The tribal rules required every boy to bring a gardenia to the girl who invited him, which he would pin to the bosom of her

gown. Too young to appreciate the bosom, I was just tall enough for my nose to be pressed into the gardenia I had brought to adorn it. The sickly smell of that flower was like chloroform as I lurched round and round the dance floor. Talk was almost out of the question; my lofty partner was just as isolated and resentful.

WILLIAM ZINSSER, *INVENTING THE TRUTH*

And the author of a report about corruption in college sports issued by the Knight Commission in June 2001 uses passionate language to convince readers that colleges and universities are damaging their institutions through commercialization. Here is an excerpt from the report:

> Major college sports do far more damage to the university, to its students and faculty, its leadership, its reputation and credibility than most realize— or at least are willing to admit. The ugly disciplinary incidents, outrageous academic fraud, dismal graduation rates, and uncontrolled expenditures surrounding college sports reflect what Duderstadt and others have rightly characterized as an entertainment industry that is not only the antithesis of academic values but is corrosive and corruptive to the academic enterprise.

KNIGHT REPORT, "A CALL TO ACTION"

In these paragraphs, the authors use vivid language to engage their readers' emotions—Zinsser to evoke a nostalgic image from his childhood ("shot up like mutants," "tribal rules," "sickly smell," "lurched round and round"), the Knight Report to stir outrage about the way money has corrupted college sports ("ugly," "outrageous," "dismal," and so on). Both are using connotation—the power of words to *suggest* much more than their bare-bones dictionary definitions include—but they're doing so responsibly and openly. That's the key: responsibility. You can use emotional language for effect, but don't conceal your position and your purpose from your readers.

AVOID STEREOTYPES AND OFFENSIVE LABELING

When you're writing college papers, business documents, articles for newspapers or newsletters, or communications that will go online, pay special attention to avoiding offensive language. Avoid gender or racial and ethnic stereotyping, and don't express contempt for people who are different from you or disagree with you.

● **SEXIST LANGUAGE**

To avoid sexist language, keep some guidelines in mind.

Instead of using the male pronouns *he* and *him* in general statements, write *he or she* and *him or her.* Often you can avoid the problem by using plural nouns, or you may switch back and forth between *she* and *he* when you're generalizing.

WHY WRITE . . .	WHEN YOU COULD WRITE . . .
The astute leader always listens to his men.	Astute leaders always listen to their followers.
Men show their true nature in times of crisis.	People show their true nature in times of crisis.
Policemen, mailmen, chairman, or businessmen . . .	Police officers, mail carriers, chairperson, or business executives . . .

Edit out language that stereotypes certain professions as male or female. Don't suggest that nurses, librarians, or secretaries are usually women, or that engineers, physicians, and military officers are usually men.

Avoid implying that men and women behave in stereotyped ways. Don't suggest that most women love to shop, that most men are sloppy, or that only men like to hunt and fish.

● **USING RACIAL AND ETHNIC TERMS CAREFULLY**

Mention race only if you make an important point by doing so. Then keep these guidelines in mind:

Use specific and accurate terminology. For Americans whose forebears come from another country, combine descriptive terms with *American: Japanese American, Cuban American,* and so on, without hyphens. The term *Asian* is so broad that it's almost useless; use *Chinese, Japanese, Indonesian, Filipino,* and so on. The term *Oriental* is no longer used to describe specific races. The term *Hispanic* is also very broad and means something different from *Latino.* When you can, choose a more specific term: *Mexican, Peruvian, Colombian, Spanish,* and so on.

The terms *Native American* and *American Indian* are both acceptable for indigenous Americans; for natives of the Arctic regions, more specific ethnic names such as *Inuit* or *Aleut* are preferred over *Eskimo.*

As far as you can, use terminology preferred by the people you're writing about. At this time, the term favored by many whose ancestors came from Africa seems to be *African American,* but *black* is still widely used. If you're in doubt, ask a friend from that group or consult a respected newspaper such as the *New York Times* or the *Christian Science Monitor. People of color* is the choice of some writers.

Be careful not to slip into subtle ethnic or racial stereotypes. Might someone construe something you've written to mean that Irish are hot-tempered or Italians are connected with crime or Scots are stingy? If so, consider revising to avoid unintended bias. Sometimes it helps to get someone else to read your work to look for such slips.

Avoid unnecessary references to age, physical condition, or sexual orientation. Be careful not to demean people for characteristics over which they have no control.

Use respectful terms for people who are sixty-five or older, and recognize that individuals in that category vary as much as those in any other group. Many such individuals do not want to be called *elderly* or *old* or even *senior citizens.* Your best bet here is to be specific; write "late sixties" or "early seventies." Mention someone's age only if it's relevant, and avoid patronizing comments like "For a seventy-five-year-old, he's remarkably alert." Of course, that doesn't mean that you can't recognize truly unusual accomplishments, as a *New York Times* article did in reporting on a performance the Russian ballerina Maya Plisetskaya gave on her seventieth birthday.

Use *boys, girls,* and *kids* only for people under eighteen. College students and young working adults deserve to be called men and women. The term *college kids* is both patronizing and highly inaccurate.

When it's relevant to mention a person's disability or illness, use specific language and avoid words like *crippled* or *victim.* Terms like *blind, visually impaired* or *paraplegic* are simply descriptive and are acceptable. A useful formula is to mention the person first and his or her disability second: "my friend Joe, who is diabetic" or "Anne's father, who has multiple sclerosis."

Mention a person's sexual orientation only when it is pertinent to the topic you're discussing, and use specific, nonjudgmental language when you do. *Gay* and *lesbian* now seem to be the terms preferred by those whose sexual orientation is toward their own sex.

Edit out language that suggests negative stereotypes such as *redneck, wetback, welfare mother, fraternity boy, country club set,* or *Junior Leaguer.* Be careful, too, with terms that have become code words suggesting racial or social stereotypes; two such terms are *underclass* and *cultural elite.*

● **MAINTAINING A CIVIL TONE**

Finally, remember that the language you use reflects who you are. So even when you're using strong language for strong purposes, keep it civil. People who call those who disagree with them names like *wacko* or *fascist* or *pinko* reveal themselves as extremists who have little interest in honest argument or productive discussion. Their language works only with those who already agree with them. They're contemptuous of anyone else. So if you want to be taken seriously, show respect for your readers even when you disagree with them. That's the only way you'll get them to consider your point of view.

● ●

Q   *When can I use contractions such as* they're *and* wouldn't *in college writing?*

A   As with most questions about writing style, the answer to this question depends on your writing situation. You need to analyze each situation in order to decide what your audience expects of you and what you want to accomplish with what you are writing. It would also be useful to think about how the writing situation *feels* to you. If it is relaxed and friendly, contractions may be appropriate. But if you feel your instructor keeps a certain distance from students, you may decide that he or she would rather you didn't use contractions.

Certainly you've noticed that we use contractions in this textbook. We do so because many years of teaching writing have convinced us that students master the craft of writing more easily in a friendly and relaxed environment; therefore contractions come naturally to us when we're addressing students in a textbook—they make the writing more relaxed and friendly. Probably each of us, however, would use few if any contractions when we were giving a formal paper at a conference of our professional peers and felt substantial distance between ourselves and our listeners. But we might use contractions frequently if we were presenting research findings to a small group of colleagues whom we knew well.

If you're writing a straightforward history paper comparing the leadership of Pericles in fifth-century B.C. Athens with that of Napoleon in eighteenth-century France, you'd probably do well to avoid most contractions. Your writing situation is not informal. If you've chosen to write the report on the findings of a group project in a psychology class, contractions would not be appropriate. But if you were writing a process paper to explain how batteries work to an audience of ten-year-olds, you'd probably use contractions without hesitation. Writing for someone who is grading your work establishes a different purpose and audience from writing simply to explain something.

So deciding when contractions are appropriate and when they're not is a judgment call, one you'll learn to make intuitively as you become a practiced writer. In the meantime, if you're in doubt when you're writing a college paper, play it safe: you'll never be wrong *not* to use them.

FOR PRACTICE

❶ Working with other students in a small group, discuss the following titles chosen from the table of contents of an essay anthology. How useful do you find them as forecasts of what to expect in the essay? As a group, decide which three titles are the most informative and which three are the least informative.

In Distrust of Movements

Earth's Eye

If You Are What You Eat, Then What Am I?

What's So Bad about Hate?

The Synthetic Sublime

The Singer Solution to World Poverty

The Joys and Perils of Victimhood

–A Son in Shadow

–In Defense of the Book

2 Working with several other students, draft some possible titles that would be both informative and inviting for these articles:

A press release about an exhibit of women students' paintings at the college museum

A newspaper editorial about a proposal to construct twenty-four skyboxes at the college stadium to be sold for $250,000 each

An article about the local Hands-On Housing program that is looking for skilled volunteers to design and supervise construction for five low-cost homes on a tract of land donated anonymously to the city

3 Working with other students in a group, evaluate the following opening paragraphs taken from newspaper feature stories. How well do you think the leads work? Do they make you want to read the story? Why? What improvements would you suggest, if any?

While we have become familiar with things like blueberries from Maine and tomatoes from New Jersey, there is some produce, like watermelon, that seems to have no origin. Watermelons are just something that you know will be there, piled high in your grocery store throughout the summer. Every day, tons and tons of them arrive in the city, just hours out of the field, and as they disperse to grocery stores, markets, and bodegas, all traces of where they came from disappear.

AMANDA HESSER, "FOLLOW THAT WATERMELON!"

In spirit, the Endangered Species Act is the noblest of the landmark environmental statutes passed during the Nixon era. In practice, it has been by far the most controversial. It is the act right-wing property-rights advocates love to hate, and once again it is under fire for allegedly protecting animals at the expense of human economic needs—this time in Oregon's Klamath Basin, where the federal Bureau of Reclamation has shut off irrigation water in order to save the endangered sucker-fish and the threatened coho salmon. The action, coming on top of the worst drought the Pacific Northwest has seen in many years, has left 1400 farmers without water, ruined crops on about 200,000 acres and inspired isolated acts of civil disobedience in which angry farmers have tried to reopen headgates blocking the water. It has also become the latest rallying cry for opponents of the Endangered Species Act.

EDITORIAL, *NEW YORK TIMES*

I knew I'd arrived at the Aransas National Wildlife Refuge when I pulled up to the visitor center and spotted two white-tailed deer grazing in a clearing. They soon were joined by two more deer, which watched nonchalantly as I got out of my car and headed inside. They seemed to know that they're safe on this 115,000-acre refuge, created in 1937 to protect the endangered whooping cranes.

SCOTT WILLIAMS, "ARANSAS OFFERS REFUGE FROM CITY LIFE"

4 Here are two long though fairly readable sentences by professional authors. How would you break them up to make them more readable without destroying their unity?

When Ben Jonson was a small boy, his tutor, William Camden, persuaded him of the virtue of keeping a commonplace book: pages where an ardent reader might copy down passages that especially pleased him, preserving sentences that seemed particularly apt or wise or rightly formed and that would, because they were written afresh in a new place, and in a context of favor, be better remembered, as if they were being set down at the same time in the memory of the mind.

WILLIAM H. GASS, "IN DEFENSE OF THE BOOK"

Blue and white canopied water taxis glide through the harbor, allowing passengers to embark and alight at the attractions that dot the waterfront: not only the glass-enclosed shopping pavilions and the Aquarium, but the kid-friendly Maryland Science Center (Imax theatre and hands-on displays galore) and the oddly provocative American Visionary Art Museum (where the displays of multimedia constructions by self-taught artists range from the striking to the bizarre) as well.

DIANE COLE, "HOW DOWDY OLD BALTIMORE TURNED FASHIONABLE"

5 Working with two or three other students in a group, discuss how you might revise the following passages to get rid of biased language:

The artist must follow his own intuition if he is to do lasting work, whether he is a painter or a sculptor. The man who tries to imitate what is currently chic will not make his mark on the culture.

The nurse who wants to work with the day-to-day patients in a hospital will often find that she has been replaced by nurses' aides because the hospital administrator has been forced to cut his expenses.

Policemen, teachers, and mailmen are often well paid in large cities that have strong public employee unions.

One can depend on good restaurants in Cincinnati because many Italians and Germans settled there.

As a 6-foot 8-inch African American, Jarvis will probably be going to college on a basketball scholarship.

The editor of an online magazine to be launched next year is a gay man with wide experience in magazine publishing and television talk shows.

Those girls have been playing bridge together once a week for at least twenty-five years.

Although the photographer has passed her seventy-fifth birthday, she still travels and does outstanding work.

FOR WRITING

Choose one of the writing assignments in this section and, before writing, complete an analysis of your readers. Include the analysis when you submit the assignment. Your analysis should answer the following:

Who are your readers?

What questions do they want answered?

What is your persona in this piece of writing?

What is your goal in writing?

What characteristics of the audience do you need to keep in mind in order to hold their attention?

1 You have a part-time job as restaurant critic for your local newspaper, and you specialize in reviews of restaurants that attract both students and faculty from your institution. Write a review of no more than 500 words (two double-spaced pages) in which you focus on food quality, atmosphere, and the service you received. Keep a moderate tone and an informal style. Be sure to mention price ranges and specialties.

2 The board of trustees is holding a hearing to help decide whether to tear down and replace low-rent student housing that was fashioned thirty years ago out of buildings at a local Air Force base that was closed down. The housing is unsightly and needs repairs; some trustees believe it may be unsafe. If it is torn down, however, there will be no low-cost student housing available close to campus for at least two years, and the housing that would replace it would rent for at least 50 percent more.

As spokesperson for the married students who are now living in the housing, prepare a ten-minute talk (no more than 750 words) against tearing down the housing. Be sure to propose some alternative solution. In the proposal suggest what measures the college might take to improve the current buildings or where substitute housing might be located and how it could be financed.

3 A charitable organization in your city called The New Career Closet seeks donations of women's clothes appropriate for first-time women job seekers who have finished a city-sponsored business training program and will be going out on job interviews. You have offered to create a Web site for the organization to help it publicize its service to both potential donors and possible recipients of such clothing. Remember, you have two audiences here: women who can donate such garments, and women who seek a reliable source for tasteful business apparel. Write copy of no more than 350 words for the Web site.

Crafting Paragraphs

8

○ *Create paragraphs that will make*
life easier for your readers.

Most of us seem to think naturally in sentences. We don't, however, think in paragraphs. They are artificial divisions created by writers—or sometimes editors—because readers need them. They break writing into chunks so that readers can process and absorb what they're reading without bogging down and having to reread. And since most of us don't have editors to help us, we have to learn paragraphing on our own. How does one do that? Partly through practice and partly through developing a keen sense of audience. The more conscious you are of your audience, the better you will become at crafting paragraphs.

You can look at paragraphing from two points of view: *external* and *internal*. When you create paragraphs from an external point of view, you're paragraphing for appearance. When you create paragraphs from an internal point of view, you're paragraphing for unity and coherence. Let's consider the external view first.

THE EXTERNAL VIEW OF PARAGRAPHING

A printed page or computer screen has its own "body language" that sends signals to readers before they ever read a word, and paragraph length strongly affects the impression readers get. Think about your response when you face a page of solid, unbroken print, whether in a book, in an article, or online. Don't the unbroken paragraphs look hard to read and discourage you before you ever get started? Although you may have to read the material anyway, you're not going to be happy about the task. If the writer had crafted shorter paragraphs and been careful to leave good margins and ample white space around the print, almost certainly you would have been more receptive to his or her message.

Of course, the terms *long* and *short* paragraphs are relative, but as a rule of thumb, let's say a short paragraph is from three to six sentences of medium length and doesn't take up more than one-third of a regular page. A paragraph of eight to ten medium-length sentences that takes up two-thirds or more of a page is definitely long, and you should look for places where you could break it. We'll give you some guidelines for finding such places in the next section.

Professional writers who have a strong sense of their audience also make paragraphing decisions on the basis of what they know about their readers. If they're writing for a broad audience of casual readers who usually read quickly—say, the readers of *Parade* magazine—they will write shorter paragraphs than they would for a smaller audience of skilled readers, such as the readers of *Scientific American.* They will also write shorter paragraphs when they're writing for young readers or for a newspaper where the writing will appear in columns. So think about who your readers are when you decide how long your paragraphs should be.

● SOME GUIDELINES FOR BREAKING PARAGRAPHS

You may not want to worry about paragraph length until you're revising and thinking how your document is going to look. That's fine—concerns about appearance can wait. But we think it's useful to develop an awareness about length as you draft your paragraphs and to get into the habit of looking for logical places to break them.

The conventional wisdom about paragraphing is that each paragraph develops a single idea, so you start a new paragraph when you come to a new idea. That plan works well when you're making a series of points and can develop each point as a paragraph. But it's not always easy to put the one-idea, one-paragraph rule into practice. Sometimes it's hard to tell when you come to a new idea, and sometimes an idea is too complex to be developed in a single paragraph. Thus it's useful to know some natural dividing places you can use for breaking up paragraphs. Here are some clues:

NATURAL DIVISION POINTS FOR BREAKING PARAGRAPHS

○ *A shift in time.* Look for sentences beginning with words like *first, next, formerly,* or *at that time.*

○ *A shift in place.* Look for sentences beginning with words like *elsewhere* or *in the meantime.*

○ *A shift showing contrast.* Look for sentences beginning with words like *however, on the other hand,* or *nevertheless.*

○ *A shift in emphasis.* Look for sentences beginning with terms like *if that happens, in spite of, another possibility,* or *not only.*

○ *A shift signaling additional information.* Look for sentences that begin with terms like *moreover, in addition,* or *besides.*

There are no firm rules on these matters. You just have to use your judgment and ask yourself, "Should I break up this piece of writing, and if so, how should I do it?" Let's look at two examples of paragraphs that are readable but that we think could be broken into more manageable chunks and still be unified. We've marked our proposed divisions by double slashes. In the first quotation, notice that we divided the paragraph before *for instance* and again when we came to a new example introduced by *also*:

> There is a tendency to exaggerate the rate at which our lives will be changed by technology. We still have a whole year to go before 2001, but I doubt that Arthur C. Clarke's vision of commercial flights to the moon is going to come true by then. Individual technologies reach plateaus beyond which further improvement is not worthwhile. // For instance, the experience of riding in commercial aircraft has not materially changed since the introduction of the Boeing 707, more than forty years ago. (The Concorde is an exception that proves the rule; it has never paid for the cost of its development.) Computer technology has not yet reached its plateau, but it will—probably when the miniaturization of the solid-state devices runs into the limits imposed by the state of the finite size of individual atoms. // Successful technologies also tend to be self-limiting once they become available to the general population. I doubt that it is possible to cross Manhattan from the East River to the Hudson River faster by automobile today than it was by horse-drawn streetcar a century ago. The Internet is already beginning to show the effects of overcrowding. I tremble at the thought of two billion air-conditioners in a future China and India, each adding its exhaust heat to the earth's atmosphere.

STEVEN WEINBERG, "FIVE AND A HALF UTOPIAS," JANUARY 2000

In the next example, we suggest that the author could have created new paragraphs at places where she introduced new examples to illustrate her main idea:

> Arranged marriage looks somewhat different from the point of view of the bride and her family. Arranged marriages continue to be preferred, even among the more educated, Westernized sections of the Indian population. Many young women from these families still go along, more or less willingly, with the practice, and also with the specific choices of their families. Young women do get excited about the prospects of their marriage, but there is an ambivalence and increasing uncertainty, as the bride contemplates leaving the comfort and familiarity of her own home, where as a "temporary guest" she has often been indulged, to live among strangers. // Even in the best situation she now comes under the increased scrutiny of her husband's family. How she dresses, how she behaves, how she gets along with others, where she goes, how she spends her time, her domestic abilities—all of this and much more—will be observed and commented on by a whole new set of relations. Her interaction with her family of birth will be monitored and curtailed considerably. // Not only will she leave their home, but with increasing geographic mobility, she may also live very far from them, perhaps even on another continent. Too much expression of her fondness for her family, or her desire to visit them, may be interpreted as an inability to adjust to her new family, and may become a source of conflict. In an arranged marriage, the burden of adjustment is clearly heavier for a woman than for a man. And that is in the best of circumstances.
>
> SERENA NANDA, "ARRANGING A MARRIAGE IN INDIA"

Remember, however, that you shouldn't chop up paragraphs arbitrarily just for the sake of appearance. By definition, a paragraph should state an idea and develop it, so you need as many sentences as it takes to do that. Occasionally you may write one-sentence paragraphs for emphasis, but use them sparingly and only when you have a specific reason for doing so. Here's an effective example:

> At the Senior Ball, teenagers in the ballroom of the Beverly Hills Hotel, beautiful teenagers in black tie and gowns, try very hard not to look like teenagers. But on the other hand, it is very important not to look like one's parents.
>
> The balancing act trick of American adolescence is to stand in-between—to be neither a child nor an adult.
>
> RICHARD RODRIGUEZ, "GROWING UP IN LOS ANGELES"

When experienced writers start writing, almost certainly they don't stop to think how they're going to organize their paragraphs. They've been using a variety of patterns for so long that they can use them without thinking how they work. But writers who are less experienced can profit by reviewing these common paragraph patterns and considering how they might use them. We offer you several of those patterns in this section and give examples that may be helpful.

Experienced writers do think about how well their paragraphs stick together and whether they focus on one point. They also work to see that sentences follow each other in logical order, each one supporting or advancing the point of the previous sentence. They're always aware that a paragraph needs to be unified.

How can a writer achieve this unity? Most of us do it by employing some version of a common pattern; that is, we start with a statement or question and follow through with support for the statement or answers to the question. Here are some typical variations on that pattern. In each example the statement or question is italicized.

● **GENERALIZATION WITH SUPPORTING DETAILS**

Perhaps the most typical way to begin a paragraph is to make a general statement and follow it up with details that support it. Here each sentence after the first provides relevant details:

> *Every big plantation was a fiefdom; the small hamlets that dot the map of the [Mississippi] Delta were mostly plantation headquarters rather than conventional towns.* Sharecroppers traded at a plantation-owned commissary, often in scrip rather than money. They prayed at plantation-owned Baptist churches. Their children walked, sometimes miles, to plantation-owned schools, usually one- or two-room buildings without heating or plumbing. Education ended with the eighth grade and was extremely casual until then. [. . .] The textbooks were hand-me-downs from the white schools. The planter could and did shut down schools whenever there was work to be done in the fields. [. . .] Many sharecroppers remember going to school only when it rained.
>
> NICHOLAS LEMANN, *THE PROMISED LAND*

Notice the use of questions in this next paragraph—first to start the whole topic off, and then to move the discussion deeper:

> *What's the difference between prison and college?* They both prescribe your behavior for a given period of time. They both allow you to read books and develop your writing. They both give you time to think and time with your peers to talk about issues. But four years of prison doesn't give you a passport to greater opportunities. Most likely that time only gives you greater knowledge of how to get back in. Four years of college gives you an opportunity not only to lift yourself but to serve your people effectively. What's the difference when you are called a nigger in college from when you are called a nigger in jail? In college you can, although I admit with effort, follow procedures to have those students who called you nigger kicked out or suspended. You can bring issues to public attention without risking your life. But mostly, college is and always has been the future. We, neither less nor more than other people, need knowledge. There are discomforts attached to attending predominantly white colleges, though no more so than living in a racist world.
>
> NIKKI GIOVANNI, "CAMPUS RACISM 101"

● STATEMENT AND ILLUSTRATION

Often a paragraph will begin with a general statement which is then illustrated by subsequent sentences. Here, all of the sentences after the first illustrate ways the author is hated by the Burmese:

> *In Moulmein, in lower Burma, I was hated by large numbers of people—the only time in my life that I have ever been important enough for this to happen to me.* I was subdivisional police officer of the town, and in an aimless, petty kind of way anti-European feeling was very bitter. No one had the guts to raise a riot, but if a European woman went through the bazaars alone somebody would probably spit betel juice over her dress. As a police officer I was an obvious target and was baited whenever it seemed safe to do so. When a nimble Burman tripped me up on the football field and the referee (another Burman) looked the other way, the crowd yelled with hideous laughter. This happened more than once. In the end the sneering yellow faces of young men that met me everywhere, the insult hooted after me when I was at a safe distance, got badly on my nerves. The young Buddhist monks were the worst of all. There were sev-

eral thousands of them in the town and none seemed to have anything to do except to stand on street corners and jeer at Europeans.

GEORGE ORWELL, "SHOOTING AN ELEPHANT"

● ASSERTION AND EXPLANATION

Another technique is for the first sentence to make an assertion and then for subsequent sentences to explain just what the assertion means:

> "The book business was an elitist, standoffish institution," [Barnes & Noble executive] Len Riggio told Business Week in 1998. "I liberated it from that." Riggio's critics have mocked his populist pose, but it should be taken seriously. Before the appearance of the chains, a relatively highbrow, urban clientele shopped at the independents, and a relatively lowbrow, largely regional one bought mass-market titles at supermarkets, price clubs, and drugstores. Now, thanks to the chains and to Internet sales, the vast territory between the two extremes has been bridged. Elitists may carp, but the truth is they are no longer quite so elite. These days shoppers in Buford, Georgia, and Rapid City, South Dakota, can pick up important titles such as Norman Cantor's Inventing the Middle Ages, Eugene Genovese's Roll, Jordan, Roll, and Andrew Motion's biography of John Keats—titles that are neither popular nor newly published—at their local Borders.

BROOKE ALLEN, "TWO—MAKE THAT THREE—CHEERS FOR THE CHAIN BOOKSTORES"

So writers can choose several different ways to follow the basic statement and follow-through pattern for creating paragraphs. Just remember that every sentence after the first must expand on or respond to the opening sentence. No detours.

● OTHER COMMON PARAGRAPH PATTERNS

You can also use several other paragraph patterns:

Reasoning from evidence
Assertion and support
Cause and effect
Comparison and contrast
Classification

Narration

Process

In the sections that follow, you'll find examples of each, along with brief commentaries. Again, the topic sentences in each are italicized.

REASONING FROM EVIDENCE

Reasoning from evidence is a particularly useful pattern when you're writing an argument. It's typical of the pattern trial lawyers use before juries. For example:

> [*Tigers*] *are not idle predators; when they kill, they kill to eat.* Even a well-fed tiger in a zoo keeps his vestigial repertoire of hunting behaviors intact. [. . .] In the zoo, tigers will stalk birds that land in their habitats, and they grow more alert than most people would care to realize when children pass before their gaze. Though stories of man-eating tigers have been extravagantly embellished over the centuries, the existence of such creatures is not legendary. In the Sunderbans, the vast delta region that spans the border of India and Bangladesh, more than four hundred people have been killed by tigers in the last decade. So many fishermen and honey collectors have been carried off that a few years ago officials at the Sunderbans tiger preserve began stationing electrified dummies around the park to encourage the tigers to seek other prey. One percent of all tigers, according to a German biologist who studied them in the Sunderbans, are "dedicated" man-eaters: when they go hunting, they're after people. Up to a third of all tigers will kill and eat a human if they come across one, but they don't make a special effort to do so.
>
> **STEPHEN HARRIGAN, "THE TIGER IS GOD"**

ASSERTION AND SUPPORT

Assertion and support is a useful pattern when you want readers to accept the reasoning upon which you base a claim. Here a feminist scholar explains in the introduction to a book about the six wives of Henry VIII why she has chosen to write about these women as representative of upper-class women in Tudor England:

> *Any look at women in Tudor England invariably begins with the wives of Henry VIII.* There are other equally engaging women—equally brave, equally tragic, equally intelligent, equally victimized, equally triumphant—

but because of Henry's glamorously bizarre behavior, those six women dominate our perception of the era's women. They hover in our imagination around the king like faithful satellites orbiting a splendid sun, and the fact that on scrutiny the sun reveals itself as a great, empty mass of hot air does little to lessen the fascination. Henry VIII's monstrous egotism and dynastic misfortune, occurring at a time when Europe was ripe for religious revolution, drew into history six women who were dramatically different from the man who controlled their destinies, and dramatically different from each other. Each became, for varying degrees of time, the most powerful woman in England; each lost that position because she was at the mercy of the most powerful *man* in the land.

KAREN LINDSEY, *DIVORCED, BEHEADED, SURVIVED*

CAUSE AND EFFECT

A cause-and-effect paragraph illustrates one of people's most common thought patterns. You can state the effect first and then follow through by giving the causes, as the next paragraph does, or you can list the causes first and conclude with the effect:

> *Many cultural circumstances worked against the likelihood of sexual satisfaction within Victorian marriages.* The inflexible taboo on pre-marital sex for middle-class women meant, among other things, that it was impossible to determine sexual compatibility before marriage. The law then made the wife the absolute property of her husband, and sexual performance one of her duties. Imagine a young woman married to a man she finds physically repulsive. She is in the position of being raped nightly—and within the law's consent. The legendary Victorian advice about sex, "Lie back and think of England," may be seen as not entirely comical if we realize that in many cases a distaste for sex developed from a distaste for the first sexual partner and from sexual performance that was essentially forced. In addition, the absence of birth control made it impossible to separate sex from its reproductive function, so that to be sexually active meant also the discomforts of pregnancy, the pain of childbirth, and the burden of children.

PHYLLIS ROSE, *PARALLEL LIVES*

COMPARISON AND CONTRAST

We all use comparison and contrast almost automatically to highlight the differences or likenesses between two things. You can draw the contrasts within one paragraph or make the comparison with alternating paragraphs. Here are two examples. In the first, a movie critic and essayist compares values in our time with those of ancient Greek society. In the second, an Arab American woman compares her taste with her brother's by describing their separate homes in separate paragraphs.

> The American reader [of The Iliad] comes from a society that is nominally ethical. Our legal and administrative system, our presidential utterances, our popular culture, in which TV policemen rarely fail to care for the victims of crime, are swathed in concern. Since many Americans believe that our society is actually indifferent to hardship, it is no surprise that irony and cynicism barnacle our attitudes toward public life. By contrast, the Greek view was savage, but it was offered without hypocrisy. Accepting death in battle as inevitable, the Greek and Trojan aristocrats of The Iliad experience the world not as pleasant or unpleasant, or as good and evil, but as glorious or shameful. Homer offers a noble rather than an ethical conception of life. You are not good or bad. You are strong or weak, beautiful or ugly, conquering or vanquished, favored by the gods or cursed.
>
> DAVID DENBY, "DOES HOMER HAVE LEGS?"

> My brother's house smells of fresh paint and packaging—those foam bubbles and peanuts that come in big boxes. It smells like carpet no one has ever stepped on. I cannot imagine the bravado of a white carpet. My brother prefers if you remove your shoes at his front door. So do I, but no one ever does it in our house.
>
> We have dusty wooden floors and raggedy little rugs from Turkey and Libya. We have throw rugs hand-knotted in Appalachia in 1968. We have a worn Oriental carpet that once belonged to my friend's reclusive father, a famous science fiction writer. [. . .] Our house smells of incense and grandmothers' attics in Illinois in the 1950s and vaguely sweetened shelf paper pressed into drawers.
>
> NAOMI SHIHAB NYE, "MY BROTHER'S HOUSE"

CLASSIFICATION

You can craft paragraphs in which you classify your ideas by categories. For example:

> Complaints about the treatment of women on-line fall into three categories: that women are subjected to excessive, unwanted sexual attention, that the prevailing style of on-line discussion turns women off, and that women are singled out by male participants for exceptionally dismissive or hostile treatment. In making these assertions, the Newsweek article and other sto-

ries on the issue do echo grievances that some on-line women have made for years. And, without a doubt, people have encountered sexual come-ons, aggressive debating tactics, and ad hominem attacks on the Net. However, individual users interpret such events in widely different ways, and to generalize from those interpretations to describe the experiences of women and men as a whole is a rash leap indeed.

LAURA MILLER, "WOMEN AND CHILDREN FIRST: GENDER AND THE SETTLING OF THE ELECTRONIC FRONTIER"

NARRATION

Often you can use a narrative paragraph to illustrate a point that you're making. It can also enliven your writing by adding a visual or personal element. This little story about email does that:

I discovered just how portable my e-mail was when a thief crept into my house and walked off with my computer. One day I had been happily communicating with the entire world, the next I was reduced to virtual silence. My anxiety at the loss of my equipment was exacerbated by my sense of all the messages I was missing. I had become dependent on my daily fix, and the burglar, as if guessing at this aspect of my psychology, had even cut the phone wire that led into the computer—a symbolic act, easily remedied by the purchase of a new wire, but one that drove home for me my feeling of violent interruption. "I feel as if I'm hemorrhaging information," I told my husband. But the information was only the half of it. All the little pieces of me that I had been feeding into cyberspace were loosed into the world, never to return.

WENDY LESSER, "THE CONVERSION"

PROCESS

Paragraphs describing a process can make a piece of writing more concrete by describing how something is done. Here a writer describes the process she goes through when she begins to write a story:

As much as I can break down the process of writing stories, I would say that this is how it begins, I find a detail or image or character or incident or cluster of events. A certain luminosity surrounds them. I find myself attracted. I come forward. I pick it up, turn it around, begin to ask questions, and spend hours and weeks and months and years trying to answer them.

JULIA ALVAREZ, "GROUNDS FOR FICTION"

Chapter 5 makes several suggestions about patterns you might use for opening paragraphs. They're important because they serve as the lead that pulls your reader into your essay. As such, they need to do several things:

◯ Introduce you to your readers and establish a first impression.

◯ Announce your topic.

◯ Set the tone for your writing.

◯ Let your readers know what to expect.

Because these are crucial functions, it's worth investing time and thought in crafting a powerful opening paragraph before you submit your final effort. An engaging and forceful opener will get you off to a strong start with your readers; a poor one handicaps you from the beginning. But remember that you don't have to get your opener right the first time. An effective opening paragraph may well take shape only with your fourth or fifth draft. Often you can't even write a good first paragraph until you're fairly well satisfied with the rest of your piece. When you do get to that point, you'll do well to come back and review this section to ensure that your opener does what it needs to do.

Here are two strong opening paragraphs from professional writers. The first is by Michael Dorris, who wrote both fiction and nonfiction:

> My father, a career army officer, was twenty-seven when he was killed, and as a result, I can't help but take war personally. Over the years his image has coalesced for me as an amalgam of familiar anecdotes: a dashing mixed-blood man from the Northwest who, improbably, could do the rhumba; a soldier who regularly had his uniform altered by a tailor so it would fit better; a date, according to my mother, who "knew how to order" in a restaurant; the person whom, in certain lights and to some people, I resemble. He is the compromise of his quirkier qualities, indistinct, better remembered for his death—my grandmother still wears a gold star on her coat—than for his brief life.
>
> MICHAEL DORRIS, "FATHER'S DAY"

The author of the second paragraph, an essayist and fiction writer, opens an engaging personal essay about working in a bakery when he was a fledgling writer trying to support himself:

I like bagels, but I have never felt in their thrall. I never craved them, never viewed them as something special, out of the ordinary, or exotic. They were a fact of life, personified, when I was growing up, by a local store that baked and sold them, B & T Bagels, on Eightieth Street and Broadway, which was open twenty-four hours a day, seven days a week. Besides selling bagels, the store performed a kind of community service by perfuming the air in its vicinity with the smell of baking bread, which gave the chaotic stretch of Broadway north of Seventy-ninth Street a neighborly, friendly feel. There is something about the smell of baking bread, in its diffuse form, that civilizes people.

THOMAS BELLER, "PORTRAIT OF THE BAGEL AS A YOUNG MAN"

As different as these paragraphs are—one dealing with a grand universal theme and the other with the aroma of baking bread—both do just what opening paragraphs are supposed to do. They engage readers' attention, they help readers anticipate what is to come, and they forecast what the tone and style of the piece will be.

● ADAPTING OPENING PARAGRAPHS TO AUDIENCE AND PURPOSE

You'll want to vary your openers according to the kind of writing you're doing. Your good sense should tell you that a provocative first sentence that might be just right for an opinion column or an article posted on *Salon* won't do for a business report, a technical paper, or a literary analysis.

When you're writing a straightforward, informative paper for specific readers who have specific expectations, announce your topic directly in the first few sentences. In this situation, your first concern should be not to waste your readers' time—they're often busy, impatient people who want to read efficiently and learn from the piece. For example, the primary audience for Eleanor Hennessy's paper about the painter Artemisia Gentileschi is the instructor and other students in a women's studies course. The author wants her first paragraph to announce her topic, state her thesis, and briefly indicate how she's going to develop the thesis.

Hennessy's first opening, written after several false starts, looked like this:

Artemisia Gentileschi, a remarkable painter of seventeenth-century Italy, defied every norm of her era—artistic, social, economic, and sexual—to become one of the best-known painters of her day. To women art historians of the twenty-first century, she has become an icon whose work disproves the allegation that there have been no great women artists. Her career gives us insight into the obstacles women painters faced in her time, but also into ways in which woman artists were sometimes able to circumvent constraints all women endured in that era.

The paragraph worked to get Hennessy started on the paper, and the first sentence meets her instructor's requirement for a thesis sentence. The paragraph also lets her readers know what to anticipate from the paper. As she neared the end of the paper, however, Hennessy realized that she hadn't included anything about other women artists of the era, partly because she didn't have space but mostly because she had found Gentileschi so interesting that she wanted to focus entirely on her. So after she finished her second draft she rewrote the opening paragraph:

Artemisia Gentileschi, a talented painter in seventeenth-century Italy, defied every norm of her time—artistic, social, economic, and sexual—to emerge as one of the most successful artists of her era. To women art historians in the twenty-first century, she is a hero whose work disproves the allegation that there have been no great women artists. But Gentileschi's story also appeals to today's women in ways that go well beyond the specialized world of art history. She has become a feminist icon because of her courage, her self-confidence, her determination, and her proud defiance in refusing to bow to the censure of a hostile and judgmental society. She would have been an amazing woman in any time and place; for her to have triumphed as she did in the sexist, repressive culture of seventeenth-century Italy seems no less than a miracle.

Notice that this opening is more tightly focused, substituting the specific word *talented* for the vaguer one *remarkable*, and finishes with a sentence that leads directly into the topic of the next paragraph.

In a book that describes a scientific experiment for the general reader, the science writer Jonathan Weiner starts an account of two biologists working in the Galápagos Islands with this factual description that gives his reader essential details:

There are two kinds of shorelines in the [Galápagos] islands, the visible and the invisible.

The visible shores are the black broken rocks and white broken waves where volcanoes rise out of the Pacific. They are the borders of the air, and the lava, wave-gnawed rings around the summits that have given Darwin's finches their homes in the middle of nowhere. These shores are defined simply by the level of the sea.

The invisible shores are the borders between the birds themselves. These shores are more intricate. They are defined by the secret codes and unwritten rules that wrap each of the thirteen Galápagos finches in a kind of self-invented isolation. These boundaries hold each species apart from the rest [. . .] so that even though seven or eight may share the same volcanic summit, feed together in mixed flocks, scrape the same cinders for the same seeds, they still breed as much apart as if they were themselves an archipelago of enchanted islands.

JONATHAN WEINER, *THE BEAK OF THE FINCH*

WRESTLING WITH CLOSING PARAGRAPHS

Conclusions are hard. Even experienced writers occasionally have trouble tying up the threads of their arguments and bringing their ideas to a conclusion without lapsing into clichés or obvious comments. Many of us struggle with conclusions no matter how long we've been writing.

For some writing tasks, endings are almost prescribed, and you can find models that will help you. For example, for technical and business reports, case studies, or grant proposals, the writer is expected to summarize the findings and, if appropriate, make recommendations. Such straightforward endings aren't too hard to write.

In other kinds of writing, such as an argument or an analysis, the writer often needs to restate the main ideas or claims he or she made earlier in order to refresh the reader's memory. Conclusions of this kind are patterned on the summations lawyers make for juries: they restate the principal claims, they summarize the evidence, and when appropriate, they make a recommendation.

● OTHER KINDS OF CONCLUSIONS

Beyond these rather by-the-numbers conclusions, we can't offer much solid advice about the best way to end an essay. In the hundreds of essays we've looked at, we've found dozens of good ways to conclude. So it's not easy to generalize. Nevertheless, we have three suggestions that may be helpful.

David Brooks summarizes his previously stated main points in concluding a section about the rise of the new intellectual class in his book *Bobos in Paradise:*

> Marx told us that classes inevitably conflict, but sometimes they just blur. The values of the bourgeois mainstream culture and the values of the 1960s counterculture have merged. That culture war has ended, at least within the educated class. In its place that class has created a third culture, which is a reconciliation between the previous two. The educated elites didn't set out to create this reconciliation. It is the product of millions of in-dividual efforts to have it both ways. But it is now the dominant tone of our age. In the resolution between the culture and the counterculture, it is im-possible to tell who has co-opted whom, because in reality the bohemians and the bourgeois co-opted each other. They emerge from this process as bourgeois bohemians, or Bobos.
>
> **DAVID BROOKS, *BOBOS IN PARADISE***

FINISH WITH A RECOMMENDATION

Cathy Young, in her essay "Keeping Women Weak," rejects the kind of feminism that wants to overprotect women and portray them as victims: Her last paragraph recommends an alternative:

> We need a "Third Wave" feminism that rejects the excesses of the gender fanatics and sentimental traditionalism of the Phyllis Schlaflys, one that does not seek special protection for women and does not view us as too socially disadvantaged to take care of ourselves. Because on the path that feminism has taken in the last few years, we are allowing ourselves to be treated as frail, helpless little things—by our would-be liberators.
>
> **CATHY YOUNG, "KEEPING WOMEN WEAK"**

TIE THE LAST PARAGRAPH TO THE FIRST PARAGRAPH

You can give your readers a sense of closure and wrap up your essay by plucking an image or reference from your opening paragraph and using it in your last paragraph. Barbara Kingsolver does this in an essay that is her tribute to a librarian:

A librarian named Miss Truman Richey snatched me from the jaws of ruin, and it's too late now to thank her. I'm not the first person to notice that we rarely get around to thanking those who've helped us most. Salvation is such a heady thing the temptation is to dance gasping on the shore, shouting that we're still alive, till our forgotten savior has long since gone under. Or else sit quietly, sideswiped and embarrassed, mumbling that we really did know pretty much how to swim. But now that I see the wreck that could have been, without Miss Richey, I'm of a fearsome mind to throw my arms around every living librarian who crosses my path, on behalf of the souls they never knew they saved.

My thanks to Doris Lessing and William Saroyan and Miss Truman Richey. And every other wise teacher who may ever save a surly soul like mine.

BARBARA KINGSOLVER, "HOW MR. DEWEY DECIMAL SAVED MY LIFE"

Eleanor Hennessy used this strategy in writing the final paragraph of her essay on Artemisia Gentileschi, picking up on the theme of overcoming obstacles that she had opened with. Here is her original paragraph:

It is gratifying to know that a woman artist whose genius was obscured for centuries by a male-dominated profession has finally received the recognition she deserves. But it is even more satisfying for a woman student today to learn the story of this magnificent woman who more than three centuries ago refused to accept the negative judgments of a narrow-minded and biased society and went on to prove her talent and succeed in a hostile world. Artemisia Gentileschi's story should inspire every young woman of today who has become discouraged as she fights against odds to establish herself.

When Hennessy reread the paragraph as she was revising, it sounded adequate but bland, particularly the last sentence. She drafted two more versions before she came up with a much stronger version that gives more important details. She took a chance by finishing an academic paper with an unconventional last sentence, but she did so to emphasize her admiration for her subject. Here is the revised paragraph:

Gentileschi has finally achieved the recognition she deserves only because in the 1970s and 1980s a handful of women art historians challenged the assumptions of their discipline, one that had never taken women artists seriously. Two of those historians, Rozsika Parker and Griselda Pollock, say, "Modern art history [. . .] identifies women artists as inevitably and naturally artists of lesser talent and no historical significance." Parker, Pollock, and others—notably Germaine Greer—did the research necessary to bring to light the paintings that demonstrate Gentileschi's genius, and to confirm her stature in her own day. Mary Garrard, in her 1989 biography, has supplemented those treasures by giving us the story of this amazing woman who went against the grain of her culture to triumph over obstacles that women of today can scarcely imagine. It's an awesome story to which one can only say, Yes! Ain't that a woman!

Q *My high school teachers acted as if "the paragraph" was carved in stone. Yet your chapter seems to suggest that a paragraph is a fairly arbitrary unit—even that the same text could be paragraphed one way in a newspaper article and another way for an academic report. What's up with that?*

A Perhaps you have oversimplified what your high school teachers said. But beyond that, you'll be doing more kinds of writing in college than you did in high school. As one looks at different kinds of writing, the variations among them become more obvious, and we notice, for examples, that newspapers usually use shorter paragraphs than academic papers, that Web pages use shorter paragraphs and more lists, and that technical reports sometimes use really long paragraphs (which we still think is bad writing, but it's pretty common in that genre). The important thing, then, is to write paragraphs that are appropriate for the kind of writing you're doing.

FOR PRACTICE

❶ Read over the following paragraph to see where you think it could be broken into shorter paragraphs:

In outline it was a good plan, but it quite failed to take into account the mentality of buzzards. As soon as they were wired to the tree they all began to try and fly away. The wires prevented that, of course, but did not prevent them from falling off the limbs, where they dangled upside down, wings flapping, nether parts exposed. It is hard to imagine anything less likely to beguile a movie-going audience than a tree full of dangling buzzards. Everyone agreed it was unaesthetic. The buzzards were righted, but they tried again, and with each try their humiliation deepened. Finally they abandoned their effort to fly away and resigned themselves to life on the tree. Their resignation was so complete that when the scene was readied and the time came for them to fly, they refused. They had had enough of ignomiy; better to wait on the limb indefinitely. Buzzards are not without patience. Profanity, firecrackers, and even a shotgun full of rock salt failed to move them. I'm told that, in desperation, a bird man was flown in from L.A. to teach the sulky bastards how to fly. The whole experience left everyone touchy. A day or so later, looking at the pictures again, I noticed a further provocative detail. The dead heifer that figured so prominently in the scene was quite clearly a steer. When I pointed this out to the still photographers, they just shrugged. A steer was close enough, after all they were both essentially cows. "In essence, it's a cow," one said moodily. No one wanted those buzzards back again.

LARRY MCMURTRY, "HERE'S HUD IN YOUR EYE"

2 What kind of follow-through in the rest of the paragraph would readers expect after reading the following opening sentences:

It is hard to see why anyone would think that religion is a cure for the world's problems.

STEVEN WEINBERG

In twentieth-century America we place so much emphasis on romance that we barely notice the other essentials of marriage that include economics and child rearing.

ANNE ROIPHE

There are fair-weather friends and foul-weather friends, and we need both kinds in our lives, especially so because each is likely to absent himself rather abruptly when the wind shifts.

EDWARD HOAGLAND

3 Working with two or three other students, discuss what kind of paragraph you could write to follow through on each of these opening sentences. Then choose the one you find most interesting and draft a paragraph together to be shared with the rest of the class.

When enrolling in a college or university, students are often unaware how much student fees will add to the cost of their education.

The average American squanders water in ways that would be unthinkable in arid countries like Israel or Morocco.

While boys are usually less fashion-conscious than girls, many of them are certainly swayed by current trends in hairstyles and body ornament.

1 As a volunteer at a city clinic, you have been asked to write the copy for a brochure that will be available to patients who come to the clinic. Your supervisor wants the brochure to explain to young women who come in with problem pregnancies what options are open to them through the clinic and other organizations. She emphasizes that the brochure should use simple but neutral language and keep a positive tone. It should not exceed 600 words. Remember that brochure text is often set in narrow columns, so keep your paragraphs short.

2 Create a Web site for an animal rescue organization for which you want to recruit new members. It could be something like a group that finds homes with private owners for retired K-9 police dogs, an association that arranges adoptions for abandoned or abused weimaraners, or an organization that finds homes in the country for saddle horses that have been retired from riding stables. Explain your organization's goals, how it operates, what successes it has had, and what kinds of volunteers it needs. If you can, include a picture to enhance the appeal of your announcement.

3 Write an article for a weekly newspaper for retired citizens in your community. Your goal is to convince your readers that they would enjoy and benefit from buying a computer and connecting to the Internet. Work at crafting an opening paragraph that will catch your readers' interest but is not patronizing. In subsequent paragraphs, explain some advantages of email, what kinds of services the World Wide Web offers—travel discounts and bookstores, for example—and mention some of the kinds of chat groups or special interest sites they might enjoy.

This article will require some research, but don't overwhelm your readers with paragraphs that include too much information. Give some specific examples to illustrate your points. Estimate costs, including those of a monitor and printer and perhaps an additional phone line, and describe two or three servers they might sign up with and at what cost. Your article should not exceed 1,000 words.

Revising

9

▸ *Think of revising as a way to develop your writing rather than as a way to correct it.*

Most professional writers who care about doing good work see revision as an essential stage of their writing and plan on revising virtually everything they write. Often they expect to develop new ideas *through* the revising process. They count on revising to help them reach three goals:

❶ To generate additional ideas as they work
❷ To help them focus their ideas
❸ To help them polish and tighten their writing

When you see revising this way, as part of your creative process rather than as correcting your work, you'll probably feel less pressure as you write. Now a draft is just a draft, a work in progress, not something you have to make perfect. If you have suggestions from other readers, you can consider how to incorporate them into your draft.

AN OVERVIEW OF THE REVISION PROCESS

We see revising as a two-stage process. In the *large-scale* or *global* stage, you make substantial changes. You may

◗ Shift or narrow the focus of your writing.
◗ Redirect your writing to better suit your audience.

- Modify the central purpose of your writing.
- Make substantial cuts.
- Expand on some points.
- Reorganize your writing to change the emphasis.

In the *small-scale* or *local* stage, you make changes that affect style, tone, and unity but usually not content. You may

- Add examples, anecdotes, and more details.
- Cut excess words and phrases to eliminate clutter.
- Add graphics or illustrations as needed.
- Consider whether you can find stronger verbs.
- Improve transitions.
- Rearrange some words or phrases to improve style.
- Review and perhaps rewrite opening and closing paragraphs.

A PLAN FOR REVISING IN STAGES

When you have completed a reasonably good first draft and are ready to start revising, consider how important your piece of writing is to you. If it's a major project that is going to count heavily, allow yourself enough time for two more drafts, perhaps three. Careful revising takes a lot of time. Don't undercut yourself by procrastinating until the last minute and turning in work that isn't as well developed or carefully considered as it could be. We recommend the following two-stage process:

STAGE ONE: LARGE-SCALE REVISION

❶ *Remind yourself to stay with large-scale changes.* Don't get sidetracked by details or start working sentence by sentence.

❷ *Print out your draft and read it slowly, taking notes as you go.* What are the major strengths? What have you left out? What helpful comments have you received from others?

❸ *Look first at the central idea of your work.* Is your main idea clearly stated? Have you narrowed your topic to one you can do justice to?

④ *Define your audience and purpose.* What are your readers like? What questions will they have? Are you giving them the information they need? What do you want to accomplish? Have you done that?

⑤ *Review your claims and assertions.* Have you stated your claim or thesis early on? Have you developed your points?

⑥ *Review your organization.* Do you have a pattern that your readers can follow? Should you rearrange some information to help your readers follow your thesis more easily?

● **STAGE TWO: SMALL-SCALE CHANGES**

① *Read your revised draft over quickly.* Do you need more examples to illustrate your assertions? Would adding charts or graphs help to clarify some points?

② *Read your draft paragraph by paragraph.* Are some sentences long and rambling? Where can you cut? Do you have too many long sentences bunched together or a series of short choppy sentences? Where could you break up the long sentences? Where might you insert a short, crisp sentence or two to break up the monotony? Are there places where you could strengthen the writing by adding people to your sentences? (See pages 62–64 in Chapter 6.) Can you recast some sentences so that they have concrete subjects and active verbs? (See pages 64–67 in Chapter 6.)

③ *Look at your word choices.* Have you used strong, direct verbs? Have you shown people doing things? Can you rewrite to get rid of some clunky sentences and deadwood nouns?

④ *Check your writing for unity.* Have you written clear transitions between sentences? Between paragraphs? (See pages 75–78.) Have you followed through on your commitments to your readers and done what you told them you would do?

⑤ *Reread your opening and closing paragraphs.* Does your opening paragraph engage readers and forecast content? Does the last paragraph tie up all the threads effectively? If necessary, rewrite one or both paragraphs so they meet these criteria. Look at the sections on opening and closing paragraphs in Chapter 8, on paragraphing, to see how (and why) Eleanor Hennessy, the author of the model paper on Artemisia Gentileschi, revised the first and last paragraphs of her paper.

Working in a group with other writers can help you develop and revise your work. Such groups work well for several reasons:

◯ They give you a chance to write for an immediate audience other than your instructor.

◯ You get the chance to discuss your drafts with actual readers who respond to your work.

◯ You get immediate feedback as you develop your work.

◯ Working with other writers can bolster your confidence. You'll see firsthand that other writers also struggle and that most writers' first drafts are less than excellent.

◯ You'll get in the habit of working collaboratively, a skill you'll find valuable in many situations.

● SOME GUIDELINES FOR WORKING IN GROUPS

Many writers are initially shy about working in groups, particularly if they've never done it before. Sometimes they're reluctant to comment on each other's work, wondering, "Who am I to criticize other people's writing?" Our answer: "Don't think of responding to a draft as criticizing. Your role is that of an interested reader who may have good questions and some useful comments to offer." Some writers who are new to this process say they don't know what to look for. The response forms we show here should help on that score; we have found such response sheets useful for responding to both large- and small-scale drafts.

We believe it's useful to start group work with certain ground rules:

◯ Agree that no one starts out by apologizing or by making excuses. Drafts are first efforts, and apologies just waste time.

◯ For first drafts, focus on large-scale concerns. Save comments on language, spelling, and details for the second draft.

◯ Concentrate on what the writer is saying; try to understand main points and how the writer develops and supports them.

○ Avoid arguing with the writer about his or her ideas or opinions. Even if you disagree with them, your job is to respond to the writing, not to the opinions expressed.

We think it's useful to respond to a draft on a separate piece of paper rather than on the draft itself. On pages 119 and 120 you'll find response sheets designed for responding to both large- and small-scale drafts.

WHEN SHOULD YOU STOP REVISING?

Some writers and editors often say that all good writing is rewriting, and mostly they're right. But in revising your writing you will eventually come to a point of diminishing returns. If you have put substantial effort into turning out three drafts, we question whether, say, two more drafts would improve your writing in proportion to the amount of time they would take. Consider these points:

○ When you have read and reread something seven or eight times, you lose distance from it and can no longer see its flaws.

○ You may be worrying too much. Perhaps you would learn more by moving on to something new.

○ You run the risk of becoming a perfectionist who can't turn loose a piece of writing because it's not exactly right. Nothing is ever exactly right.

So do some cost accounting. Are you willing to write and rewrite and get feedback, then rewrite again to turn a piece of B work into A work? Would an extra six or eight hours be a good investment? Writers who ask themselves these questions may decide to settle for less than their best because they have other priorities. That's a legitimate and often sensible decision. But it's good to know that most competent writers can become excellent writers if they have the time, will, and energy to do so. And revising is the key.

You can also work on internalizing some sentence patterns that will strengthen your writing and cut down the time you spend on revising. We suggest developing these habits:

- Start your sentences with a subject that is a concrete noun.
- Put people in your sentences when you can.
- Avoid passive verbs unless they're absolutely necessary.
- Avoid long introductory clauses.
- Avoid strung-out noun phrases.
- Break your writing into readable chunks and short paragraphs.

The more you're aware of these elements of clear writing, the better your first drafts will be.

RESPONSE SHEET FOR LARGE-SCALE REVISION

Writer's name _____

Title of draft _____

Name of person responding to draft _____

1. What are the strong points of this draft? What works particularly well?

   _____

2. Who seems to be the audience?_____

   How well does the writer keep that audience in mind?_____

3. What does the writer's purpose seem to be?_____

   How could it be clarified?_____

4. How well is the draft focused on a central topic?_____

   Any suggestions for improvement? _____

5. What questions do you have for the writer? _____

6. Should the writer expand on any points?_____

   If so, which ones? _____

7. What two suggestions would you make for improving this draft?

   _____

8. What general comments do you have?_____

RESPONSE SHEET FOR SMALL-SCALE REVISION

Writer's name _____

Title of draft _____

Name of person responding to draft _____

1. What is especially effective about this draft?_____
    What specific details do you like? _____

2. How well does the writer keep his or her audience in mind?_____
    Suggestions?_____

3. Is this draft tightly focused?_____ Suggestions?_____

4. Where might additional examples add to the draft?_____

5. Where might visuals improve the paper?_____

6. Where might the draft be improved by cutting?_____

7. Might some word choices be improved? _____
    If so, where? _____

8. Might transitions be improved in places?_____
    If so, where?_____

9. How effective is the opening paragraph?_____ Suggestions?_____

10. How effective is the closing paragraph?_____ Suggestions?_____

11. General comments:_____

Q *What to do when I have to revise under a tight deadline? Are there ever times when you just* can't *revise?*

A Absolutely not. Bad writing costs too much, especially on the job. That's why it's worthwhile to develop writing habits that will serve you well when you're short on time. Two suggestions: (1) Always plan to do at least two drafts. Try to write the first one quickly but keep your audience in mind as you write. Why are they reading? What do they need to know? (2) Print out a copy and read it carefully, marking places where you *must* revise. Check for spelling and punctuation and run the spell checker to catch typos. Make your final copy. As this chapter has spelled out, there are certainly more revising activities you can carry out, but in a tight situation, these two steps are the bare minimum.

FOR PRACTICE

1 Exchange a paper or writing project that you turned in for a course with another person who's working on improving his or her writing. Using the large-scale revision sheet on page 119, go over each other's piece of writing and make suggestions for revision.

2 Make a similar exchange with another person. Using the small-scale revision sheet on page 120, go over each other's piece and make suggestions for revision.

Editing 10

▷ *You show your good manners as a writer when you edit carefully.*

Professional writers who want to make a good impression on their readers discipline themselves to edit their writing carefully. And careful editing does take discipline. It's tedious to go over a piece of writing line by line, consider word choice, eliminate repetition, verify spelling, and take care of other picky details. But when a lot depends on a piece of writing you're submitting, careful editing can make a difference. Leave yourself enough time to work through the necessary steps systematically.

SOME GUIDELINES FOR EDITING

- ▷ Review any specifications.
- ▷ Check for accuracy and inconsistencies.
- ▷ Check for awkwardly repeated words.
- ▷ Check for common errors.
- ▷ Check spelling and run your spell checker.
- ▷ See if you could improve your document's appearance.
- ▷ Proofread.

We believe that it's most efficient to work from a printed copy at this stage—it's too easy to overlook lapses and inconsistencies when you're scrolling copy up on a screen. And if you can, get another reader to look over your work, particularly if the document is important to you. That fresh eye can often spot mistakes or omissions that you may not see when you're reading something for the third or fourth time.

● REVIEW ANY SPECIFICATIONS FOR YOUR DOCUMENT

Before you start editing, check to see that you've done what you were asked to do. If it's an academic assignment, is a certain length specified? Does the assignment call for a certain type size and margins of a specific width? A separate title page? Running heads at the top of each page? Does the assignment ask for an annotated bibliography rather than just a "works cited" page? If the assignment is a brochure, have you covered all important points and included mailing address, email address, and phone number? If you're writing a column for a newsletter or newspaper, have you stayed within the word limit?

● CHECK DETAILS FOR ACCURACY AND CONSISTENCY

Have you gotten names, places, and events right? Are the names correctly spelled? For instance, is it Carol or Carole, Marian or Marion? If you've given dates, are they accurate? Check to see if you've been consistent about details—called someone Willie in one place but Will in another, or used the form *e-mail* in one place but *email* in another.

● CHECK FOR AWKWARDLY REPEATED WORDS

Sometimes repetition works well, particularly to unify a paragraph with a series of parallel phrases or clauses or to repeat a term for emphasis. But repetition can sound monotonous when a writer uses the same term too often or even in various forms. For instance, "They *know* that their *knowledge* is outmoded," or "Their performance featured a *variety* of dances and *various* instrumental solos." Such constructions look clumsy and are easily fixed. For example, you could write, "They realize their knowledge is outmoded" or "Their performance featured a variety of dances and solos with different instruments."

● Check for the Most Common Errors

Read over your writing, watching for major grammar errors. Many instructors suggest that their students keep a list of editing problems that recur frequently in their writing; for example, forgetting to insert commas after long introductory phrases, or to see that items in a list are in parallel form. If you keep such a list, perhaps in a file on your hard disk, you can refer to it quickly when you're editing.

● Check Your Spelling and Run a Spell Checker

If you've come this far in your education and are still a poor speller, it may make you feel better to know that you have a lot of company. Many highly intelligent people are poor spellers. Most of them, however, are also careful to see that any writing that goes out under their name isn't marred by misspelled words. They know how damaging spelling errors can be in the academic or business world or even on a Web site.

If you're a poor speller, there are two things you can do. First, recognize that you have a problem with spelling. Don't apologize and think people will forgive your lapses; just resolve to spell correctly. Second, develop a set of habits that will overcome your handicap. Here are some suggestions:

○ As you edit, check or circle words you're uncertain about or that you know are tricky—for instance, *harass, liaison, villain, bourgeois.* If you often confuse *accept* and *except*, mark those. Mark words that end in those pesky suffixes *-ible* or *-able* that sound exactly alike. You may have to look them up several times.

○ Buy a good college dictionary and use it. No excuses. When you're editing, look up any word you're unsure about.

○ Buy a word list, that inexpensive, pocket-size reference that lists the words most commonly misspelled, and use it.

○ If a specific, hard-to-spell term occurs frequently in a project you're working on—*Gentileschi* was such a word in the model paper—pick an abbreviation for it, such as *Gt.,* and use it every time the word occurs in your essay. When you finish the essay, use the Find and Replace feature on your computer to fill in the correctly spelled term everywhere the abbreviation occurs.

○ Develop some memory gimmicks for tricky words—for instance, "Emma is in a dilemma" to remember the double *m* in *dilemma*, and "Remember the gum in argument" to remind yourself there's no *e* after the *gu*.

○ Watch out for words that sound like contractions but are not; for instance, *your* for *you're*, *there* for *they're*, *were* for *we're*, or *its* for *it's*. Remember, the spell checker won't know the difference, so it's up to you to spot them!

○ Run your spell checker, but don't count on it to catch all your spelling errors. It won't distinguish between *cite* and *site*, *passed* and *past*, or *reel* and *real* because all those words are in its stock of correctly spelled words. It will, however, catch many misspellings and most typographical errors. Misspelled words that the spelling checker would have caught—for instance, *thare* or *wich*—may be the most damaging of all, for they show your readers that you don't care enough about your final product to use a simple tool to improve it.

○ If you can, get one of those lucky people who seem to be naturally good spellers to check your writing for spelling errors. Fortunately, when you're working with a computer, errors are easy to correct.

● CONSIDER THE WAY YOUR WRITING LOOKS

How does your document look? Open and spacious, or crowded? Do you need to look for ways to add white space? Are the paragraphs too long? Can some information be set out in lists? If the document is long, should you break it up with headings? If you've composed a Web page, is it easy to read and is the navigation clear? (Consult Chapter 11, on document design, for helpful advice about appearance.)

Break up your text with graphics and illustrations when they're appropriate. They can do a great deal to make your writing easier to read and to understand. Present statistics in charts and graphs when you can, in color if possible. They add impact and can make the data easier to understand. You can also highlight special information in boxes or set it off with a light screen. Your computer manual has instructions on how to create these visuals, and they can enhance your work.

When you finish editing, do a final proofreading. One good method is to read down a page slowly, sliding a six-inch ruler or straightedge under each line as you go. This method keeps you from reading too quickly and helps you to catch errors. Another way to make yourself slow down and read carefully is to touch each word lightly with a pencil as you read.

As you proofread, keep these specific things in mind:

◗ *Check your punctuation:* Have you put apostrophes in contractions and possessive nouns? Have you put periods, question marks, or exclamation points at the ends of sentences? Have you set off nonrestrictive elements with commas? Have you put quotation marks around direct quotes? Have you capitalized all proper names and nouns, even when they're used as adjectives such as *German* or *Machiavellian*? Are all parentheses and quotation marks paired?

◗ *Check for omissions:* Have you left out words such as *to* or *for* where they're needed? Have you failed to delete words you intended to omit? Have you left out explanatory notes or dates where they're needed?

◗ *Check titles and quotations:* Are titles of books, plays, and movies underlined or italicized? Are chapter titles or the titles of short works in quotations? Are long quotations set off and indented?

◗ *Check all citations:* Do notes and citations follow the proper form? Are notes and citations accurate?

Finally, run your spell checker one more time. You may turn up additional typos. Such meticulous editing is a pain, to be sure, but the consequences of turning in or publishing sloppy work can also be painful.

Q *I can't believe that once I get out of school anyone is going to care whether I leave out a comma here and there, or misspell an occasional word, at least not the way my English teachers do. Isn't it true that people in business have better things to worry about than punctuation and spelling?*

A We know it's hard to believe. But there's good research to show people in business in fact do get pretty upset by seeing the kinds of errors in their employees'—or clients'—writing that seem to represent carelessness or lack of education. As one of our former students, who joined a very big and competitive engineering firm, reported to us after a year on the job, "Anyone who can't write doesn't stay around here very long. And here the word *writing* very much includes making your report or letter as nearly perfect as it can be." Or as our friend Harry Bruce (former CEO of the Illinois Central Railroad) said to one of us, "If you make one mistake per page in a thirty-page report, that's thirty mistakes! And if you're making that many mistakes in little things like grammar and spelling, what's your boss going to think about how you're likely to be handling the big things?"

FOR PRACTICE

1 Trade drafts of a paper you're working on with someone else in your class. Edit your partner's paper following the suggestions in this chapter. After you're finished, sit down with him or her and compare notes on what you did. Look in particular for things you did with his or her draft that are different in important ways from what you would do with one of your own. Look also for things your partner did with your paper that are different from what you would have done with your own paper. Take some time to think about any such differences—and what they might mean.

2 It's hard to draw a hard-and-fast line between revising and editing. One fairly common definition is that revising is something you have to do for your own writing yourself (although others can certainly give advice), while editing is something that's relatively easy for someone to do for someone else's writing. Think back on your own experiences as a writer (and, presumably, as an editor of your own writing)—what are your strengths as an editor, and what are your weaknesses? Be prepared to discuss what those are.

3 One of the oldest and most respected newsletters for professional editors is *The Editorial Eye,* from EEI Communications in Alexandria, Virginia. Articles from their past issues are available free on www.eeicommunications.com/eye/. Check out this Web site and read two or three articles that look appealing to you. Come to class prepared to report on their contents to your classmates.

Considering Design 11

> ◗ *When the design of your projects looks good, you're off to a good start with your readers.*

Now that most of us write on computers, we are able to make all kinds of choices about the design of our writing projects. We can use different fonts and sizes of type, justify pages right or left or both (or center the text), scan in images, add charts and graphs and tables, use colors other than black, turn the text and visuals sideways on the page—the list goes on and on. Readers in college and in the professional world have come to expect that those design elements will be used effectively to make what they read more accessible and attractive. Just to list a few examples, many readers have become impatient with large, solid blocks of text, whether in the form of an 8½-by-11-inch report page with no paragraph breaks or headings, or a PowerPoint slide showing hundreds of words of straight text, or a Web page that's so poorly designed they cannot find what they want on it. Thus it's in your best interest to learn the basics of document design. They are not that difficult, and they can serve you well.

Many writing projects benefit from effective design. A few examples would include management or marketing reports containing charts and graphs, architectural or scientific proposals featuring sketches and drawings, PowerPoint slides that graphically reinforce the key points in a presentation, Web sites that make users smile with their accessibility, church newsletters that tell their stories clearly and attractively, and résumés that help you stand out from the crowd in a positive way.

You don't need the latest software or hardware to design effectively. Effective design comes more from knowing and meeting the needs of your readers than from applying dazzling technology. In fact, the worst kinds of document design today often come from pushing the computer's abilities to the limit without thinking about the information needs of the audience. For example, before you worry what a newsletter should look like, think carefully about what readers the newsletter addresses and what they want to get out of it. This chapter will help you consider such questions, and the directory of model documents at the end of the book provides good examples.

A FEW USES OF DOCUMENT DESIGN

All writing is designed. Even the simplest choices, such as using 12-point type instead of 10-point type, or using $1^1/_4$-inch margins instead of 1-inch margins, are design decisions. Here are just a few of the ways you can use the processes and principles of good document design:

⊃ Add headings and subheadings to your writing to help your readers find the information they need. See Model 3.

⊃ Add visuals to your papers and thus change their impact upon your readers. Charts, graphs, tables, drawings, clip art—all are available to today's computer users. See Model 2.

⊃ If your instructor doesn't require that you follow exactly the style and format prescribed by an authority such as the Modern Language Association (MLA) or the American Psychological Association (APA), you can create a format of your own for your academic report. (Similarly, if the company you work for does not dictate style and format for its written projects, you can create your own.)

⊃ If you combine different fonts and type styles, break your paper up with headings and subheadings, include visuals to support your points, and use different page layouts (maybe designing all the pairs of pages as two-page spreads, for example), you can lift the appearance of your work up out of the ordinary. See Model 4 for an example of variable page layout in a two-page spread.

○ For a class project or a business presentation, you can create effective slides to augment or reinforce an oral presentation, showing them on an overhead projector or on a computer screen. Such slides will help you hold your audience's attention and do a better job of selling your idea or product. See Model 7.

○ You can create a Web site to display your work. A growing number of teachers are encouraging students to create their work as Web pages, thus reinforcing the vital link between today's classrooms and tomorrow's professional communication needs. See Model 5 for the Web design of a sample page from the paper on Artemisia Gentileschi discussed and shown in Chapter 12.

○ If you're conscious of a few design principles when you create your résumé, you can turn any version of it—print or HTML—into a more effective document. See Model 11.

○ Your letter of application for a job can be more attractive if it follows a few basic design principles. See Model 9.

○ In a newsletter for your office, your neighborhood, or other group, you can combine news stories, announcements, and pictures in an attractive format that will catch people's attention and keep them informed. Such newsletters can also keep clients and donors up-to-date on performance and financial needs. See Model 13.

○ In brochures, you can use graphics and text to educate readers or promote a product or a service. See Model 14.

○ Your announcements or news releases and a variety of other kinds of documents can all profit in their own ways from the processes and principles of document design. See Models 13 through 19.

○ You can create informational brochures to educate clients and sponsors or as part of a fund-raising campaign. You can make these simple, in black and white, or you can use colorful graphics and pictures. See Model 14.

○ You can compose posters and flyers to announce events and draw people to them. See Models 15 and 16.

◗ You can produce an attractive program to enhance the audience's enjoyment of a performance. See Model 17.

PLANNING A DESIGN

When professional communicators talk about "document design," they mean both the *process* for arriving at the design of documents and the *look* of the resulting documents. It's an all too common rookie mistake in producing a document (whether a print document or a Web page) to invest the time and money for using technology to the fullest but to fail utterly to plan for meeting readers' needs. No amount of technology can make up for a lack of such planning. Design thus begins with a set of planning questions, continues with sketching out a preliminary design, and then moves into estimating costs.

QUESTIONS TO ASK AS YOU PLAN A DESIGN

Always start with a plan. Since your project will probably incorporate several elements, you have to think ahead about each element:

◗ *Who are the people in this audience?* What are their key characteristics? Do you think they expect a conventional design? Or might they like something *different?*

◗ *What are the information needs of the people in this audience?* Are they only looking for information? Do they want in some way to be entertained? Or do they need to be persuaded? Beyond that, what kinds of content do they want and need from this document—personal views, facts, problem analysis, arguments, illustrations, links to other sources, or something else? You can try to guess, but the best way to find out the real information needs of the people you are trying to reach is to ask them, directly.

◗ *What is your own purpose in producing this project?* What do you want to get out of it? What kind of effect do you want to create? Do you mean to create a *serviceable* document, or a *showcase* document? Are you just trying to get the boss off your back by getting the newsletter out, or are you particularly trying to impress someone?

○ *What tone do you want to convey?* What kind of impact do you want this document to have? For example, a personal home page that you expect only your friends and family to see will probably be vastly different in tone from a professional home page, one you expect to represent you on the Web to clients, customers, peers, and prospective employers.

○ *What components are you working with?* Mostly words? Or will you include visuals—and if so, what kinds (illustrations, charts, photographs)?

○ *Is this a print document, or will it be on the Web?*

○ *What constraints are you under?* How much time do you have? How much money can you spend? What are the limits of your expertise, and what kind of technical help will be available?

If you were creating a fund-raising brochure for a children's museum, your working plan based on this analysis might look like this:

Audience: Civic leaders who I hope will support the children's museum, and interested citizens who might become donors. From this brochure, they can learn about a worthwhile project to support.

Purpose: To show that the museum is an educational and cultural asset for our community and thus worthy of both public and private support.

Tone: Informal and friendly—I want them to like the museum. (Use a lighthearted type and open layout with borders.)

Components: Information about what the museum offers. Some graphics—if possible, pictures of children enjoying the museum— but cost might be a real constraint.

Print or Web: Only a print document for now, but we need to save the disk files so that eventually this material can be the beginnings of a Web site for the museum.

Constraints: Two weeks to produce the brochure. Inexpensive is good. As a nonprofit, we shouldn't look as if we're spending a lot of money, so design should be simple.

Using pencil and paper, sketch out a preliminary design. Eventually (as discussed later in this chapter) you will need to worry in more detail about what type to use (fonts, styles, and sizes), where and how to use headings, what colors of print and paper to use, and how the elements of the layout (movement, white space, chunking, graphics, and artwork) will work together. But for this preliminary step you just want a rough sketch that will help you decide where to put headings, blocks of text, charts, pictures, and so on.

If you need ideas for the basic design, visit any travel agency, or your local chamber of commerce, or any office that has lots of brochures you can look at. You'll most likely find one you want to imitate. Or you can look up samples on such Web sites as the Microsoft Office Template Gallery (officeupdate.microsoft.com/templategallery/), which will not only show you designs, but also allow you to download and use them, inserting your own text and visuals.

For example, a sketch of one possible layout for your museum brochure might look like this:

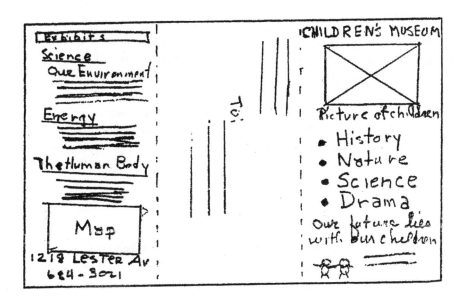

If you are preparing a Web page or site instead of a print publication, you should still work from a pencil-and-paper sketch. In this case, however, you will have to sketch out the layout of each individual screen and the way the screens lead one to another. Will you design your document as basically one long page, relying on the reader to scroll down and down and down (see "Philosophy & Literature" at www.philosophyand literature.com for an example)? Or will you use a more hierarchical (top-down) design, with a navigation page for the first screen, where users can choose from a number of different paths (for an example, see the Library of Congress site, at www.loc.gov/). These options are discussed in more detail in the section on Web site structure and Web page design later in this chapter.

Once you have a preliminary sketch or sketches, it's important to get someone else to look at them and give you feedback. If possible, get feedback from people who are members of the eventual audience for your project. If that's not possible, be sure to tell the readers of your preliminary sketches something about that audience. Coming up with a preliminary design is nice; getting a meaningful review of it by members of the target audience is wonderful.

● ESTIMATING COSTS

Think about costs. Once you've made preliminary decisions (in the case of a print document) on size, illustrations, two or four-color versus black-and-white, and (in the case of Web materials) on the basic design, get an estimate of costs, whether for printing or for Web site hosting. That estimate will affect your final decisions. Work out your cost estimates, in as much detail as you can. You may need to visit a printer for a reliable estimate, or to talk with a more experienced Web site developer. Remember, if you're building a Web site, someone has to *host* it and to *maintain* it as well.

● ● ● CONSIDERING TYPE

You don't need to know the fine points of working with type that would concern a book or magazine designer or a graphic artist. For your purposes, you need to consider only three elements of type: *font, style,* and *size*; all word processing programs give you options with all three:

- *Fonts* are typefaces—Times, Helvetica, Garamond, and so on.
- *Styles* are such variants as *italic*, **boldface**, outline, shadow, CAPS, SMALL CAPS, or L E T T E R S P A C I N G.
- *Sizes* are measured in points—8 point, 14 point, on up.

● FONTS

If you're using a sophisticated word processing program, such as Microsoft Word or WordPerfect, you have a wonderful variety of fonts available to you, ranging from routine, serviceable fonts to dramatic display fonts and graceful or playful decorative fonts. (In Word, for example, just click on the Format button on the toolbar, and the first option is a drop-down box with Font as the first item. Click on that and you'll see the fonts you have available.) You can also download, often free, inexpensive supplemental font packages that will provide you with dozens more. There are four categories of fonts: serif, sans serif, decorative, and symbol.

- *Serif fonts:* These are the fonts that have little feet (*serifs*) attached to the ends of letters. Some common ones are Times, Courier, Palatino, New Century Schoolbook, and Bookman. These fonts work well for extended passages of print because the serifs help move the reader's eye along from one word to the next. They have a traditional look and are comfortable to read because people are used to seeing them in newspapers and magazines.

- *Sans serif fonts:* These are barer, more modern-looking fonts, and are more commonly used on Web pages. Some of the more popular ones are Helvetica, Futura, Univers, and **Chicago.** Sans serif fonts work well for *display* type—headlines, headings, titles, and such—because they have an assertive, no-nonsense quality. They don't work as well for long blocks of print because they're not quite as easy to read as serif fonts (except on the Web, where they're easier to read than serif fonts).

- *Decorative fonts:* These come in a dazzling variety, ranging from ultra-old-fashioned to jazzy and brash. Just a few examples: 𝕱𝖊𝖙𝖙𝖊 𝕱𝖗𝖆𝖐𝖙𝖚𝖗, *Regency Script*, **Belwe Medium**, Gill Sans, Avant Garde, *Mistral*, and ᎪᏁᏁᎪ. These—and there are many, many more—are special effect fonts. They are fun to play with, but should be used sparingly; they're attention getters and often don't combine well with their less flashy fellow fonts. Their appropriateness really depends on two key factors. First, using too many fonts in *any* document is a mistake, but the number you can use, say, in a college or professional report is certainly different from the number you can use in invitations to a child's birthday party. Second, some fonts combine well visually with other fonts, and some fonts don't.

◗ *Symbol fonts:* Sometimes called *dingbats*, these fonts provide you with a broad range of icons, ornamental signs, and geometric symbols—for example, ©, ™, ⇔, ⊕, %, ↑ , ◁⁾⁾, ⤵, ♉, ⊜, and ⊞. These fonts include an assortment of arrows, geometric figures, and mathematical symbols. You will also find items you can use for borders, bullets, decorations, identifying pictures, or separating chunks of text. Look under Zapf Dingbats, Monotype Sorts, or Wingdings in your word processor's fonts menu. (You can also find symbols in other places on your word processor. For example, in Word you can click on Insert, and then on Symbol in the drop-down box, and you will see many more symbols to choose among.)

Fonts have distinctive personalities, and those personalities will help you set the tone of your document. When you're thinking which fonts to select, consider what tone you want to convey and then choose accordingly. For most academic projects, your basic font for body text needs to be a serif font from the "workhorse" category (Times or Courier, for example), and your headings and figure captions need to be a workhorse sans serif (such as Arial). On page 137 is a Sampler of Type Fonts you can use to begin your considerations.

A SAMPLER OF TYPE FONTS

Workhorse: Usually serif fonts, the workhorses, do most of the routine work in documents and hold up well for the long pull. They're unobtrusive and easy to read. For routine academic projects, these should be your choices.

Authority: These display fonts command attention and work well in headlines and on announcements. You might use these on a title page for a report, as well.

Show-off: These are the cutups that make a point of being different. They're fun, but a little goes a long way. They can be used for light-hearted posters and brochures—but sparingly.

Elegant: Lighter, more delicate fonts will give a touch of class. They work well for invitations and courtesy notes (for example, thank you cards).

Script: Script fonts are graceful, flowing fonts, useful for quotations, invitations, or programs. If you put very much text into such a font, it becomes hard to read.

Workhorse	Authority	Show-off	Elegant	Script
Courier	**Chicago**	Missive	ᑫᑎᑎᑕ	*Regency Script*
Palatino	Gill Sans	FUNKY Fresh	AUGUSTEA	Nadianne Book
New Century Schoolbook	Century Old Style	Lambada	CASTELLAR	*Mistral*
Times	**Helvetica Black**	EAST BLOCK OPEN	Centaur	***Zapf Chancery***
Futura	**Poster Bodoni**	**Dolmen**	Belwe Medium	*Freestyle Script*

Note that type sizes aren't uniform among fonts. For example, 10-point type in Courier, **Helvetica**, and Bookman is quite readable, but 10-point type in *Mistral,* Futura, or *Vivaldi* looks tiny. You'll need to adjust type sizes as you see your fonts appear on the page or the screen.

COMBINING FONTS

Here's what part of a student paper looks like in just one font:

> Once the possibility of a cochlear implant begins to be considered, various kinds of audiological tests can be used to determine more about the level and kind of hearing loss. Various kinds of hearing aids and other such devices can be temporarily fitted to test whether these devices might be beneficial. If these tests suggest that the person might indeed be a candidate for a cochlear implant, additional medical tests are then performed. For example, X-rays are taken to see if the cochlea can take an implant. Another very specific procedure, called a promontory test, may also be used to determine whether electrical stimulation of the auditory nerve (such as might be produced by an implant) will in fact result in sound.

By today's standards, this use of just one font looks very flat. But typography experts recommend that you use only two fonts, or at most three, in any document. Any more than that can look jumbled and confusing. In most student writing projects, you might see a traditional serif font for the body of the report or article and then a sans serif font for the display type—headlines, or headings and subheadings. Here is an example (in this case, a straightforward news announcement) with a headline in the sans serif font Arial and the body in the worker-bee serif font Times New Roman:

Emotional Intelligence Author to Speak

On Tuesday, December 5, at 7:30 p.m., Daniel Goleman, author of the best-selling book *Emotional Intelligence,* will speak at City Auditorium. Dr. Goleman, who is a social science writer for the *New York Times,* will outline the principles of his book and explain why parents should be more concerned about helping their children develop emotional intelligence than about trying to get them enrolled in prestigious colleges.

Here is a less formal combination of fonts for an announcement about an upcoming event. It combines Lucida Sans for the headline with Bookman Old Style for the text.

Edgar Winner to Talk about Writing Mysteries

On Sunday, May 17, at 2:00 p.m., Mary Willis Walker will read from her novel of suspense *Under the Beetle's Cellar* in the third-floor atrium of Book People. Ms. Walker, who won the coveted Edgar award for her 1994 mystery *The Red Scream,* will also talk about her experience of working with other writers in critique groups, a practice she considers essential to her own writing process.

The example on the following page shows what happens when there are too many fonts. Each line clashes with the one above it and the one below. The effect is overkill.

On April 9 you'll have the privilege of hearing

Ronald E. Dickson

of

Harvard University

author of the autobiography It Ain't Necessarily So

The title of Dr. Dickson's talk will be

"Trying to Tell the Truth—It's Not Easy"

BASSET HALL   THIRD FLOOR   7:30 P.M.

There are no actual rules about using specific fonts or for combining fonts—just guidelines. And there is plenty of literature—but no consensus—about how the effects of various fonts may change as one moves from print documents to Web documents. Once they get past the rule of thumb—stick with two or three basic fonts for the entire document—different experts go in different directions. For some good examples to follow, look over the front page of a major newspaper such as the *New York Times* or the *Los Angeles Times,* or the introductory pages of a news magazine such as *Time* or *Newsweek*, either in print or on the Web. Model your own documents initially on others you see that are successful, but then play around and experiment a little bit with yours, also. You have a wealth of possibilities open to you that no one would have dreamed of a few years ago. Get creative when you have the opportunity.

● TYPE STYLES

The basic type style choices are between roman and italic, and between boldface and lightface. Lightface roman type is the most simple, straightforward, and unembellished. It is the one most people call "normal"— the standard type style from which boldface and italics are the variations.

Boldface type stands out. Use it in headlines, headings or subheadings, or other displayed elements. For brochures, newsletters, or posters you can boldface borders or dividing lines. But keep these cautions in mind:

   ◗ Using too much boldface, like using too many exclamation points, reduces its impact.

○ Large amounts of boldface make a document look dark—eventually too much boldface just cancels itself out.

○ For Web pages, if you boldface words for emphasis, readers might think those words are hypertext links (especially if the bold is another color, such as blue) and try to click on them—and become frustrated when it turns out they are not links.

Italic type is conventional for several uses—the titles of books, plays, magazines, and papers, and for foreign words and phrases. You can also use it *sparingly* to emphasize selected words or phrases—for example: "Julio's *manners* are fine. It's his intentions I question." On the Web, bold italic is used for emphasis more often than alone, because on the Web italic by itself can be hard to read.

Underlining can also be used to mark words for special use, or (as in MLA style) to mark titles. But underlining entire lines (much less paragraphs) should be avoided because it makes a passage of print hard to read. On the Web, underlining, like boldface, can be mistaken for hypertext links. As a rule, confine underlining to papers (or articles for publication) that must conform strictly to a style manual that requires it.

● TYPE SIZE

Decisions about type size need to be based on both the purpose of your project and any readability concerns there might be (such as whether it's a Web project, a 2-by-3-inch calling card, or an academic report). And of course, the type sizes can vary within documents—headings may be bigger than body text; captions and source notes may be smaller.

For academic papers and any manuscripts you may be submitting to an editor, use either 10- or 12-point type in a readable font. For notes or a script you need to read in front of an audience, 14-point type works well. For anything that needs to be read on a poster, 24- or 36-point type works best.

In other settings, type size in general correlates with purpose. Headings and subheadings in reports and academic papers should be only slightly larger than the print in the body of the paper—perhaps two points larger (see Model 3). On the Web, viewers can make the size of type pretty much whatever they want, but the sizes of different kinds of type stay in the same proportional relationship to one another—what you make big stays big.

Headlines require special attention, especially in such documents as announcements, newsletters, and brochures. A headline needs to catch readers' attention. Make your headlines three to four times as large as the type in the body of the article. Think of headlines as sentences to be read quickly. Use no more than three lines—one or two would be better.

● **COLOR**

Different colors of type may be used to highlight particular words or phrases in some settings. In general, however, a very little variation goes a long way. Certainly there are exceptions—birthday invitations for seven-year-olds come to mind, or some commercial brochures, perhaps— but for most academic publications, you're well advised to stick to black type on white paper. Some designers will use *one* other color, such as blue or green for words that need to be emphasized or for headings, or red for cautions and warnings, but that is about as far as you want to go in a college paper.

The use of color in visuals—in charts, graphs, diagrams, or other kinds of illustrations—is common in today's professional world and is rapidly becoming more common on college campuses (as more and more students have access to color printers). A good general guideline is to consider whether the color is being added to enhance the meaning somehow, or just for decoration. Color just for decoration should be avoided. But color can be used to highlight special elements of a graphic (one line among several on a line graph, for example) or to enhance meaning by symbolizing a concept (such as showing profits in green and losses in red). Once again, however, the caution needs to be sounded that a little color goes a long way: the fewer colors you use, and the more consistently you use them, the easier it may be for readers to take in your meaning.

Choosing color for Web pages can be difficult, because different Web browsers have different color settings, so that there's never any guarantee that the color you choose will be the color your users see. For corporate or professional pages, use of color should be restrained—the page still needs to look professional. Hot pink type on a yellow background will cause Web viewers to click on their browser's Back button as fast as they can. For text on the Web, a little color again goes a long way. If you look at some of the most heavily trafficked pages on the Web, such as the Microsoft, Yahoo!, or Google home pages, you'll see that other than putting the basic text in blue rather than black, they employ very little other color—most often one other color (such as green) is used to emphasize one word or set of words (often links), and that's it. On the other hand, for visuals, graphics, drawings, photos, and so on, color is one of the Web's strongest features.

CONSIDERING LAYOUT

You do not have to be a professional graphic designer to create an effective and engaging layout. Four simple principles can help you arrange text effectively:

- Move readers in the right direction.
- Use white space effectively.
- "Chunk" information.
- Position graphics and artwork carefully.

DIRECTION

Readers of English expect to read from left to right and top to bottom. Thus you should arrange the elements of your document to lead readers in those directions. If you use more than one column, lead readers from top to bottom down the first column, then up, then down again. If you're using a chart or photograph, you can put it at the top of the second or third column or in the middle of the first column (see Model 13). Put supplementary information such as phone numbers or addresses in smaller print at the bottom.

If you are going to incorporate several elements—for instance, a title, a photograph, two or three short pieces, and borders or boxes—sketch out a model of how the resulting document might look before you start. Again, you need to make sure the reader will move through the piece in the right direction. It's also useful to use the Page Setup or View command on your word processor, which lets you see a page in miniature as you work. Doing so will show you how it's going to look from a distance and make it easier to see which way the movement is directed.

When you're creating a document like a brochure or booklet that involves several pages, plan two or more pages at a time so you can see how they will fit together. Make sure that the important information is given appropriate placement in featured positions.

● WHITE SPACE

White space includes the margins, the vertical space between columns, the horizontal space between paragraphs or lines of type, the space above and below headings, the open areas around graphics, and the space at the top and bottom of a document. How you arrange this white space strongly affects the look and readability of your document.

For most documents, assume that you want an open, spacious, and uncrowded page. (This is even more important for Web pages than for print documents.) Keep this assumption in mind especially for brochures, announcements, newsletters, posters, or anything else you want your audience to take in at a glance. But it's also important for academic papers, reports, or proposals. You want them to look readable too. Some specific advice:

> ◗ Leave plenty of white space around titles and headings; generally, more above than below.
>
> ◗ For reports or academic papers, make side margins of at least one inch.
>
> ◗ Leave three-eighths to one-half inch between vertical columns.
>
> ◗ In academic papers, double-space within paragraphs.
>
> ◗ Leave a space around graphs, photographs, or artwork. On an 8½-by-11-inch page, you need at least one-half inch of space between visuals and other text.
>
> ◗ For presentations, double- or triple-space between lines.
>
> ◗ If necessary, cut text to avoid crowding.

● CHUNKING INFORMATION

Readers absorb information better when it is arranged into meaningful units and blocks. In printed documents, you can create such units in several ways (in addition to the use of headings and subheadings). Here are just a few:

○ Display items in lists (like this one). Number items if their order is important; bullet them if it is not.

○ Use boxes or screens to highlight key information.

○ Set off items for emphasis with borders or lines.

● POSITIONING GRAPHICS AND ARTWORK

While there are no hard-and-fast rules about placement of graphics and illustrations, here are some helpful guidelines:

○ Put photographs toward the top of the document, especially in newsletters or posters.

○ Try to put charts and graphs close to the place in the text where they are discussed; if you can't do this, clearly point readers to the correct location (by numbering and cross-referencing figures). Readers should not have to hunt to connect a graph or chart with text.

○ Avoid putting too many illustrations on any one page; one or two illustrations on a page will have more impact than five or six.

○ If your document has several pages, try to put at least one illustration on the first page.

○ When you can, place illustrations so that the text wraps around them. They will look more integrated into the document.

○ Leave adequate white space around illustrations.

○ Be sure every illustration connects directly to the information in the document; never use graphics just for decoration.

○ Make the size of each graphic proportionate to other graphics in the document, to the page size itself, and to the importance of that graphic to that document. It makes no sense to illustrate a minor point with a full-page graphic, nor does it make sense to have a 1-by-1-inch graphic illustrating a major point. Sometimes you can shrink (or expand) an entire graphic (especially a downloaded graphic) to fit the need. Other times you may need to *crop* (cut a part off) the graphic to get it to the right size.

While there is more to effective design on the Web than can be explained here, we suggest a few basic principles that can help you create Web sites and pages that are both attractive and effective. Even if you do not create Web pages, knowing these principles will help you understand and explain to other people why some Web sites and pages work better than others.

Effective design on the Web is design that responds to the real information needs of the people who visit the site. Your first decision must be about the *purpose* of the Web site: for example, entertainment, advertising, or advocacy—see the discussion in Chapter 12, on research writing. Beyond that, many of the principles of good Web design are the same as those for print publications—movement, white space, chunking, and placement of graphic elements. The following sections build on those principles, with specific attention to the interaction between Web site structure and Web page design.

● How the Web Is Read

People do not read Web sites in the usual sense of the word—rather, they *scan* or *browse* them. Thus designing for the Web calls upon you to adjust traditional print publication practices accordingly. Visualize how you yourself use the Web—one hand holding a cup of coffee, the other on the mouse, scanning, scrolling, and clicking (forward *and back*). This is the situation effective design on the Web must respond to.

WRITING FOR THE WEB

When you write for the Web, you need to meet the needs of readers who browse or scan. In general, this means using more lists, headings, and open spacing than might be the case in a paper document; highlighting keywords; and writing shorter paragraphs whose main thought almost always falls in the first sentence and which stick closely to just one idea each. Here are some specific tips for writing for the Web:

> ◗ Keep your screens simple. Crowded or jumbled screens drive users away fast.
>
> ◗ Rely more on bulleted or numbered lists than on paragraphs.
>
> ◗ If you must use paragraphs, keep them short (five lines or so), and

make sure you put the main point of every paragraph in the first line (that's all most readers will look at).

○ Try to use fewer words. Cut out the deadwood in your prose.

○ Write headings and subheadings carefully, and leave enough space around them so that a scanning reader will see your key points easily and quickly.

○ Highlight keywords. Bold italics work well on the Web. Remember that combining boldface or underlining with color will make readers confuse your highlighted keywords with hypertext links.

○ Try to write anything longer than two or three screens as a series of linked pages, each with its own heading(s). (At this point, Web page design becomes Web site structure.) The first page needs to be a summary of the whole site, with links to the other pages.

○ Make each of your pages reasonably self-contained and self-explanatory. One good test is to print out each page by itself and look at it carefully. Does it make sense without the context of the first page? If not, you need to work on the site some more.

VISUALS ON THE WEB

It's hard to generalize about how to use visuals on the Web. As with print publications, keeping the visuals as close as possible to the corresponding text is critical. Be careful with color graphics—the ones that are too big or complicated are slow to load. These need to be simplified or rendered in black and white. If you're writing an academic report that relies on words more than graphics, you might use a layout like that of the introduction page from the NASA report at the end of this chapter. On the other hand, if your document is advertising a new product, people need to see the product as well as read about it. The next sections of this chapter discuss the integration of words and graphics in more detail.

● WEB SITE STRUCTURE AND WEB PAGE DESIGN

If a Web site is more than one page long, both the structure of the site and the design of each page need to accommodate its length. Thus on the

Web, *page design* flows into *site structure.* The following sections briefly explain two popular structures.

THE ENDLESSLY SCROLLING SITE

One easy way to structure a site is to set it up as just one page, but a page that can be very long. You can see a good, simple example at the very popular refdesk.com site. There are three columns, and readers have to keep scrolling down to see all that is in the page or in any of the columns. The site's creators must judge carefully what readers should see on the first screen to open and what they will have to scroll down to get to. Notice also the way small graphics are incorporated into the design. In each case, clicking on the graphic takes users to other sites.

Here's how that first screen (just the top part of the site) looked on September 22, 2001:

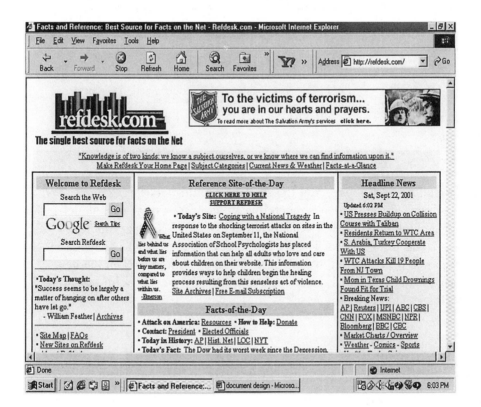

The endlessly scrolling site is a very simple but effective structure. Students (and others) often use this design for newsletters, for schedules of events, or for putting résumés on the Web.

THE HIERARCHICAL SITE

A more complicated structure is the hierarchical site, a structure that would be more appropriate for a long résumé, a student organization's Web site, a long report, or a corporate Web site. In the abstract, such a site's design looks like this—a home page connected by hypertext links to major subpages:

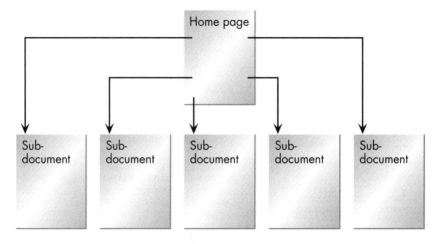

See on the facing page how the structure would work for a résumé. The first page of the site looks much like a one-page résumé (see Model 11 for an example), but each résumé heading is also a hypertext link to one of the pages on level two. The second level of the site would then consist of separate pages linked to each of the headings introduced on the first page: here perhaps "Education," "Work Experience," "Volunteer Work," "Honors," and "References":

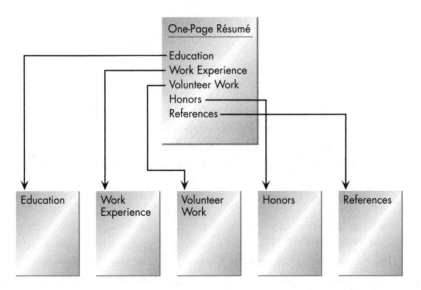

In still longer documents, each of the level-two pages becomes a sub-menu—it links to further pages for items within its category. Graphics can easily be worked in as separate subdocuments linked to the main page. Thus the effect is hierarchical: the reader starts at the top and then navigates down through the levels to find the desired information.

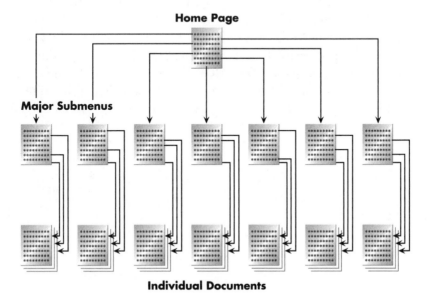

A student's report for an academic class, or a complete multipage résumé, or a student organization's Web site, could be set up in either the endlessly scrolling or the hierarchical structure.

Some people who specialize in Web page design and site structure belittle the endlessly scrolling site as too simple, but when designing your page you cannot allow your choice to be dictated by the highest technical level available to you—your Web site design needs to be governed by the purpose of the site, the needs of users, and the nature of the site's content. If a simpler design will do the job, the simpler design is better.

HTML OR PDF?

There are those who argue that for academic, corporate, or government reports, the typical HTML (Hypertext Markup Language) Web page, with its emphasis on graphics, color, short paragraphs, and the like, may not in fact be the best choice. An alternative is to convert the files for your print document into PDF (Portable Document Format) files using Adobe Acrobat. What you will get on the Web are pages that look much like print pages, but offer you much of the flexibility of HTML—hyperlinks, color, searching, and so on.

For interesting examples of PDF pages, check out the NASA public reports available on the Web from www.nasa.gov/siteindex.html. Simply click on "Public Reports" under "News and Information" on that page, and you will see reports done in the form of screens that have the look of traditional reports—complete with full-color graphics and hyperlinks—but in fact are Web pages set up in PDF. In settings where that more traditional look is desirable, PDF provides a good alternative. (The Adobe Acrobat Reader is needed for viewing PDF pages, but the reader can be downloaded for free.)

Here is the cover page of the *NASA Performance Report for Fiscal Year 2000,* from a PDF file—a spectacular visual (the original is in startling color—a golden space station, bright blue skies).

Notice how the page looks like a classic cover from a traditional report.

Here's the next page:

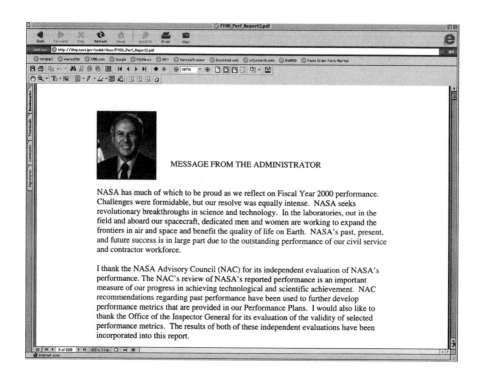

MESSAGE FROM THE ADMINISTRATOR

NASA has much of which to be proud as we reflect on Fiscal Year 2000 performance. Challenges were formidable, but our resolve was equally intense. NASA seeks revolutionary breakthroughs in science and technology. In the laboratories, out in the field and aboard our spacecraft, dedicated men and women are working to expand the frontiers in air and space and benefit the quality of life on Earth. NASA's past, present, and future success is in large part due to the outstanding performance of our civil service and contractor workforce.

I thank the NASA Advisory Council (NAC) for its independent evaluation of NASA's performance. The NAC's review of NASA's reported performance is an important measure of our progress in achieving technological and scientific achievement. NAC recommendations regarding past performance have been used to further develop performance metrics that are provided in our Performance Plans. I would also like to thank the Office of the Inspector General for its evaluation of the validity of selected performance metrics. The results of both of these independent evaluations have been incorporated into this report.

Although this NASA report behaves in most ways like a Web document (interactive, searchable, etc.), the look of the page and the way the paragraphs are written is right out of the most traditional style of print publications. Later in the report, though, once the pages have begun to incorporate technical graphics, the pages look like hybrids between print and Web publications, as the report's page 9 shows:

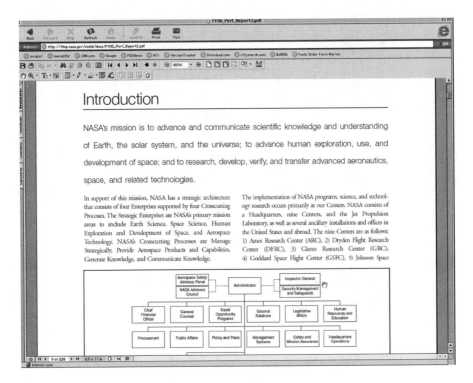

● MODEL TEMPLATES FOR WEB PAGES

A number of sites on the Web offer templates for typical Web sites and pages. A few of the current ones are www.freelayouts.com/, www.4templates.com/, and www.freesitetemplates.com/. Use your favorite search engine and look for "Web site templates" to find more. Here are templates of the basic designs behind the sites we've seen in this chapter. The endlessly scrolling site can be all one column, or, as shown on the following page, multiple columns:

The endlessly scrolling site		
Column 1	Column 2	Column 3

The hierarchical site can consist of two, three, or more levels:

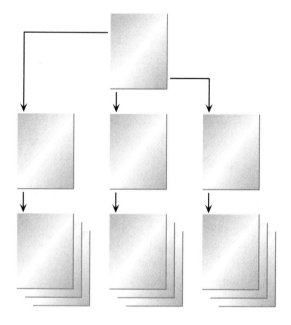

① Find a Web site whose structure is of the endlessly scrolling type, and analyze its strengths and weaknesses. As part of your analysis, make a sketch of the site's structure as it would look if the site were recast to fit a hierarchical design.

② Find a Web site that is set up according to the hierarchical structure, and analyze its strengths and weaknesses. How does the design of individual pages adapt to that structure? How has the designer kept the site from seeming as disorganized as the following illustration?

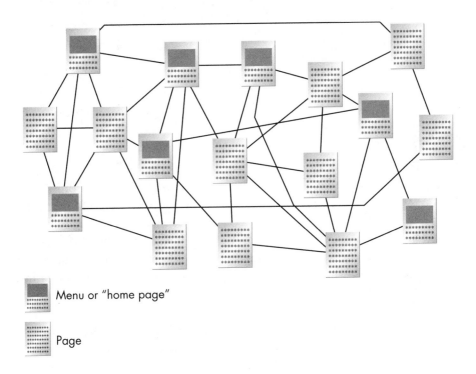

Menu or "home page"

Page

Writing Research Papers 12

◗ *The point of writing is discovery.*

Research today is easier, more exciting, and more rewarding than ever. With access to electronic encyclopedias, the Internet, and services like ProQuest and LexisNexis, you have an enormous world of information at your command. Not only is finding that information easier, but communicating with others about your research is also easier than ever—whether using email to ask experts questions, sitting in on electronic discussion lists, or sending drafts out as attachments for others to review.

But researchers using the Web or other computerized sources can quickly find themselves overwhelmed by too much information, much of it dubious. So with more information come more responsibilities: to sort carefully, to focus tightly, to evaluate critically, to credit your sources honestly, and to create an effective report. We'll discuss these issues and more in this chapter.

The general approach for writing research papers, whether for a course, a magazine, an employer, or a client, includes three basic steps:

❶ Selecting a topic
   Pick a good topic

Define your purpose

Identify your audience

Formulate a research question

❷ Researching your topic

Set up a general search strategy

Use primary and secondary sources

Do original research

Make a research outline for using the library and the Web

Find things out for yourself

Be open to serendipity

Take notes

Manage sources and quotations

Manage and evaluate electronic sources

❸ Writing your paper

Get started

Choose a plan of organization

Write a draft

Get responses

Finish your paper

● ● SELECTING A TOPIC

A research paper requires a major investment on your part. So why not be good to yourself right from the start? If you choose a topic that truly interests you, one that will be fun to explore, you'll write with more of a sense of purpose. A good research paper topic has the following qualities:

◎ *The topic is interesting to you.* You'd really like to know more about it.

◎ *The topic has an argumentative edge.* You have a point you'd like to make with your reader.

◎ *The topic is tailored to a specific audience, or audiences.* You have in mind an audience that wants or needs to know more about the topic.

○ *The topic is narrow enough.* You have focused it on something you can cover adequately within the specifications given (see Chapter 3).

● Pick a Good Topic

When you have a range of choices, pick an area you already know something about and would enjoy exploring further. Here are examples of the kinds of topics students might choose to start with:

> You might want to learn more about the Mayan civilization because last summer you went on an archeological dig at the Tikal ruins in Guatemala.

> You might want to write a paper on Nelson Mandela, the civil rights leader who became president of South Africa after spending more than twenty-five years as a political prisoner in that country.

> Some aspect of the life of that remarkable medieval queen, Eleanor of Aquitaine, might make a good topic for you.

> Perhaps you can gather statistics on how many major symphony orchestras are conducted by women versus how many by men, and then go on to explore the causes for that disparity of numbers.

> Or maybe you wonder why in most historical periods of painting, there are so few women artists represented.

● Define Your Purpose

Know the purpose behind your research. Perhaps your instructor has specified that purpose in the assignment by using a term such as *analyze, explain, investigate, compare, prove,* or *discuss.* As you work on your draft, keep checking to see that you're doing what the assignment specifies.

Then think about your own purposes. Most readers want you to take a position on your subject, then use the information you collect to support and amplify that position. Remember that research papers are always better pieces of writing if they have an argumentative edge.

In this early stage of planning your paper, it's useful to get down a tentative *thesis sentence* that sums up the main points you plan to make and thus expresses that argumentative edge. For example,

Artemisia Gentileschi, a talented artist in seventeenth-century Italy, overcame formidable cultural, professional, and sexual obstacles to produce some of the finest art of her day; some of that art reveals a strong feminist theme.

Any such thesis is only a working statement; almost certainly you would want to revise and refine it for the final version of your paper.

● IDENTIFY YOUR AUDIENCE

Whether you are writing on an assigned topic or on a topic you've chosen, begin by considering who your readers are and what they want to get from your paper. First is your professor. Professors always hope to learn something new from their students—that's one of the bonuses of teaching. But in addition to reading for content—new information and interesting ways of looking at familiar information—professors read your research papers with several other concerns in mind:

◖ To evaluate your knowledge of your subject matter

◖ To determine your ability to make a valid claim, find information that will support it, and present your case in a clear and organized fashion

◖ To see how you got to the claim your paper makes, how you found the information you use to support it—to see enough of the workings of your research process itself so they can evaluate its strength

◖ To assess your mastery of the formal conventions of research writing in a given academic field; for example, the format recommended by the Modern Language Association (MLA) for an English paper, or the format recommended by the American Psychological Association (APA) for a paper in sociology or psychology (see "Mastering the Conventions of Documentation," pages 271–87).

To create a good research piece, it's useful to identify another audience besides your professors, an additional group of readers you would like to influence or inform. You could choose a magazine or other kind of periodical that might publish something about the topic you're writing on. For example, a travel magazine might be interested in an article on your visit to Tikal, the Mayan site in Guatemala. Today there are many online publications, such as *Salon* (salon.com), that you can browse right at your own computer; select one of those and write your research paper as an article for it. (You can see a full listing at www.metagrid.com/.) Who knows—you might even decide to submit your piece to be considered for publication. At the very least, assume that you are writing for other students in the class for which you're writing the paper.

Whatever audience(s) you decide to write for, ask yourself these questions:

- ○ What do they already know about my topic?
- ○ What would they like to know?
- ○ What kind of details are likely to interest them?
- ○ What's in this topic for them—what might their stake in it be?

If you are writing your paper in a class where students respond to each other's rough drafts, asking yourself these questions as you are writing will be particularly helpful. Asking your peer reviewers these questions as they review your draft(s) will give them good ways to begin to respond to your work constructively.

● FORMULATE A RESEARCH QUESTION

Once you have decided on a tentative topic, you can begin to formulate a question (or questions) about your topic to answer through your research. You may, for instance, want to find out the answers to questions such as "What can the average citizen do on a daily basis to help protect the natural environment?" or "Why is California the site of so many earthquakes?" or "How do the film versions of Jane Austen's novels, such as *Sense and Sensibility,* compare with the novels themselves?"

If you were writing a paper on Artemisia Gentileschi, you might phrase your question like this: "Why have women painters from earlier centuries than the nineteenth received so little attention until now?" or "Why are painters like Artemisia Gentileschi so little known today?" or "How did Artemisia Gentileschi go about transcending the limitations which her culture and her personal history placed upon her?" You need to formulate your research question early in your research, and continue to reformulate, refocus, and sharpen it as you move through every step of the research process.

Resist the temptation to begin your research with questions that are built upon unproved assumptions or that lead to obvious or foregone conclusions. A question like "How has commercialism corrupted professional sports?" is inappropriate if the underlying assumption—commercialism has corrupted professional sports—cannot be convincingly established. When you are researching and writing about topics that are controversial or surrounded by debate, your first task may well be to show that you're arguing from valid assumptions. If you're going to have to spend half of the paper just establishing the validity of those assumptions, as you would have to in the topic of commercialism and professional sports, then reconsider your choice of topic.

How do you go about creating a research question? How, for example, do you get from "Artemisia Gentileschi" to "What is unique about the career of Artemisia Gentileschi?" or from "phytoplankton in Wilson Inlet" to "In what ways does the growth cycle of phytoplankton in Wilson Inlet allow us to anticipate the growth cycle of phytoplankton in the Ross Sea?"

One way to make that transformation is to ask these six questions about your topic: *Who* has noticed the work of Gentileschi? *What* is unusual about it? *Where* can her work be seen? *When* did she live? *How* did events in her life affect her work? *Why* was her work neglected? Each of these questions can help get your topic moving in the direction of being a question to be answered and an argument or arguments to be made.

Another technique for creating or discovering a research question, also one used by the authors of this book, is to look for *anomalies*, things that don't make sense, within the subject you are examining. Here are some examples:

"Why is it that Gentileschi's work was considered unimportant, yet some of her paintings were mistaken for the work of acknowledged masters such as Caravaggio?" What is the anomaly there?

"Why is it that city X continues to spend millions of dollars developing the buildings, parks, and sidewalks along the river that flows through the middle of town, but continues to do nothing about the terrible and deteriorating condition of the water quality in that river?" What is the anomaly there?

When students begin research, the *key mistake* they often make is going straight to the Web or straight to the library catalog to try to find the information they need. That step is properly in fact a *middle* step in a larger research and writing process. The parts of that larger process—including how to use both the Web and the library—are explained in the following sections.

● SET UP A GENERAL SEARCH STRATEGY

Only when you have defined your purpose, considered your audience, and formulated (or begun to formulate) your research question are you ready to begin your research. As you plan your research strategy, keep several important principles in mind:

❶ *Make a plan for your time, working backward from your due date.* For example, if you receive your assignment on March 15 for a paper due on April 20, you might plan your time like this:

April 20: Submit revised final paper to instructor.

April 16: Receive annotated draft from instructor.

April 12: Give draft to instructor.

April 8–10: Revise and rewrite draft.

April 1–7: Write first draft. Confer with classmates or a second reader for feedback.

March 24–31: Refine and focus topic; do additional research online and in library. Make notes and rough out an outline.

March 16–23: Select topic; do preliminary research on the Internet, in ProQuest, and in LexisNexis.

It helps to set deadlines for yourself and post due dates in some prominent place where you'll see them every day.

❷ *Remember that everything will take longer than you think it will.* Electronic sources are wonderful, but it's very time-consuming to search the Web and be appropriately critical of the results, or to search library databases and indexes (like LexisNexis, *Humanities Abstracts, Art Abstracts,* or the *Applied Science and Technology Index*) and then follow up on materials you find. Taking careful, thorough notes on index cards or on your laptop, downloading articles and highlighting relevant passages, or making photocopies and annotating them is also slow going. Inevitably you'll run into snags—copy machines don't work, your Internet server goes down, or you can't locate a source. All are good reasons for delay, but your instructor doesn't want to hear excuses when the paper is due.

❸ *Make some sort of research outline that tells you what sources you need to consult and the order in which you need to work through those sources.* In particular, if you are going to need to send away for information, set up interviews, or conduct surveys, take care of these time-consuming research tasks *first* so that you will have time to complete them and to think about your information before you begin to write your paper. Then if your research takes longer than you anticipated, you won't find yourself having to begin writing your paper without having consulted your most valuable sources. (Writing your paper is explained in more detail later in this chapter.)

❹ *Set a deadline when you must stop researching and begin drafting your paper.* Sometimes it's tempting to keep looking for more information, especially when you discover new leads. However tantalizing these leads are, you may not be able to follow up on them, simply because you are running out of time. If this is the case, you might mention the potential value of these sources for further study in your conclusion or in an informational note.

● USE PRIMARY AND SECONDARY SOURCES

After setting up your research strategy, you can begin collecting material. Two types of sources will concern you: *primary* and *secondary*. Primary sources are those that deal most directly with your topic—reports of eye-witnesses, articles or letters from those directly involved in a situation, fact-finding reports, and so on. Secondary sources generally comment on and help you to interpret your primary sources.

In a research paper for a history course, for instance, your primary sources might be newspaper articles or government documents, letters or diary entries written or published during the historical period you are writing about, even photographs taken at the scene. Your secondary sources might be books or articles written by historians who have also consulted those same primary sources. Remember that you need to bring a fresh perspective to those secondary sources.

In a research paper for a literature course, your primary sources would be the literary texts that you are interpreting or criticizing, or the letters or journals of the author whose work you are investigating. Secondary sources would include books, articles, lectures, and reviews by literary critics on the subject of your paper. In a scientific research paper, your own observations and experiments might be your primary sources, whereas reports of other scientific investigators on the same or a closely related topic would constitute your secondary sources.

● Do Original Research

If you are asked to do *original research,* you must work almost entirely from primary sources. For example, suppose you were asked to do original research on student protests against the Vietnam War in the 1960s. First, you would probably go to an encyclopedia to find out when and where such protests took place; then you would pick a period and place on which to focus your attention—perhaps the protests at Kent State when four students were killed, or the protests at the Democratic National Convention in 1968. You would then go to indexes of newspapers like the *New York Times* and the *Los Angeles Times* to find news stories from those dates that would tell you what happened at such protests, writing your paper from the information you found in those papers or in magazines such as *Time* or *U.S. News and World Report.* You would not use more recent articles or books that reflected on the protests or tried to interpret them, although you might want to read such articles for your own enlightenment.

If you were asked to write a paper based on original research in an American literature course, you might pick a topic such as the images of women in Willa Cather's novels. You could then select four novels—perhaps *My Ántonia, The Professor's House, The Song of the Lark,* and *A Lost Lady*—read them carefully, analyze the way Cather portrays her women characters, and write a paper identifying and reflecting on her handling of the women characters. Resist the temptation to see what other writers have said—the professor who asks for original research wants to know *your* response, not that of the critics.

● MAKE A RESEARCH OUTLINE FOR USING THE LIBRARY AND THE WEB

This section presents a comprehensive outline for the research you do in the library and on the Web (see Figure 1). You will need to adapt this outline for your own project. Depending on the scope of your research paper, you may choose to skip some of the steps, and it's inevitable that some steps will prove to be more useful than others.

FIGURE 1: Steps in a complete, integrated search process

Step 1:
Move from *keywords* to *subject terms*.

Step 5:
Consult *search engines* (general, meta search, and specialty).

Step 2:
Consult *general* and *specific* reference tools.

Step 6:
Search *indexes* and *databases*.

Step 3:
Consult *subject trees* on the Web.

Step 7:
Search *additional databases* and *other archives* online.

Step 4:
Consult your *library catalog*.

Step 8:
Find *firsthand information*.

STEP 1: MOVING FROM KEYWORDS TO A SUBJECT SEARCH

Often a student will say something like "I want to do a paper on recycling," or "I want to do something on arbitration." In that case, the student's search process is beginning with *keywords* (the keywords are *recycling* or *arbitration*). *Keyword* is the name for any word you might normally use to describe your topic. The first step in a good research process is to move from the keyword stage to a search based on the right *subject terms.* If you start by looking up your keywords in your library's card catalog (or on the Web), you may waste hours of valuable time sorting through useless information and never even find the right information for your paper.

Maybe all you know is that you want to write about a popular American novelist, or about painters, or recycling, or arbitration. How do you get from those words to subject terms—the terms librarians use to index books and articles—and from subject terms to a research question? Here are some of the ways:

○ Read about your topic; talk to people who know about it; look for more information; try to find out through reading and conversation what the subject terms relevant to your topic might be.

○ Go to the *Library of Congress Subject Headings List*, a multivolume bound book (the "big red book") available at most library reference desks (to be discussed in more detail in step 4). It will help you translate your keywords into the right subject terms.

○ Many online databases make available lists of "descriptors" (their name for subject terms), and you can consult such lists directly to find a particular database's way(s) of naming your subject. For example, the *Thesaurus of Descriptors* for the Education Resources Information Clearinghouse (ERIC) database yields subject terms that make searching that database more effective. And if you use the ProQuest database and text retrieval service, one of its search screens will show you its list of subject terms.

○ You can go to a *subject tree*, such as the one on the bottom of the Yahoo! home screen (www.yahoo.com/), or the one at The Virtual Library (www.vlib.org/), and by clicking on the word from the first screen that most nearly matches your interest, let the computer take you further and further into your search. (Subject trees are discussed in more detail in step 3.)

These techniques helped a student writer get from *arbitration* to *Shearson v. McMahon*. They can also be used to get from *women painters* to *Artemisia Gentileschi*, or from *contemporary novelists* to *Richard Russo*.

Another good way to find subject terms for your topic is to ask an expert. Yet another good way is to use a trick called *backward searching;* if you can find one good "hit"—one article or book exactly on your topic—then you can look that article or book up in your library catalog or in the databases or indexes appropriate for your field (see step 4), find out what subject terms are used to index that item, and then feed those terms back into the database or library catalog you are using and see what else might be listed under them.

STEP 2: REFERENCE TOOLS

A really thorough research process begins with consulting reference tools—general encyclopedias, specialized encyclopedias, and other kinds of reference tools that may be particular to your topic's own field. Whether you access these reference tools as bound volumes in the library or you access them on the Web, an important early part of any thorough research process is learning what sources such as *Encyclopaedia Britannica* (www.britannica.com/) say about your topic, or about the subject heading that is closest to your topic. Start with general encyclopedias, then go to specialized encyclopedias and/or dictionaries (there's a great list of online encyclopedias and dictionaries at refdesk.com), and then in the library go to your field's entry in Balay's *Guide to Reference Books* to discover what other specialized reference tools there are for you to consult.

Starting your research by consulting general reference tools and then moving on to specialized ones gives your research paper a kind of background depth and texture that is hard to come by any other way. Researchers who start by diving right into the Web or the library catalog often write papers that, by comparison, are much more shallow. Often it is the information on the periphery of a subject—potential questions about the real economics of recycling, for instance, or about the history and authenticity of Gentileschi's paintings—that makes for the most interesting research papers. Students who dive right into the middle of their topics may miss these potentially rich shadings of their topics entirely.

STEP 3: SUBJECT TREES

Ultimately, your topic and your research question will determine what kinds of research resources are most helpful to you. For topics that are very timely (for instance, legislation currently being discussed or enacted by Congress, or the latest developments in computer technology), newspapers, periodicals, government documents, and government sites on the Web, such as *Thomas: Legislative Information on the Internet* (thomas.loc.gov/), are more likely sources of information than books or reference works such as encyclopedias, which require considerable lead time for publication. For the most up-to-date topics, the Web probably provides the most up-to-date information.

While you can access many encyclopedias directly on the Web, the Web's own evolving version of an encyclopedia may well be the search tool known as a *subject tree*. If you've ever looked at the bottom half of the Yahoo! search engine's home screen, you've seen something that looked like Figure 2. Most search engines have a similar function, or you can find a subject tree by itself at the WWW Virtual Library (www.vlib.org/). By entering *"subject tree"* into the text box of your favorite search engine, you can find lists of more subject trees (such as the one sorted by fields of study at bubl.ac.uk/link/menus.html).

Use a subject tree by finding the entry that most nearly matches your topic (for instance, if you're researching artists in general, you could start with "Arts & Humanities," go from there to "Art," and then follow

FIGURE 2: Simple subject tree found on Yahoo! home screen	
Agriculture	**Arts & Humanities**
Agriculture, Gardening, Forestry, . . .	Literature, Photography, . . .
Business & Economy	**Computing**
Economics, Finance, Shopping, . . .	Internet, E-Commerce, Languages, . . .
Education	**Entertainment**
Education, Applied Linguistics, K–12, . . .	Movies, Music, Humor, . . .
Government	**Health**
Elections, Law, Taxes, . . .	Medicine, Diseases, Drugs, . . .
Recreation	**Regional**
Sports, Games, Gardening, . . .	African, Asian, Countries, US States, . . .
Science	**Society**
Animals, Astronomy, Engineering, . . .	Political Science, Religion, Social Sciences, . . .

down the succeeding choices until you get to a list of artists. Clicking on their individual links, or the history of art, or various movements in art such as the baroque period, will usually lead you somewhere interesting. You might want to try your topic in several different subject trees because different topics are treated more completely on different trees.

STEP 4: THE LIBRARY CATALOG

The library catalog stage of your research is much more rewarding if you have done the previous steps outlined here, and successfully moved from a vaguely formed idea of a research topic to a fairly sharply focused research question. If you are still working on the basis of a topic name alone, you absolutely must use the *Library of Congress Subject Headings List* to find the right words (the subject terms) to look up in the catalog. For example, a student starting her research process might be distressed to learn her university's library apparently contained no information on *madness, mental disorders*, or *mental diseases*. With the help of a librarian and the *Subject Headings List*, she was able to realize that the term she needed to be researching was in fact *mental illness*; the *Lists* entry for *mental illness* also told her what many of the related topics were (diagnosis, evaluation, treatment, and so on).

As you do your research in the library catalog, perhaps by using specific subject headings, or by using the names of particular authors, books, or journals you are already aware of, remember you can also search *backward*. That is, if you find one "hit," one source that is exactly on your topic, you can often use that item's catalog entry to tell you how that item is indexed. Then you can feed the index terms you find back into the catalog's search function as search terms, thus discovering new materials that will often shed new light on your subject.

You can also *search sideways*, finding other sources by the same author, or even looking for other books on the same shelf as one you find that looks useful. You can also do a sideways search for books via an unusual commercial search tool, Amazon's "Customers who bought this book also bought" function (www.amazon.com). Give it the name of one reasonably current book on your topic, and see what other, similar books it suggests.

You can also *search deeper*, checking out your subject terms in the catalog of the Library of Congress itself (www.loc.gov/). If you've started your research early enough, your own library may be able to borrow those other books for you through interlibrary loan.

Search engines are Web-based computer utilities that allow you either to access a subject tree (discussed under step 3) or to type your own search terms—whether keywords or subject terms—into the search engine's text box and let the search engine find results for you. Popular search engines include Yahoo! (www.yahoo.com/), Alta Vista (altavista.com/), and Google (www.google.com/), among many others. You can find a very full listing and more detailed discussions at Search Engine Watch, www.search enginewatch.com/. Working your subject through a variety of search engines, and a variety of types of search engines, will yield many results. Later on in this chapter we will discuss how to broaden those results, how to narrow them, and the essential task of making judgments about their reliability.

Two kinds of searches and three kinds of search engines concern us here: basic searches and advanced searches; and general search engines (such as the ones listed above), meta search engines (which search several search engines at once), and specialty search engines (which search only in one area, such as law, medicine, or science).

BASIC AND ADVANCED SEARCHES. Most search engines allow both kinds of searches. A basic search involves simply typing your search term or terms into the search engine's text box. Thus, on Alta Vista, a student interested in Pocahontas can type *Pocahontas* into the text box. Unfortunately, that yields 154,000 hits! Adding more terms to the basic search is one way to *narrow the search*: *"Pocahontas descendants"* (you must use the quotation marks to let the computer know you want the words considered as a phrase) brings the number of hits down to 91.

You can do narrower or broader searches even better by switching to the advanced search screen, which lets you use words like *AND, AND NOT,* and *NEAR* to refine your searching. Thus you can rule out the references to Disney's movie about Pocahontas by switching from the basic search (*Pocahontas*) to the advanced search (*"Pocahontas AND NOT Dis-*

ney"). The resulting 90,000 hits would still need narrowing, however, so you could also scroll down on the advanced screen and limit your search to items posted within the last month, which brings the number of hits to 9. Most search engines have these same capabilities, although they all work a little differently.

GENERAL SEARCH ENGINES. General search engines such as those listed above compete with each other to cover the biggest part of the Web and to "rank" their results most effectively. Imagine a search that yields 150 hits—wouldn't it be nice if those hits were presented in something other than random order? Search engines use many sophisticated methods for this ranking, such as ranking by how many other pages link to a particular page (having more links moves the page up the rankings) or by how many people click onto a site when they see it in the search engine results. Some search engines rank highest the pages whose owners have paid a fee to the search engine. Obviously, these ranking systems are often unreliable, maybe even useless, for scholarly research. So, because different general search engines search different parts of the Web and rank their results different ways, it's always a good idea to do your search on several different search engines (Google, Alta Vista, and Fast Search, for example).

META SEARCH ENGINES. Wouldn't it be nice if there were search engines that searched multiple search engines for you? Meta search engines do. Ixquick Metasearch (www.ixquick.com/), for example, searches eleven general search engines. A search for "Pocahontas descendants" that yielded 9 results on Alta Vista yields 39 on Ixquick. Other popular meta search engines include Dogpile (www.dogpile.com/) and Metacrawler (www.metacrawler.com/index.html). (There's a complete listing on the Search Engine Watch site mentioned earlier.)

SPECIALTY SEARCH ENGINES. Specialty search engines focus on one area—travel, science, law, art, population statistics, or medicine, for example—and search that area more deeply. If you intend to do research in a particular field for several years (for example, if that field is your major in college), it's well worth knowing if there is a specialty search engine just for that field. You can find a short list of specialty search engines on the Search Engine Watch site and much fuller lists at the ZDNet Search IQ site (www.zdnet.com/searchiq/subjects/).

The next step in your research is to find articles in periodicals. Periodicals are materials such as magazines, newsletters, and professional journals that are published periodically—for example, monthly, seasonally, or annually. Because of their publication schedules, they often contain more up-to-date material than you can find in books, and so they are an extremely important source of information for researchers. Usually the most recent issues of periodicals are shelved unbound in libraries, while older issues are bound into individually indexed volumes. Some heavily used periodicals, such as news magazines, are often stored on microfiche instead of or in addition to bound volumes. Today more and more periodicals make at least some part of their contents available either on databases that students can access through their libraries or directly on the Web.

Finding articles in periodicals requires that you consult special guides or indexes to periodical literature. The most general of these, and one that is apt to be found in even very small libraries, is the *Readers' Guide to Periodical Literature.* If you didn't learn to use this reference work in high school or in an introductory college writing course, you can easily teach yourself how to use it now, or you can ask your reference librarian for assistance. However, other, more specialized guides and indexes to periodicals are likely to be more useful to you as a college-level researcher. Many of these are available online, whether through CD-ROMs the library has or directly on the Web. A few of the major indexes of this sort are the following:

Applied Science and Technology Index

Art Index

Biography Index

Biological Abstracts

Book Review Digest

Business Index

The Education Index

Engineering Index

General Science Index

Humanities Index

Index Medicus
MLA International Bibliography
PsycINFO
Public Affairs Information Service (PAIS)
Social Sciences and Humanities Index
Web of Science

Your library probably gives you access to many more specialized indexes and bibliographies; these can be located by consulting the subject entries in a special catalog for reference works (such as Balay's *Guide to Reference Books*) or by asking a librarian. Most libraries today have computerized card catalogs that allow you to search from a computer terminal for articles in the library's periodical holdings. Usually, guides to using online indexes are provided at terminals in the library. They will tell you what indexes are available to you online and will give you instructions for accessing the available indexes and for conducting various types of searches. Sometimes libraries give short courses to help you learn to use online search tools. If you are taking a class that requires writing a major research paper, consider signing up for such a short course. It could save you lots of time in the long run.

All of these computer databases and indexes work by subject terms (or *descriptors*, as librarians call them). So if you were doing research about prenatal care among teenage mothers, the descriptors to punch in for your search would be *"prenatal care"* and *"teenage mothers"* (note that you probably need the quotation marks to link the separate words into phrases for the search). If you were particularly interested in the correlation between adequate prenatal care for teenage mothers and the high school attendance record of these mothers, you could add *"high school attendance"* as a third descriptor. The computer then does a three-way search, narrowing its search to articles that address all three issues. Sometimes you have to be imaginative about your descriptors. For instance, if adding the term *"high school attendance"* doesn't seem to work, try *"high school dropouts"* as an alternative.

The list on the next page includes just a few computerized indexes. If none of these meets your needs, ask the librarian for others. More indexes are becoming available all the time.

TOPIC	INDEX
Astronomy	*INSPEC*
Business	*ABI/INFORM; InfoTrac*
Contemporary events	*Newsbank*
Contemporary periodicals	*Academic Index; InfoTrac; PAIS (Public Affairs Information Service)*
Economics	*PAIS*
Education	*ERIC*
General information	*Wilsondisc* (covers same material as *Readers' Guide*)
Humanities	*InfoTrac*
Literature	*MLA Bibliography*
Mathematics	*MATHFILE*
Psychology	*Psychlit*
Public affairs	*PAIS*
Social science	*InfoTrac*

When you find a citation in an index or bibliography for an article that sounds helpful to you, *copy down the full citation.* This will not only help you locate the article itself but will also save you time later on, when you need to compile a bibliography for your paper. The same is true, of course, for citations of materials from other sources as well—newspapers, documents, books, pamphlets, TV and radio broadcasts, documentary films, the Web, interviews, and so forth.

While using bibliographies and indexes is an efficient way to locate periodical articles, you will find that current issues of most periodicals are often not indexed. If up-to-date information is essential to your investigation, check the most recent issues on the periodicals' display shelves or check to see if there's an online version of the journal that may include the current issues. You can also ask a librarian if an online index and full-text retrieval service such as ProQuest is available; tools such as ProQuest contain a wide variety of fairly current articles that you can read on-screen. Often you can print out an article from ProQuest on a library printer, or even email it to yourself at home so you can work on it electronically at your leisure there. At many universities, services like Pro-Quest are available to all faculty, staff, and students, regardless of where those individuals may be logging in from.

The procedure for locating newspaper articles is similar to that for finding information in periodicals. The major indexes for newspaper articles on national and international topics include the following:

The New York Times Index

National Newspaper Index—lists articles from the *New York Times*, the *Christian Science Monitor*, and the *Wall Street Journal*

The Newspaper Index—lists articles from the *Chicago Tribune*, the *Los Angeles Times*, the *New Orleans Times-Picayune*, and the *Washington Post* (these four papers also give regional news for their areas)

Printed versions of these indexes often do not arrive in libraries until some time after their publication, so computerized indexes are your best bet if you are researching current news stories. You'll find some of the most useful computerized search tools in Newsbank, which indexes a microfiche collection of stories from over 400 U.S. newspapers.

Yet another source of national and international news stories is the Web, which allows online access to current articles in most major newspapers published in this and other countries. Search engines such as Moreover (www.moreover.com) or Excite's News Search (www.excite.com/search/news) can help you find deeper access to news stories than general search engines offer. Of course, you can always search the newspapers themselves online (there's a great list at refdesk.com). Many of them let you read their current issues free; most let you search their archives free; and some even let you have copies of archived articles free. Others request a small fee (usually only a couple of dollars) for reprints of archived articles.

GOVERNMENT DOCUMENTS. Most large libraries contain a special section for U.S. government publications, a type of source that can be especially useful to you if you are writing a research paper for history, political science, law, or social science courses. Some government publications are indexed in the public catalog and are shelved according to the Library of Congress or Dewey decimal numbering system. Other, uncataloged documents are kept in the government documents section of the library, arranged according to Superintendent of Documents numbers. Still others are kept on microform in collections called microform sets. These, too, are filed according to Superintendent of Documents numbers.

Here is a list of a few of the major indexes you can use to locate government document publications. In many libraries you will find a number of other indexes as well; ask a librarian for assistance if you have difficulty using them.

> *Monthly Catalog of United States Government Publications*
> *The Federal Index*
> *Index to U.S. Government Periodicals*
> *C.I.S.U.S. Serial Set Index*
> *Washington Information Directory*

Searching for government documents online can be done via specialty search engines such as FirstGov (firstgov.gov/), which provides access to all online federal government resources, or through sites like Google's "Uncle Sam" (www.google.com/unclesam), which returns links only to government sources. There's a thorough discussion of searching government documents, and many more links, starting at the Web site of the National Archives and Records Administration (www.nara.gov/alic/rayd/govdoc.html).

STEP 7: DATABASES AND ARCHIVES

Many university libraries now have integrated search systems that make use of the World Wide Web. And many, perhaps most, college students can access many additional databases, indexes, and archives right from their own personal computers. Some of that access may be through their library's own Web site, but much of it is directly through the student's own Internet service provider.

In addition to the many search engines, databases, and indexes already listed and discussed in this chapter, there are also many other kinds of sites that archive various kinds of documents, such as the government documents in the Archives Library Information Center (www.nara.gov/alic/rayd/govdoc.html). The following list is only a sampling, selected to show you some idea of the range of sources available:

Alex Catalogue of Electronic Texts (www.infomotions.com/ alex/). Specializes in English and American literature.

Electronic Text Center (www.etext.lib.virginia.edu/). An enormous collection of documents at the University of Virginia.

Internet Public Library (www.ipl.org). You can look up your field of study, or your topic, in this comprehensive online library.

Liszt (www.liszt.com). A huge directory of electronic discussion lists.

Project Bartleby (www.bartleby.com/). Another huge collection, this one at Columbia University.

Project Gutenberg (www.gutenberg.net). A huge electronic library.

Refdesk (refdesk.com). This is not only an excellent collection of links to online reference tools, it also contains great lists of other kinds of resources accessed by the name of each individual field. So if you're looking, for example, for other Web-based materials on computer science, you can click on Refdesk's "computer science" link and find many more resources.

Tile.Net (tile.net). Allows for searching discussion lists by topic.

Voice of the Shuttle (vos.ucsb.edu). A subject-based guide to text archives.

"Webliographies." A "webliography" is a bibliography of Web sites. Over 7,000 of these exist already. You can find out if there's one for your field of study or your topic by typing your field's name or one or another of your subject terms into a good search engine's text box accompanied by the word *webliography*.

● FIND THINGS OUT FOR YOURSELF

Although a great deal of academic research takes place in the library and on the Web, these are by no means the only places where you can collect data and information for college research papers. There are times when other sources can provide more direct, specific, and useful material.

Suppose, for instance, that you wanted to find out how your own community was responding to a water shortage brought about by the summer's drought. Because your question refers to a local situation, it is unlikely that you would turn up much useful information in the sorts of national and international publications that make up the bulk of a university library's holdings. Instead, you would want to gather information locally—perhaps looking for materials such as announcements published by city officials, walking around the reservoir, or arranging interviews with city council members, employees at the local water works plant, or members of local citizens' action groups. Local news broadcasts on radio or television and locally published newspapers are other potential sources of information. Keep in mind that firsthand research can be especially effective when used in combination with library and Web research.

Experts whom you consult in person can sometimes provide you with brochures or in-house publications on your topic that are not readily available in libraries or on the Web. Other potentially helpful sources include television and radio broadcasts, documentary films, and informational pamphlets published by professional organizations or special interest groups.

● BE OPEN TO SERENDIPITY

Cultivate serendipity. Experienced researchers know the value of lucky accidents and stay alert for them, glancing at the titles of books shelved right next to the ones they are seeking, or running their eyes over the table of contents in the issue of a periodical that contains an article on their prepared list. Unplanned breakthroughs in research investigations can be prompted by conversations, by media broadcasts or news stories, or by casually skimming materials in the library, in a bookstore, or on the Web. The key is keeping your mind open to the unexpected source; your best piece of information may be one you stumble onto while you are looking for something else.

You may also want to join electronic discussion groups relevant to your topic, particularly if you can find a group that's highly focused—for instance, a group that is conversing about a new kind of insulin pump for diabetics might contribute valuable, up-to-date information. Such groups can give you useful names and references. But the interchange on discussion groups can also be discursive and trivial, not worth your precious research time, and many professors look at information derived from discussion groups with a pretty skeptical eye unless it is well supported from other, more reliable sources.

● Take Notes

Sometimes the chore of taking notes for a research paper looms so large that you are tempted just to print out or photocopy *everything* you find, then worry about making sense of it after you leave the library. That's not a good idea. This practice encourages you to rely too heavily on the original words of your sources before you have digested their ideas. Wholesale photocopying of everything you find is often a shortcut that actually defeats the whole purpose of research, and in addition can lead to inadvertent plagiarism.

Many people prefer to take their notes on index cards because cards are easier to sort and reorganize than sheets of notebook or typing paper. Others, however, prefer to keep all their notes in a notebook because in this form the notes are easier to carry around and are less likely to get lost. Still others take notes at the computer and organize them in files; an advantage to this method is that you can make backup files to guard against lost notes and outlines.

Whatever method you choose, be sure that you always include full details about the source along with the information. And *always* write down the page numbers for *all* the information you record, whether you directly quote that information or simply refer to it in a summary or paraphrase; for Web pages, always write down the date you accessed a page. If you don't keep track of page numbers at this stage, you will have to go back to your sources to hunt for them. If you don't keep track of access dates for electronic sources, you will have to hope your field's documentation style does not require that information in citations of Web pages.

● Manage Sources and Quotations

Whether you are working in an academic setting or a professional one, your readers will want to sense from the way that you handle your sources that you have done responsible research. How you handle those sources depends in part on whether you are writing a piece of popular appeal (such as a magazine article) or a piece of academic interest (such as a term paper).

INFORMAL CITATIONS

Writers of books, magazine articles, or newspaper columns usually cite their sources informally. For example, the columnist William Raspberry might mention a government report he read recently and name the agency that published it, but he might not bother to give the date or location of the report. Another magazine author might cite statistics on the growth of legalized gambling revenues for the last five years but not give the source of that statistic. These authors assume their readers will accept their claims as sound ones.

FORMAL CITATIONS

In an academic paper, your instructor wants all the facts that are connected with your claims, and part of your responsibility is to learn how to present those facts. You're obligated to leave a careful and accurate trail so that readers can follow the path of evidence you're presenting and verify that evidence if they wish. You also need to name your sources so readers can judge for themselves what interests those sources might represent. If you were citing the statistic about the increase in legalized gambling, you would need to present the information like this:

> In an article in the Autumn 1999 issue of the *Wilson Quarterly*, Professor Jane Smith says that between 1994 and 1999 legalized gambling revenues in the United States nearly doubled, from $10 billion to about $20 billion annually.

Then you would give a full citation for the article in the Works Cited portion of your paper so the reader could easily find the article if he or she chose to.

When you attribute opinions or theories to an organization or movement, you need to specify the group that has expressed those opinions or theories. You might write,

> The communitarian movement, as described by its founder Amitai Etzioni in his forthcoming book, *The Golden Rule: Community and Morality in a Democratic Society*, holds that there are four basic principles of social justice: equality, mutuality, stewardship, and inclusion.

You would then include full information about Etzioni's book in your Works Cited page.

Give the exact source of every direct quotation. You can do this with footnotes, endnotes, or parenthetical notes within your paper, depending on the style your instructor specifies. (See "Mastering the Conventions of Documentation," pages 271–87, for more on these options.) Integrate quotations of three or four lines or less into the body of your paper, using terms of attribution such as *asserts*, *claims*, *argues*, *writes*, and so on, and enclosing the integrated quotations in quotation marks.

Indent longer quotations and type them without quotation marks. For example:

> In *Great Books*, David Denby says,
>> Accepting death in battle as inevitable, the Greek and Trojan aristocrats of the *Iliad* experience the world not as pleasant or unpleasant, nor as good or evil, but as glorious or shameful. We might say that Homer offers a conception of life that is noble rather than ethical—except that such opposition is finally misleading. For the Greeks, nobility has an ethical quality. You are not good or bad in the Christian sense. You are strong or weak; beautiful or ugly; conquering or vanquished; living or dead; favored by gods or cursed. (39)

In student papers, quotations like these should be double-spaced so they're easy for the instructor to read. Notice that indented quotations put the parenthetical citation outside the final punctuation mark.

If you omit something from a quotation, you must insert ellipsis marks within square brackets [. . .] to indicate that something has been left out. For instance:

> After all, Western literature begins with a quarrel between two arrogant pirates over booty. At the beginning of the poem, the various tribes of the Greeks [. . .] assembled before the walls of Troy are on the verge of disaster. Agamemnon, their leader, the most powerful of the kings, has kidnapped and taken as a mistress from a nearby city a young woman, the daughter of one of Apollo's priests; Apollo has angrily retaliated by bringing down a plague on the Greeks. (Denby 34)

Of course, your omission must not alter the sense of a quotation.

Finally, give additional information in brackets for any term within the quotation that needs further explanation, or for any other kind of interpolation or substitution:

> The crux of the poem [the *Iliad*] comes in Book IX, well before Achilles re-enters the war. As the Trojans await at their night fires, ready to attack at dawn, the Greeks, now in serious trouble, send three ambassadors to Achilles with promises of gifts. The three warriors [. . .] beg Achilles to give up his anger. This is what they offer: tripods, cauldrons, horses, gold, slave women, [. . .] and even the return of Achilles' slave mistress, whom Agamemnon swears he has never touched. What more can Achilles ask for? (Denby 48)

USE QUOTATIONS SPARINGLY

Don't overload your paper with quotations. You don't want your paper to look as if you patched it together from other people's ideas instead of giving your own opinions and interpretation. Each quotation should be used for a definite reason:

- ○ To support an important point you are making
- ○ To illustrate a particular writer's point of view
- ○ To cite examples of experts' contrasting opinions
- ○ To illustrate the flavor or force of an author's work
- ○ To give an example of the author's style

Usually you'll do better to summarize an opinion or point of view rather than illustrate it with a quotation, particularly if the quotation would be long. Readers tend to skim over long quotations because they want to find out what the author herself is saying. Assuming you can do the original justice in a succinct summary, that's the preferable course of action.

● MANAGE AND EVALUATE ELECTRONIC SOURCES

Once you become adept at searching electronic sources, two problems present themselves: you either find way too much information (and thus you need to *narrow your search*), or way too little (and thus you need to *broaden your search*).

A major problem with using the Web is narrowing a search so that it will yield a manageable number of items to consider. Using a search engine such as Google or Alta Vista, you may type in what seems like a fairly specific term only to find it will bring a staggering number of citations. The phrase *"Lewis and Clark,"* for example, brings up over 200,000 entries! You can't begin to examine or assess the value of that many entries, so it's important to find very specific terms (*subject terms* versus *keywords*, as discussed earlier in this chapter) that will give highly focused and limited results.

Sometimes even your best efforts at finding very specific subject terms produce thousands of hits. When that happens, try adding more terms to your search. Remember that on a basic search screen you can simply group words inside quotation marks, so that you are searching for phrases, not the separate words; additional words and phrases will further narrow the search. Thus *"Lewis and Clark" maps* will produce many fewer hits than *"Lewis and Clark,"* and *"Lewis and Clark" maps Oregon* (search engines usually assume an *and* exists between words not grouped inside quotation marks) will produce fewer hits still.

On most search engines, you could also switch to an advanced search screen, thus enabling you to use words such as *AND, AND NOT,* and *NEAR* (discussed earlier in this chapter). Thus, switching from *Pocahontas* to *Pocahontas AND NOT Disney* eliminates lots of Pocahontas hits. As discussed earlier, there are other ways advanced search screens let you limit searches, such as by date, by what part of the Web you want to search, or by what kind of item you are searching for (an entire Web site devoted to the topic, Web sites that simply mention the topic, or an image, for example).

When searching the Web (step 5, earlier in this chapter) just seems to get you tons of junk but not the kind of results you need, you need to search the more academic kinds of databases (step 6), whether you do that search online through your own Internet service provider or through your university library's online facilities. If your interest in Lewis and Clark is historical, try searching a database relevant to the field of history, such as *America: History and Life,* or *Historical Abstracts.* If your interest is in geography, try searching a database relevant to that field, such as the *Applied Science and Technology Index.*

Depending on your topic, sometimes you will find too little information. On the Web, one solution is to try more search engines. Because different search engines search different parts of the Web in different ways, you can never take "the search engine found no hits on your subject" as a final answer. If you search three or four search engines and still get no hits, try searching on a meta search engine or a specialty search engine, as discussed earlier. If you still get no hits and you want to keep searching the Web, you might try using a more general term instead.

Ultimately, though, if you've tried several different forms of your search, using several different search terms, on several different search engines, you will probably have to switch from search engines to more academic kinds of databases, indexes, and archives. Once again there is a premium on knowing which databases, indexes, and archives you can gain access to on the Web or through your library, and which of those are relevant to your topic. If you cannot find such a resource relevant to your topic, then seek the help of a good librarian.

EVALUATING ELECTRONIC SOURCES

Using the results of electronic searches in such a way as to be intellectually honest has become a subject that concerns everyone. Remember that no one is in charge on the Internet; there are no editors, instructors, or censors who have approved what's "published" on it. Anyone can contribute to the store of information available online, and as a result the Web is full of trash, in addition to enormous amounts of legitimate factual information, scholarly conversations, and valid, well-considered ideas. Confronted with this staggering array of unmonitored sources and unedited information, you have to learn to evaluate the sources you find on the Web.

Traditional means of evaluating *printed* sources include considering the reputation of the author, the reputation of the publishing house, and the date of publication. These hold only indirectly for *electronic* sources. Here are some general principles that you can employ to help you evaluate online sources:

❶ *Who is responsible for this page's existence?* Look for details that show the credentials of the person who put out the information. Does she have an academic title? Is he a member of some reputable organization like the Smithsonian Institution or the American Museum of Natural History? Does he or she work for a well-known foundation? Can you find the author in a bibliography related to his or her discipline? And if you cannot find the name of the page's author (or at least the page's sponsoring organization, whose credentials you can also check), the page's reliability goes way down.

② *Is the information presented in reasonable terms, not highly connotative or exaggerated?* Are claims supported? Be skeptical of overstatements or unsupported allegations.

③ *What kind of page is this?* Web pages generally fall into just a few broad categories—personal pages, often indicated by a tilde (~) in the address; corporate pages, often indicated by the ".com" in the address; educational pages (thus, ".edu"); and government pages (thus, ".gov"). You can learn more about the different *domain names* (the part of the Web address after the "dot") by checking out the Glossary of Internet Terms (at matisse.net/files/glossary.html). But judging the category (and hence potential reliability) of a Web page by its domain name can be misleading, more so as the variety of domain names increases. Try to decide which of the following purposes the page is serving, and judge the page's reliability as much on the page's purpose as on its domain:

Advocacy. People love to put pages relating to their favorite causes on the Web. You can often detect these pages by their zealous tone, even if the page's stated sponsorship is not as unambiguous as the Save the Whales Foundation or the National Rifle Association. You might be able to start your research by getting rough ideas from such pages, but you must mistrust any such advocacy page's presentation of what "the facts" are. Claims on such a page that this or that species of whale is "headed for extinction," or that this or that law will "threaten our democratic way of life," simply cannot be taken uncritically. Basing your research on information from an advocacy page is extremely unwise; you might start there, but you'll have to do some serious fact-checking in better kinds of sources to convince academic readers.

Business, marketing, and commercial. Perhaps the majority of Web sites today are devoted wholly or in part to buying and selling. As with advocacy pages, these pages' contents usually do not make for good sources of research information.

Entertainment. Movie pages, music pages, e-book pages, game pages—how many different kinds of entertainment pages are there on the Web today? Again, it's not a good idea to base your research on those pages' claims.

Information. Pages that present technical reports, scholarly articles, or government (and other) statistics can, of course, be great sources of information. If you want the facts about health problems, go to the National Institutes of Health pages (at www.nih.gov) or the Centers for Disease Control and Prevention pages (at www.cdc.gov). The point is not particularly that these are "government" pages (although they are), but that they are information pages.

Personal. Personal pages have several subvarieties: those that are *really* personal, such as those listing hobbies, showing pictures of one's pets, and so on; and those that are in fact personal/professional, including one's professional résumé and, in the case of researchers, perhaps even copies of articles. Personal/professional pages can be great sources of information, despite the tilde in the address; truly personal pages are best left out of research papers.

If skeptical consideration of a Web page's nature or claims causes you to doubt the reliability of the page's information, do as any good journalist would: find an independent source or sources whose own credibility is much higher to corroborate that doubtful information. Otherwise, your academic audience will call your research into serious question because you proceeded on the basis of such unreliable information.

USING THE RESULTS OF ELECTRONIC SEARCHES HONESTLY,
GIVING FAIR CREDIT TO THE ORIGINAL AUTHOR(S)

Giving proper credit to the sources of borrowed material in research papers—whether that material is artwork, facts, or words—is an important issue for researchers at any level. Charges such as plagiarism or academic dishonesty hurt everyone involved, and if proven can be cause for dismissal, either from a school or from a job. "Mastering the Conventions of Documentation," pages 271–87, includes more detailed instructions on how to cite sources. The key issue for this chapter, however, is more limited.

Nearly every college professor we know has had a growing number of instances in recent years of students who download whole passages (not just a word or a phrase, but strings of sentences, complete paragraphs, even whole pages of writing) of material off the Web and incorporate it unchanged into their papers as their own—with no attempt by the researcher to rewrite the material into his or her own words, no source citation of any kind. That is dishonesty (in this case, academic dishonesty, or plagiarism), pure and simple. Not to put too fine a point on the subject, but if the original passage published on the Web says *this* (taken from www.deafblind.com/cochlear.html):

> The implant centre conducts a careful evaluation to determine if an individual is an appropriate Cochlear Implant candidate. Audiological tests establish the level of hearing loss. Hearing aids and other devices are fitted to establish whether or not these devices might be beneficial.

and if a student's paper says *this*:

> The implant center conducts a careful evaluation to determine if an individual is an appropriate Cochlear Implant candidate. Audiological tests establish the level of hearing loss. Hearing aids and other devices are fitted to establish whether or not these devices might be beneficial.

then that is plagiarism, plain as day.

If the student had at least cited the source *somewhere*, the situation might be just a tad less severe (although it would still be dishonesty). But stealing text from another source (in this case, downloading text from the Web) and incorporating it into your research reports without any effort at paraphrase and without any source citation is a major, major ethical lapse, one that seems to be occurring with more and more frequency because it has become so very easy to do. At most colleges and universities (as in most businesses and most government agencies), the penalties for such dishonesty are severe. The fact that the Web makes such dishonesty easier does not lessen the fault. (And of course students who make this mistake ignore the fact that if they can find this material on the Web, their instructor can find it too.) Sites such as the Center for Academic Integrity (www.academicintegrity.org) or Student Judicial Services at the University of Texas at Austin (www.utexas.edu/depts/dos/sjs/academicintegrity.html) discuss these issues fully. English departments also have access to specific Web sites that make tracking plagiarism much easier.

WRITING YOUR PAPER

While the process of writing has been thoroughly covered in other chapters in this book, writing research papers can present some unusual problems. We present the process here in five general stages:

- Getting started
- Choosing a plan of organization
- Writing a draft
- Getting responses
- Finishing your paper

GET STARTED

If you have been taking notes in your own words and playing with systems for organizing your notes, you have already begun the process of writing your paper. If you find you are having trouble getting past the hurdle of that first paragraph, you may want to take some time to return to your original research question and informally write something down about what you have learned since you began looking for answers. How do you understand your topic differently now from when you started out? What seem to be the most important things you've learned, and why do you believe they're important? What are the most interesting things you've learned, and why do you find them interesting? Such *freewriting* may help you focus your thoughts and could produce some chunks of text that you will want to incorporate into your draft. Other forms of preparatory writing may include outlining or brainstorming on paper (see Chapter 3).

CHOOSE A PLAN OF ORGANIZATION

Probably the best way to get all of your material under control is to make a rough outline. You may find that doing so will establish the broad claims you are going to make in your paper and show a logical way to order them. For a paper on Gentileschi, for example, perhaps you found information on the background of the period in which she wrote, information on her own life, information on works she painted, and information on her reputation as an artist (in her own day, in the intervening centuries, and today). Write down your major claims and make notes about subpoints you want to cover under each. Often you will find that once you start writing at all—even if it's only summarizing your research results and dividing them among sections of the paper—the actual writing of the paper comes easier.

You can also write an abstract for your paper. If carefully done, an abstract or summary can give you substantial guidance for organizing your paper and for beginning to articulate some of the points you want to make. Supplemented by a list of secondary or supporting points, a comprehensive abstract will serve you just about as well as an outline.

You can also write a "discovery" draft of your paper. Perhaps you might start this first write-up out as a kind of informal chronological retelling of the research process you went through. You might start with, "When I first decided to do my research paper on women artists, I had never heard of Artemisia Gentileschi. Then as I narrowed down my range of choices, I began to find that. . . . Next I discovered that. . . . Then I went to the Web and looked at. . . ." And only at the end of the discovery draft you might decide what claim you want the whole paper to make. Once you have come to realize through the discovery draft process just what your paper's claim is to be, then you can begin your actual paper's first real draft with a paragraph that ends with that claim, now expressed as your paper's thesis sentence.

Whatever plan of organization you choose, having something written down that will serve as an anchor as you work will make the process of writing go more smoothly; it will also give you something to check your subsequent drafts against to be sure you've covered your main points.

● WRITE A DRAFT

Most students find that the faster they actually do their drafting, the better it goes. Generally speaking, while you're writing your first draft it's much better to focus on just getting the material down any way you can, and to worry about making the writing *good* later. This is especially important when writing about research, because research papers often are longer and more demanding than other assignments. Certainly making the writing smooth and polished is still of great importance; you just may find you cannot do that at the same time as you focus on getting all the material down on the page, and getting it into some kind of order.

● GET RESPONSES

An essential step in writing a successful research paper is getting responses to a good, middle-level draft. A good, middle-level draft has all its factual content in place and has complete sentences organized into well-structured paragraphs but may well not have all the headings and subheadings, visuals, title page, references, etc., that writers typically only put in place during finishing. And a good, middle-level draft is typed and double-spaced. Once you have such a draft, it's essential to get responses to it, ideally on at least two levels: a peer review, and a review by someone at the level of your report's intended main audience (here probably someone at the level of your course's instructor).

What you want to avoid in any such review situation is offering the reviewer a vague, open-ended prompt. Something like "just look this over for me and tell me what you think" leaves the reviewer no good options. It's too easy for the reviewer just to take two minutes skimming the draft and say, "It looks fine." You need to give your reviewer a specific prompt (or prompts), as the next two subsections here illustrate.

PEER REVIEW

One review needs to be done by someone at your own level, someone either in the same class, or who has taken the same class, or who is at least at the same level in college as you. Here are just a few of the things you could ask such a reviewer to look for (you should pick just one or two of these per reviewer):

> ◐ Does this piece flow naturally—does it have a clear-cut beginning, middle, and ending that hang together to make a whole?
> ◐ Are there any places in the report where you get lost, or where it seems I've left something critical out?

○ What part of this draft is strongest, and why?

○ What part of this draft is weakest, and how might it be made stronger?

○ (For persuasive reports) At the end of the report, have I at least started to persuade you to see these issues my way? If not, do you have suggestions for what else I might do?

○ (For technical reports) At the end of the report, are you left feeling I've provided enough detail to give you a sufficiently clear picture of the subject I'm describing? If not, what suggestions do you have for additions?

REVIEW BY A HIGHER-UP

An important second level of reviewing needs to come from someone who is not a peer—either your instructor, or a writing center tutor, or perhaps a more experienced writer. Such a person may even ask you a couple of questions before agreeing to undertake a review, so that in addition to being able to answer "What about this paper would you especially like me to comment on?" you need to come prepared to answer questions such as "What do you yourself think you did well in this paper, and why?" or "If you could do one more thing in this paper, what would it be?"

Here are some prompts you could offer to a reviewer at this level:

○ Does the paper have enough substantive content to satisfy the assignment? Or does it seem too thin? What suggestions might you have for additional areas or sources for more good content?

○ Does the paper have the appropriate tone for this setting? Does it seem to take too casual an approach to its subject, or does it sound too stuffy and hence artificial? If there are places that sound inappropriate for this writing situation, will you please circle them?

○ While this isn't a final draft and hence will still need some polishing for grammatical correctness, if you see a number of grammatical errors of any one or two particular types (comma errors or spelling errors, for example), would you please let me know?

○ If I were to do one more thing that would make this a better piece of writing, what would that be?

These are just a few of the kinds of questions you can ask your reviewers to answer. Remember that just as it's important to offer *some* guidance to reviewers (as opposed to saying "tell me what you think about this paper"), so it's also important not to ask too much: pick just one or two questions you really need that reviewer to answer about that draft. If you have other questions, find another reviewer.

● FINISH YOUR PAPER

If you take the "quick and dirty" approach to your earliest drafts, just to get the content down, you need to allow plenty of time and energy for polishing your research paper before you turn it in. Once you've gotten an early couple of drafts done, polished the writing (as described in Chapter 9), reviewed the content yourself, and gotten some kind of outside review (whether from classmates or from your instructor), here are other things that remain to be done:

> ◐ Insert any charts or illustrations you're going to use, being sure to give credit for each one.
>
> ◐ Check your documentation to see that it conforms to the standards appropriate to the field in which the paper is written (see the appendix on documentation).
>
> ◐ Remember to include a Works Cited or References list at the end that gives full information on all the works you cite in the paper.
>
> ◐ Check for strong transitions from one paragraph to the next and from each section to the next.
>
> ◐ Review your opening paragraph and your conclusion. Do they work together to frame the paper? They should.
>
> ◐ Insert headings and subheadings to divide the paper into digestible parts. If your instructor likes the idea, you might even incorporate a pull-quote or two. But ask before doing so.
>
> ◐ Check to see if you have a focused thesis sentence in the first paragraph or two (see Chapter 5).
>
> ◐ Underline the first or second sentence of each paragraph and review the underlined text to see if it acts as a kind of skeleton for the paper. If you see that you're leaving out an important point, insert it.

○ Finally, before you turn the paper in, make sure you have a spare copy. And when you turn the paper in, try to do so in person.

Q

My problem with writing research papers is a killer—I just can't come up with a good topic. The teacher always says, "Pick a topic you're at least a little bit interested in." But then the paper has to be "something about Shakespeare" if it's a Shakespeare class, or "something about South America" if it's a Western Civ. class. How can I pick a specific topic I'm "interested in" if the course is something I'm only taking because it's required?

A

We think you have to know a little bit about a subject before you can find anything interesting in it to write about. If you're in a Shakespeare class, a good way to start looking for a research paper topic is to look at lots of examples of topics others have written about when writing about Shakespeare. Your librarian can probably lead you to good places to start. This does not mean you have to read a number of complete scholarly articles. What you want to do is browse them, flip through them, starting to fill in some gaps in your own general knowledge of the subject along the way. It wouldn't hurt to read some general introductions to your topic, as well. If you're writing about Shakespeare, or South America, try starting out your topic search with reading the *Encyclopaedia Britannica* entries on it. Then try looking in some periodical indexes for pieces, not to read and study, but to browse and flip through. The more you begin to educate yourself on general background concerning your broad subject area, and the more you survey others' research approaches, the more likely you will be to come up with a specific topic that you might be interested in yourself. Interest does not appear in a vacuum; it appears in a mind stocked with information.

Q

I am just no good using the World Wide Web (and not much better with computers in general), and so everything you say about doing research on the Web is just lost on me. Is there any hope for a student who does not want to surf online to do research?

A Yes, absolutely! We recommend you explore the really rich middle ground that exists today in most college and university libraries of using computers to facilitate research without ever necessarily using the World Wide Web. Chances are strong that in your university library's reference room there are rows of computers that read compact disks—not any more complicated than the CD player in your car, really—and provide tons of information on topics as widely diverse as American literature since 1900 and aerospace engineering. Doing your research this way, using, for example, the SilverPlatter series of CDs (probably the most common ones libraries own), you may well find most of the materials for your research paper right there on the computer sitting in front of you. No need to search the Web at all.

● ● ● **A SAMPLE RESEARCH PAPER**

On the following pages is the final version of "Artemisia Gentileschi: Artist against the Grain," the research paper referred to throughout this book. It was originally written at the University of Texas for a women's studies course on women in Europe from 1400 to 1800. Since this paper was written, Gentileschi has received new critical attention, with a major exhibit opening in 2002 at the Metropolitan Museum of Art in New York City.

Eleanor Hennessy

Professor Adams

Humanities 252

10 May 2002

Artemisia Gentileschi: Artist against the Grain

   Artemisia Gentileschi, a talented painter in
seventeenth-century Italy, defied every norm of her
time--artistic, social, economic, and sexual--to
emerge as one of the most successful artists of her
era. To women art historians in the twenty-first
century, she is a hero whose work disproves the
allegation that there have been no great women artists.
But Gentileschi's story also appeals to today's women
in ways that go well beyond the specialized world
of art history. She has become a feminist icon
because of her courage, her self-confidence, her determination, and her proud defiance in refusing to
bow to the censure of a hostile and judgmental society.
She would have been an amazing woman in any time and
place; for her to have triumphed as she did in the
sexist, repressive culture of seventeenth-century
Italy seems no less than a miracle.

   In seventeenth-century Italy, women had almost no
rights. Except for a few wealthy women from noble
families, they could not own property. Indeed, they
were considered property themselves. Anything they
produced belonged to their fathers or husbands; even
a woman's children belonged to her husband. The cul-

ture found reinforcement for such attitudes in the writings of several male writers who asserted that by natural law women were morally and intellectually inferior to men. Both the Catholic Church and society as a whole were so obsessed with women's chastity that unmarried women were not supposed to go out alone or have any contact with men outside their families. Any hint of sexual lapses could ruin a woman's reputation and her chances for marriage. So no matter how talented a woman was, it was virtually impossible for her to pursue a career or assert her independence.

   The talented Gentileschi--appropriately named Artemisia for another powerful woman, a tribal queen who fought beside the Persian king Xerxes in the fifth century BC--was fortunate in being born into a painter's family in Rome in 1593. Her father, Orazio, was a friend of the painter Caravaggio and well established in the artistic community of Rome; the family lived in the artists' quarter of the city surrounded by other painters. Thus from childhood Artemisia breathed the ambience of the artist's workshop and absorbed the traditions of the heroic school of painting of the day that emphasized myth and legends from the Bible and the classical era. From her early teens she worked in her father's studio, which would have been considered the family business, developing her expertise in mixing paints and preparing

canvases, and benefiting from the opportunity to draw
from models that was essential for any serious
painter of the day but almost impossible for women
artists to attain unless they came from a painter's
family.

The sheer size of the canvases required for the
history paintings so highly valued in the Renaissance
posed problems for women. They were expensive, and
most women had no independent source of income. Moreover, an artist trying to work on such a large scale
needed an apprentice. Almost no woman apprentices ex-
isted, and male apprentices didn't want to work for
a woman. If a woman painter did succeed in engaging
a male apprentice, inevitably there were prurient ru-
mors about a sexual relationship between them.
Painters of historical subjects, either biblical or
from myth, needed models; not only were they expensive, but women painters weren't allowed to draw from
nude models.

As the daughter and working apprentice of an established painter, Artemisia escaped those constraints, but her apprenticeship made her vulnerable
in another way. In 1611, when she was seventeen, her
father asked Agostino Tassi, a visiting artist from
Florence, to take Artemisia as an apprentice so she
could learn more about perspective. During the course
of those lessons, Gentileschi suffered an assault
that was to mark her indelibly and, in many ways,

shape her character and her direction as an artist
for the rest of her life. While she was studying
with Tassi, he raped her, assuring her afterward that
he would marry her. He did not, but continued to
press her for sexual relations. In March of the next
year Orazio filed suit against Tassi for injury and
damages, alleging that Artemisia was now damaged
property and it would be difficult for him to find
her a husband.

    An ugly seven-month public trial followed, with
Artemisia testifying under oath about Tassi's seduc-
tion and giving details of his betrayal. Doubting her
story, the court ordered her to undergo torture with
a thumb ring, but she refused to alter her testimony, crying from the witness stand, "You promised me
a ring--look at what you gave me!" She maintained
that she had struggled with him to the point of
wounding him with a knife. A witness agreed. Details
about previous incidents in which Tassi had been
charged with sexual offenses damaged his credibility,
and the charges against him were upheld. Nevertheless, he spent only eight months in prison, and the
case was later dismissed.

    Of course the scandal against Gentileschi herself
was never dismissed. Like other rape victims through
the centuries, she was somehow blamed for her own
violation, and rumor and innuendo about her supposed
lustful nature persisted throughout her life and for

centuries after her death. But the trial seemed to have hardened her and strengthened her resolve to defy her critics and succeed on her own terms. The feminist art historian Germaine Greer in her book <u>The Obstacle Race</u> puts it this way:

> The abortive trial had left Artemisia with nothing but her talent, but it also removed the traditional obstacles to that talent. She could no longer hope to live a secluded life; she was notorious. [. . .] She refused to deal in pathos [and] developed an ideal of heroic womanhood. She lived it, and she portrayed it. (Greer 193)

Within a month after the trial, Gentileschi surmounted the designation of "damaged goods," married a fellow artist, and moved to Florence. There the artists' community quickly recognized her talent, and in 1616 she became an official member of the Florence Academy of Design, which had never admitted a woman artist since its founding in 1563. Her acceptance was a remarkable achievement for a woman who had seemed irrevocably disgraced only four years earlier.

In Florence, she and her husband seem to have separated after their daughter was born in 1618, but she became a shrewd businesswoman on her own, undertaking those tasks required for any independent artist who hopes to make a living. She worked at securing commissions from the wealthy and well-connected, including Michelangelo Buonarroti the Younger, great-nephew of the famous Michelangelo. She succeeded in gaining the support of the powerful Medici family, and she won several commissions to paint portraits, assignments that required working alone with men outside her family. She also traveled, going as far as England on one occasion; argued forcefully with her patrons when necessary; and managed her own business affairs. As one way to promote herself she painted a striking self-portrait that even today highlights her artistic gifts.

Gentileschi portrays herself dramatically in her self-portrait, which she titled <u>La Pittura</u>, or <u>The Spirit of Painting</u>. It shows her as a handsome, buxom woman with the edge of a creamy bosom revealed above the top of a lace-trimmed silk gown. She is totally engrossed in her work, lips slightly apart and strands of dark hair curling at her temples. She radiates vitality, and everything in the painting reveals her talent--the warm flesh tones, the expressive eyes, the details of the delicate lace trim, the lights and shadows that highlight the sheen of the fabric, and the delicate gold chain at her neck.

The portrait, which projects self-confidence and a sexual awareness, seems a deliberate challenge to a society that decreed women should be subservient, self-effacing, and modest. Along with those other behaviors that asserted her autonomy, it established

Gentileschi as a <u>femme forte</u>, a historical term that defines a woman of notable strength and character. As Greer puts it, Gentileschi developed an ideal of "heroic womanhood. She lived it and she portrayed it" (123).

Gentileschi's anger toward men comes through in several of her most famous paintings. <u>Susanna and the Elders</u>, based on the story from the Apocrypha and painted in 1611, the year she was raped by Tassi, shows the young wife Susanna shrinking in fear as the two elders who plot an assault on her lean over her shoulder. Another remarkable painting done two years after Artemisia's rape is <u>Judith Slaying Holofernes</u>, taken from the story in the Apocrypha of Judith and her maid killing the invading general Holofernes. This violent and compelling picture is especially remarkable because it shows a handsomely dressed Judith and her maid almost calmly decapitating the struggling Holofernes--a <u>femme forte</u> indeed! Art historians have been quick to see a parallel to Gentileschi's taking her revenge on Tassi; the figure of Judith even resembles the artist.

Gentileschi's biographer, the art historian Mary Garrard, takes the parallel further, saying,

> In her paintings of Judith slaying
> Holofernes [she completed five], Artemisia
> appears to have drawn personal courage
> from her subject, to go farther than any

woman artist had ever gone--or would go
before the twentieth century--in depicting
a confrontation of the sexes from a female
point of view. [. . .] Beneath the rational veneer of the moralized tale lies a
lawless reality too horrible for men to
contemplate. Holofernes [. . .] is Every-
man; and Judith and her servant are, together, the most dangerous and frightening
force on earth for man: women in control
of his fate. (279)

Gentileschi also created several paintings depicting women who were betrayed by men. They include
one of Lucretia, the Roman matron who stabbed herself
after she was raped by a Tarquin general and whose
plea to her husband to revenge her triggered the re-
volt that drove the Tarquins from Rome. Another shows
Bathsheba being seduced by King David, who then had
her husband killed so he could marry her.

Although only thirty-four of Gentileschi's paintings have survived through the centuries since her
death in 1652, her standing in the world of art history has risen very significantly in the last three
decades, a period in which more women scholars have
entered the field. The Internet has played a key
role in publicizing her life and her work. Several
biographies are now available on various Web sites,
as well as copies of her most famous paintings, es-

pecially <u>Susanna and the Elders</u>, <u>Judith Slaying Holofernes</u>, and the self-portrait, <u>La Pittura</u>. A Web site from the University of Arizona calls her "the most important woman painter of Early Modern Europe by virtue of the excellence of her work and the originality of her treatment of traditional sub- jects." Her paintings hang in the Metropolitan Museum of Art in New York City and in several European art museums.

Gentileschi has finally achieved the recognition she deserves only because in the 1970s and 1980s a handful of women art historians challenged the assumptions of their discipline, one that had never taken women artists seriously. Two of those histori- ans, Rozsika Parker and Griselda Pollock, say, "Mod- ern art history [. . .] identifies women artists as inevitably and naturally artists of lesser talent and no historical significance." Parker, Pollock, and others--notably Germaine Greer--did the research necessary to bring to light the paintings that demonstrate Gentileschi's genius, and to confirm her stature in her own day. Mary Garrard, in her 1989 biography, has supplemented those treasures by giving us the story of this amazing woman who went against the grain of her culture to triumph over obstacles that women of today can scarcely imagine. It's an awesome story to which one can only say, Yes! Ain't that a woman!

Works Cited

Corbell, Rebecca, and Samantha Gay. "Artemisia Gen-
     tileschi and the Age of Baroque: The Life Biog-
     raphy of Artemisia Gentileschi." 12 Apr. 2002
     <http://rubens.anu.edu.au/
     student.projects/artemisia/Lifebio.html>.

Garrard, Mary. Artemisia Gentileschi: The Image of
     the Female Hero in Italian Baroque Art. Prince-
     ton: Princeton UP, 1989.

Greer, Germaine. The Obstacle Race: The Fortunes of
     Women Painters and Their Work. 1979. London:
     Tauris Parke Paperbacks, 2001.

McBride, Kari Boyd. "Artemisia Gentileschi, 1593-
     1652." 3 June 2001 <http://
     www.u.arizona.edu/ic/mcbride/ws200/
     gentil.htm>.

Parker, Rozsika, and Griselda Pollock. Old Mis-
     tresses: Women, Art and Ideology. New York:
     Pantheon, 1981.

Sending Electronic Communications

13

▷ *Sending a message faster does not necessarily mean communicating better—but it should!*

According to NUA.com, an organization that specializes in Internet surveys, there are more than 177 million people online in the United States and Canada, and more than 418 million in the world. Virtually 100 percent of U.S. college students use the Internet; nine out of ten use email daily. And Internet use among college seniors averages eleven hours a week. As a college student, you are probably already doing most of your written communication electronically, not just doing your writing on a word processor, but also sending that writing off over the Internet. If you aren't, you probably will be soon.

Obviously, the online community is enormous—and getting bigger. As with any new medium of communication, there are some things about communicating electronically that need to be done a little differently. And as with any large community, the online community needs a few codes of behavior in order for everyone to get along. This chapter will help you become more aware of some of the important characteristics of online writing—the creation of documents that are meant to be read online (whether in the form of Web page content, reports, or email)—and it will fill you in on a few tricks of the trade for handling those documents as well.

The foundation for much of this chapter relies on your understanding how readers looking at material on a screen behave in different ways from readers looking at material that is printed out. (This subject is also covered, in more detail, in Chapter 11, on document design.) The section on email do's and don'ts also describes how to handle email and attachments, and gives specific regard to privacy issues, harassment and other kinds of unwanted email, and viruses.

WRITING FOR ONLINE READERS

When you write for people who will most likely be reading your text on a screen, your writing needs to be adjusted to their situation in many ways. Reading online is more difficult, both visually and cognitively. So whatever you can do to make the text on the screen more easily accessible to the reader's eyes and brain is probably a good idea. Reading online also takes a little longer than reading on paper, and thus people want online documents to be shorter as well.

Here are some tips for adjusting your writing for online readers:

- Keep the visual appearance of your documents simple—crowded or jumbled screens drive readers away fast.
- Where you can, rely more on bulleted or numbered lists than on paragraphs.
- Make very full use of headings and subheadings, and leave enough space around them so that someone scanning your document will see them easily and quickly.
- Keep your paragraphs short (five lines or so).
- Make sure you put the main point of every paragraph in the first line (that's all many readers will look at), and that your paragraphs stick really closely to just one idea each.
- Use fewer words. You do not need to be "telegraphic" (omitting, *a, an,* and *the*); just be rigorous about cutting the deadwood out of your prose.
- Highlight keywords in the text (making it easy for a fast-scanning reader to find the section he or she wants to read more closely). Italics work well on the Web, but boldface or underlining will make readers confuse your highlighted keywords with hypertext links.

All of these adaptations apply to email as well, with the addition of a strong emphasis on brevity—no one wants to read a piece of email that runs on for more than the equivalent of about 40 lines (one or two screens, on many computers). Further guidelines for email are explained in the rest of this chapter. A fuller discussion of these points and additional guidelines specifically about writing content for Web pages are presented in Chapter 11, on document design.

EMAIL DOS AND DON'TS

How you handle email depends on whether you are writing casual correspondence (to friends, relatives, and so on) or professional correspondence (to clients, prospective employers, government agencies, and others you need to be a little bit more formal with). Three larger issues cut across those personal versus professional boundaries: privacy, "snap" responses, and dealing with unwanted email.

● PRIVACY

Whether you are engaging in casual correspondence with friends or working out secret arrangements for your company's takeover of a competitor, the fact of the matter is that email is almost never totally "private." Once you hit Send, your document exists forever, somewhere in cyberspace, and anyone with enough power and computer resources can find it and read it. Email can also be printed out and saved or circulated with one keystroke, and it can be forwarded an infinite number of times the same way. In all these ways, email may seem more momentary than print mail, but the truth is actually the opposite.

Email sent on your school's computer system is always subject to the school's scrutiny. Email sent on a commercial system is subject to the controls of that system's own administrators. Email sent on your employer's system (or even just on your employer's computers) is always subject to your employer's scrutiny—and people have lost jobs over that. Off-color jokes sent on the company's system need to hit only one person wrong, and you're in trouble. Office romances are never secrets anyway, but when they are planned and carried out over company email, they can seriously damage the individuals involved.

Even deleted email still exists on some server somewhere. Not long ago one of us needed to retrieve some email that had been deleted two months earlier from an individual account in our university's system. A simple visit to the university's computing help desk, and the files were restored in fifteen minutes—that's all it takes.

If you put something into email that you do not want others to be able to see, you are probably making a mistake.

If you really need to protect your correspondence, consider using one of the *privacy programs*, such as Pretty Good Privacy (PGP), that are available free at many sites on the Web. There are also services (called *encryption* services) that will in effect lock each piece of your mail shut for you as it travels through various computers on the way to the addressee. Typical encryption services include HushMail (at hushmail.com), PrivacyX (privacyx.com), Anonymizer (anonymizer.com), or Freedom (freedom.net). Each of these provides a basic free service (or 30 days of free service), with upgraded service available for a fee. With such encryption, no one other than your intended recipient can read your mail. Of course, any administrator who wants to can still see that you're sending and receiving encrypted mail, which could be a problem in itself. But no one else can read it.

● SNAP RESPONSES

There's another way email may seem like casual conversation but in fact is not: snap responses. In some situations, for you to respond instantly may well be a mistake. One such situation is the experience of receiving a piece of email that is just infuriating—and instantly sending a response you will very quickly come to regret.

In a professional setting, the scenario often goes something like this. On August 25, a client who *had* told you the deadline for your work is October 15 sends email saying the deadline has been moved up to September 10, blithely assuming you have absolutely nothing else to do during the interim—no other clients, no other pursuits—and that the work can in fact be done in that short a time even if you work 24 hours a day, 7 days a week on just that project. If that email comes at the end of a long day, or on a Monday morning, you may well be tempted to pound out a red-hot reply instantly. Still in the adrenaline rush of the moment, you hit Send. Two seconds later you think, "Oh-my-gosh-what-have-I-done!"

Or you read something on one of the email discussion lists you belong to—maybe the one for your women's studies class—that really sets you off. You write a blistering response—meaning to send it only to the original message's author, not to the whole list—and hit Send. A split second later you realize that because of the way that particular list is set up, anything *not* specifically designated to go to only one person automatically goes to the entire list. But in the heat of the moment you didn't make that specification. And now that "flame" you sent out will not only be read by everyone on the list, but also will live forever in cyberspace.

Many of us have made such mistakes. You can help yourself out a lot by instituting a policy of never ever responding instantly to email that provokes you in any way. If you read it in the morning, wait until after lunch to respond. If you read it at the end of the day, wait until the next day. Over and over again, even in many situations that are not quite as extreme as these but that still require some reflection before a response, you will find this policy helps you avoid dangerous mistakes, whether due to bad temper or just bad judgment.

● Unwanted Email

With so many people on the Web, perhaps it is not surprising that there are such things as unwanted email (bulk mail sent electronically, often referred to in the Web community as "spam"), even mail that is used to harass someone (mail that is sexually offensive, or physically or sexually threatening). Certainly you do not want, in either your personal life or your professional life, to be involved in sending such mail.

Many people like to send jokes, chain letters, prayers, and so on to others on the Web. From the amount of such mail we ourselves receive, there must be people out there somewhere who welcome it. We believe, however, that the vast majority of recipients do not want such mail. The evolving etiquette seems to require senders to ask their would-be recipients first whether they mind receiving jokes (or inspirational stories, or surefire investment schemes, or whatever) from time to time.

Mail that is intended to be sexually offensive or that is physically or sexually threatening (called "harassing mail" on the Web) is a much more serious issue. Some college students who have sent offensive mail to casual acquaintances or even to strangers have apparently been surprised to learn such behavior will get them expelled (and perhaps arrested). Even though the email is casual (i.e., not professional), just sending it can have serious consequences.

What do you do if you receive such mail? Obviously, that depends on how bad the content is. In some less severe cases, simply deleting it may well end the matter. If the mail is repeated, you can save that piece of mail for record-keeping purposes and then send something like this to the sender:

> On [date] you or someone using your account sent me unsolicited email which I found offensive. I am putting you on notice that I do not wish to receive any further correspondence of any type from you. Continuing to send me messages may constitute harassment that is a violation of state and federal law. Again, do not send me any further email or contact me in any other manner, electronic or otherwise.
>
> [Signed, your login name]

If there are repeated instances, you can then go to authorities (your school's system administrators, your Internet service provider, or even the police) for further assistance. It's easy to delete something without even reading it if you recognize the sender's address as one that has been sending you harassing or threatening email, but there is a strong argument that people have a civic responsibility to deal actively with harassment and threats (but in ways that are safe) rather than passively endure them. If the threatening nature of the mail or its offensiveness seems great, you need to save the email and take it to the appropriate authorities.

● ● ● **HANDLING CASUAL CORRESPONDENCE**

When you use email to correspond with friends and others you know well, you can keep your writing informal. And do think twice before sending all your friends chain letters, pyramid scheme letters, or long lists of jokes that have already been forwarded to millions of people—or at least try to make sure they do not resent such email.

When it comes to email between friends, there are still a few issues of form to observe, such as not typing on ALL-CAPS (which makes it look as if you're screaming), and not typing the entire letter in lowercase (which makes it hard to read). In casual mail, the use of various emoticons—such as the happy face :) or the sad face :(—and of common Web abbreviations (such as *IMHO* for "in my humble opinion" or *ROTFLOL* for "rolling on the floor laughing out loud") is common. So, too, are "sig files" and "taglines"—the additions to your email software that automatically add your name at the bottom of a letter and a favorite quote as well. Do be sure, though, that when you switch to writing academic or professional letters, you turn that function off. Most of the sig files students use when writing to each other would not be appropriate in more formal academic or professional settings.

In the issue of taglines, as in many other issues, the key point is to make a very clear distinction between your casual correspondence and your academic or professional correspondence. Academic and professional correspondence needs to be handled much more carefully, as the next section explains.

HANDLING ACADEMIC AND PROFESSIONAL CORRESPONDENCE

Professional correspondence (and academic correspondence with professors, deans, etc.) has its own set of rules—rules concerning the level of formality, how to handle requests, good news, bad news, and so on. Such rules are about the same in academic or professional email as in "snail" mail. The problem is that for people new to email, or new to professional life, it's so easy to forget the difference between casual correspondence among friends and more formal correspondence. But in academic and professional correspondence, form matters, style matters, content matters, grammar matters, and timing matters. The best thing you can do is to treat correspondence via email the same way you would if the same piece were being sent via snail mail. Here are some specifics about form:

> *The subject heading.* Your subject line is especially important in email. Many people receive much more email than they can easily handle, and so they screen their incoming mail by who it's from and by what the subject line says. If the subject line is too vague (for example, it says "something new" or "Hello"), your letter might get put at the bottom of the cue. If the subject line is specific (it says "contract on its way" or "new writing project"), your reader will pay attention. Try to make your subject lines as specific as possible so that your readers will know what your email is about.

○ *The salutation.* This works just as it does in regular mail: "Dear Bob Smith," "Dear Professor Adams," or "Hello Bob," depending on your level of familiarity. If you do not know the name of the recipient, use the individual's title instead: "Dear Personnel Manager."

○ *The body of the email.* Email correspondence usually is more concise than print correspondence. So, if the letter is good news or a routine request, you want the first paragraph to get right to the point: give the good news, make the request. Then the second paragraph can elaborate on that good news or that request, and the third paragraph can explain what you hope will happen next (how the shipment is to be delivered, what you hope will happen next in the employment process, and so on). As explained at the beginning of the chapter, people reading online are reluctant to have to scroll down to finish your document, so if you can do the letter in one screen, that's a real plus.

○ *The signature block.* In addition to adding your name at the end (after "Sincerely" or "Best" or whatever other closing is appropriate), include your phone and fax numbers and any other necessary contact information (such as your snail mail address).

Model 10, in the documents appendix, shows a typical email letter concerning professional matters (in this case, it's a student requesting an internship).

Email letters that are conveying bad news or making unusual requests might well require a little bit more complicated structure, but the basic elements of form are the same. In such letters the first paragraph should explain the background leading to the bad news or the unusual request, which should then be in the second paragraph.

● RÉSUMÉS

In the case of the student applying for the internship, mentioned previously and shown in Model 10, the writer chose to use just an abbreviated résumé, and so simply included it with his letter. He could also have included his résumé as an attachment (a self-enclosed file attached to the email). That would allow him to use a résumé that is fully formatted, but it takes the chance either that the recipient cannot open the attachment, or that the recipient chooses not to open an attachment from a relative stranger because of the risk of viruses (see the next section, on attachments, for more on both of these points). Bob also could have simply referred his reader to his Web site, where his résumé could be seen (perhaps along with his portfolio). The advantage of putting the résumé right in with the email is that the recipient is not required to do any extra keystrokes to see it immediately, and as Web merchants have learned, asking users to make extra keystrokes loses users.

In our experience, many students present their résumé in a combination of ways. For a one-page résumé, there's no real reason not to have a version you can send via email. You need to remember for your email résumé that in email most typography above the basic level disappears—things like different typefaces, boldface, italics, underlining, centering, and so on are not going to show up reliably on your recipient's screen. (Depending on the software you use, and what your reader uses, it *might* show up, but you cannot rely on that.) A two-column list (such as a list of courses) may well get scrambled on email as well. So an email résumé should be a fairly plain document—everything aligned at the left margin, and no typographic emphasis except the underline before and after a word that substitutes on email for underlining an entire word.

Model 12, in the documents appendix, shows the email résumé of Bob Smith, the student whose letter was mentioned previously.

While this kind of bare-bones résumé will work for email, you may want to keep other versions available as well, including a fully formatted version that can be sent on request as an attachment, perhaps an HTML version on your own Web site, and maybe a version available with an on-line job search service such as Monster.com. Some prospective employers or placement services will also request a "scannable" résumé, one that can be run through a scanner and entered into a database electronically. Such a résumé resembles an email résumé—no fancy formatting, everything at the left margin, and so on. Of course, the printed-on-paper résumé is still important as well. Thus you may prepare the same résumé—with more or less formatting, and in longer and shorter versions—in many different forms.

When you want to send a document electronically and retain its formatting (such as a report to a professor, or a résumé to a prospective employer), you need to send an email *transmitting* the report along with an attachment *containing* the report itself.

The content of such an email (called a *letter of transmittal*) is pretty standard. The first paragraph says something like "Dear Professor Kilgore: Here is the final report you requested for English 360, on the types of advocacy pages on the Web. I hope you will find it conforms to your requirements in terms of its . . . ." The second paragraph is actually a three- or four-line summary of the attached document. The third and last paragraph makes clear what you hope will happen after your recipient reads the document and opens a channel for further communication: "I understand that after you have read the report you will notify me to schedule a conference at which we will discuss your evaluation of my report. While the most reliable way to reach me is always via email, I also welcome your phone call at 555-1234."

Then the report itself, fully formatted, with tables, graphs, and so on, goes with that email as an attachment. As always, it is important for such an email to have a subject line identifying it clearly (such as "Final Report for E. 360"), and for the receiver to be expecting to receive the report from you in the form of an attachment. The problem of viruses has led many people to refuse to open email containing an attachment that they did not expect.

Computer viruses are a major problem on email today, and many viruses spread themselves through attachments. Once the host computer opens the attachment, the virus can send itself to everyone on that computer's email list. So you will get email from someone with whom you've had previous correspondence and whose name you may well recognize, but the attachment will contain the virus. About the only clue you might have is that the virus usually cannot customize either the subject line (so it will be something generic like "Check this out!") or the email message itself (so it will be something like "I thought you would be interested in this"). If you open the attachment, your machine becomes infected with the virus, which then starts using your address list to replicate itself.

Excellent antivirus software exists (such as Symantec's Norton Antivirus at symantec.com, or VirusScan at mcafee.com), but some people will not open unsolicited email with attachments. Therefore if you want to send someone an attachment, it is a good idea to send him or her another email first (or first call on the phone) saying that you are about to do so. And of course, running good virus protection software on your own computer will be doing everyone a favor.

You may also face *compatibility problems* with attachments. Many PCs still will not read attachments done on Macs, and some attachments done with the latest software are difficult or impossible to read with three-year-old software. One way around such problems is to send your attachment the second time (after the recipient sends you the "I can't read your attachment" message) in an older version of some very common software program (something like WordPerfect 5.1 for DOS, for example). You could also save and send the file as an ASCII (plain text) file (this, however, will lose much of the formatting), or as an RTF (Rich Text Format) file. (In Word, all of these options for saving a file in another format can be accessed by clicking on File, then on Save As, and selecting the appropriate option from the menu that opens.) For many, the easiest scenario is simply to paste the entire document into the body of an email (thus losing just about all the formatting, visuals, etc.) and then send the document as email.

Q *Is it really true that things like style matter in email? I stay in touch with friends and family all over the world via email, and the way we write to each other is pretty much the way we talk—not formal. Is writing that way in email wrong?*

A That kind of writing isn't wrong. It's appropriate for the setting you're in—casual communication with friends and family—and it obviously serves its purposes well: staying in contact, swapping bits of your lives, exchanging information. But that style and tone of writing would not be appropriate, for example, in a term paper for your English class, or a research report for your marketing class, or a white paper for your political science class. And it would not be appropriate for use in your professional life. Whether you become a commodities trader or a doctor, a lawyer, or an accountant, when you are using email to communicate with clients and employers and peers—in a professional setting, on professional topics—your writing needs to be a little bit more formal and more carefully done in terms of grammar and organization than it is when you're writing to your friends. We're not talking about stuffy or uptight—good business or professional writing doesn't need to be that—we're talking about clear, straightforward, economical, efficiently organized, plain English. If you want to be able to use your writing—including your email—to get ahead in your area of employment, you need to be willing and able to do *that* kind of writing.

● ● ● **FOR PRACTICE** ●

1 Using the guidelines explained in this chapter, adapt the text of a report you have already written—either for your composition class or for some other class—for online reading. (You may also want to consult Chapter 11, on document design.) Make the adaptations you think are appropriate (if you wish, you can easily simulate the look of an HTML document with your word processor) and submit both versions to your instructor. Along with those two versions, submit a short report explaining the thinking behind the changes you have made.

2 Write an email letter of transmittal for a report you have already written, and send the letter and the report (as an attachment) to your instructor.

Giving Oral Presentations

14

> ◐ *The quickest way there is to make a good, lasting impression.*

Sooner or later, you'll have to give an oral presentation. It may be in college, as part of a class project. Or it may be on the job, when your boss asks you to explain at next Monday's staff meeting what you learned on your visit to a client in Cincinnati last week. You'll do best in such a situation, and feel much less anxiety over it, if you first do a thorough job of careful preparation. That's what this chapter is about.

There are whole books and courses, of course, on "how to give an effective speech." Here we're talking about the kind of five- or ten-minute talks that most of us are typically asked to do. Following these eight steps will help you give a short but effective talk:

1. Size up the situation.
2. Write out a rough draft of your talk.
3. Outline your talk from your draft—start planning your visuals.
4. Decide on props and visuals.
5. Practice.
6. Deliver the talk.
7. Answer questions carefully.
8. Get feedback.

The first step in planning a good short oral presentation is to size up the situation. You need to know where and when the talk will be, who the audience will be, and what the purpose of your talk is.

● FIND OUT WHERE AND WHEN THE TALK IS SCHEDULED

What are the name and address of the building and the number of the room where you will be speaking? How big is the room? A talk that works well for 20 people in a small meeting room will not work well for 200 people in an auditorium. If the room is small, you can probably be more informal. If the room is large, you will probably need to assume a more formal stance.

What kind of sound system is available in the room? Is there a fixed microphone, perhaps on a stand or on a lectern, or are you able to wear a lavalier microphone? Is the room so small that no amplification is necessary? What are the sound characteristics of the room? Will there be any distracting noises—jackhammers in the street, students in the hall changing classes?

Determine what capabilities the room has for props and visuals. Is there an overhead projector, a digital projector, a Web hookup, a flip chart, a blackboard? Before deciding what props and visuals you might want to use, you'll need to figure out what props and visuals you will even be *able* to use.

Of course, you also must find out specifically *when* your talk is scheduled. Find out the date and time, and write them down.

The very best way to size up the situation is by talking with the person who has asked you to give the talk. Have that person answer the foregoing questions in your conversation. Then, if at all possible, go see the room where you're going to be talking. Check the sound, the lighting, the noise inside and out, and, especially, what different kinds of visual aids you can use. For a short and informal talk, you will want visual aids that are quick to set up and relatively simple and foolproof to use. If the room already has a digital projector and screen in it, that is one thing—but if it would require running an extension cord to another room just to have electricity beyond the lights, that is another thing entirely.

If you cannot see the room before the day of your talk and cannot have a face-to-face meeting with the person making the arrangements, be sure to ask all these questions in an email or a phone call.

● FIND OUT WHO YOUR AUDIENCE IS

As with any piece of writing, the more you know about who your real audience is, the better you will be able to reach it in your talk. We've all seen and heard "canned" talks—the university functionary who gives the same talk to the incoming students every year; the politician who gives the same campaign speech to union workers, lawyers, farmers, and the PTA; the traveling scholar who reads the same speech from the same yellowed note cards to big campuses, small campuses, and prep schools. That is *audienceless speaking*. What you want, instead, is *audience-rich speaking*.

Who are the people in your audience? How many of them will there be? What do they already know about your subject? Are they generalists or specialists? Can they be expected to sit and listen quietly, or should you expect them to challenge you or ask questions? What can they hope to gain from your talk? Is there anything they might be worried about in connection with your talk? The more you know about your audience as you plan your talk, the better a talk you will be able to plan.

● DETERMINE THE PURPOSE(S) OF YOUR TALK

Perhaps the most important decision you need to make at this point concerns the purpose of your talk. "Purpose" here really is twofold: the purpose of the person who asked you to give the talk, and your purpose in giving it. These two may not be identical, but they need to be complementary.

Teachers assign short talks for all kinds of reasons: to have students introduce themselves to one another at the beginning of the term, to assess students' progress on a project by hearing a short report, to hear the final results of students' research. Obviously, you need to know the teacher's purpose in asking you to give a talk—and how it will be evaluated. Will it be graded?

Employers request short talks for different reasons: for you to introduce yourself during your first week on the job, for you—the junior executive—to explain to others in the firm the reasons why the Cincinnati client is so unhappy, for you and your team to practice a pitch to a potential new account. Again, the purposes for which you are asked to speak are very different from one situation to the next. Are you presenting new ideas or information to this group, or is your talk just one in a continuing series on closely related subjects? Are you expected to *inform, instruct,* or *persuade*?

And finally, you need to think about what you yourself hope to gain. Maybe you want the other people in the class to feel good about you, or maybe you want to show the teacher that your project is going well, or maybe you just want to receive an A. On the job, you may want to make a good first impression, or maybe you want to convince coworkers that your analysis of the Cincinnati situation is the right one, or maybe you want to be an important part of the team that landed that big new account.

All your answers to these questions about the purposes of your talk—the purposes for which you are asked to speak and the purposes for which you do the speaking—will play a part in all your remaining decisions about your talk.

● ● ● WRITING OUT A ROUGH DRAFT OF YOUR TALK

When you give a talk, you have one chance to get the message right, and to get it across effectively. It's rarely a good idea to just wing it. You owe it to your audience to do a good job—not to forget to say important things, and not to ramble. The best way to prepare even a short talk is to write out at least one full draft ahead of time. We do *not* recommend, however, that you then *read* to the audience what you've written. But the only real way to make sure you cover exactly the points you want is to write them all down ahead of time.

Writing out your talk will stimulate your thinking, and may well help you come up with additional, even better points to make. Because no one but you will ever see (or hear) the exact words, sentences, and paragraphs you put in this rough draft, you do not need to worry about its mechanics. Once you have a draft of the talk, ask yourself these questions:

○ Have you included all of the *content* you need? (Are all the major points covered? Have you covered the right number of points?) Remember that in a five-minute talk, for example, you can make at the most three major points. It's better to do a good job on fewer points than to have to rush through too many points, perhaps not making any of them clearly or effectively.

○ Does your talk have a *structure* that will help people follow what you are saying? (Something simple, like past-present-future, or background–problem statement–analysis–solution, works best.)

○ If you were to read this talk out loud, slowly, would it fall within the established *time constraints*?

Keep working on your draft until it meets these criteria. Remember, this is not a script; you're just trying to get all of the pieces of your talk together and into some kind of reasonable structure. You'll actually be speaking from an outline, described in the next section.

OUTLINING YOUR TALK—AND PLANNING YOUR VISUALS

No one wants to listen to any speaker *read* a speech word for word. If you think you can read your speech in such a way that no one knows it, think again. It makes much more sense to create an outline of your talk and then to present the talk from that. The outline could be on a sheet of paper, on note cards, or on a laptop computer. But however you do it, remember that people expect a short informal talk to have some of the spontaneity, the eye contact, and the flow of normal speech.

Remember too that on the day of your talk you may well encounter less than ideal conditions. You might want to use 14-point type for your notes—in case the light is not good. If you are using multiple note cards or sheets of paper, be sure to number them. Many speakers like to collect their notes in a binder, so that all they have to do is turn pages and not worry about pieces of paper falling on the floor or getting out of order. Find a system that lets you easily look back and forth between your notes and your audience. The more effortlessly you can seem to do that, the more comfortable the audience will be with your presentation.

Many speakers who use PowerPoint or some other kind of presentation software find these programs to be helpful at the planning stages as well. Because you will often use your PowerPoint slides to call out your major points, it can make sense to prepare your outline and your Power-Point slides at the same time.

The content of the visuals you choose will obviously be controlled in part by the content of your talk. Here are some ideas for the content of your visuals:

○ An outline of your talk (or, if you are summarizing a written report in your talk, an outline of that report)

○ Key concepts or points

○ Definitions of key terms

○ Tables, charts, graphs, and diagrams

○ Pictures, photographs, or drawings

For a short talk, you usually don't need too many props or visuals. And in most situations, the simpler the better. If your technology overwhelms your ideas (or if the technology fails, or works only after time spent fiddling with it), people may remember the technology, not the ideas. What is appropriate will, of course, vary from situation to situation. An architect (or architecture student) presenting ideas for a new riverfront condominium development will be expected to bring some visual renderings of the project for people to see. But an English major giving a talk on versions of Jane Austen's *Sense and Sensibility* can probably get by with a simple one-page handout to distribute to classmates.

Here are some possible kinds of visual aids:

○ *An outline on a blackboard.* In a classroom setting, this is the bare minimum.

○ *Handouts.* Keep them simple and low-tech. Make sure you have enough, and that they are distributed before you and any other speakers begin to talk. Also make sure to put your name and the date on all handouts.

○ *Poster boards.* Some of the best uses of poster boards we've seen have involved making visuals in PowerPoint, blowing them up and printing them out poster board size, and attaching them to the poster boards. Most copying services can do this directly from your computer files.

○ *Flip charts.* You can make these up in advance, or you can use the blank flip charts for an interactive presentation in which audience members brainstorm ideas for discussion. You can appoint a scribe to write the ideas down, and tape the sheets up on the wall. Then you have all the ideas visually displayed around the room to guide the discussion.

○ *Demonstrations.* Sometimes you'll want, or need, to show something to your audience—how it works, how the parts fit together, etc. Do be careful, though, to anticipate how much time this will take.

○ *Samples and models.* For some topics, there's no substitute for bringing a sample of the object or product, or a model of the construction. Remember, though, that if you want to pass something around during your talk, it is going to cause some distraction.

○ *Overhead transparencies.* A tried-and-true technology available just about everywhere, overhead projectors do not even require a screen—just about any wall will do. Again, you can use presentation software to make your own transparencies at a nearly professional level.

○ *Digital graphics.* With a laptop and a digital generator, you can create marvelous graphics. But the technology can overpower a short talk. Remember, the focus needs to be on you and your message, not on the technology.

The setting, the audience, your topic, and the purpose(s) of your talk will all help determine what visual aids you use. Do keep in mind that you need to leave each visual up for a minute or two. So for a seven-minute presentation, four visuals might be the maximum.

● SOME GUIDELINES FOR USING VISUALS

○ *Make sure everything—including the lettering—is big enough to be clearly legible, even from the back of the room.* If you are printing lettering on poster boards, the letters will need to come out at least two inches high (that means 24-point type, at least; 36- or 48-point is better). The same size considerations apply no matter what medium you use—on a screen, the letters also need to be at least two inches high. (Model 7 in the Model Documents appendix shows typical slides.)

◗ *Keep it simple.* Each visual must focus on just one thing. Your audience cannot absorb more than that in the time they have to see it. And be careful not to include too much text—four or five lines of text, with six or seven words per line, is about all anyone can read on a screen. Remember, too, that it is never a good idea to put up a transparency of a typewritten page; you want your audience *listening*, not *reading*.

◗ *Do not put your whole presentation in your visuals.* The visuals and props are there to reinforce your major points, not to duplicate your presentation. You do not want people trying to read lengthy visuals as you speak. You want people to glance at the visuals, but to pay attention to you. One terrible misuse of presentation graphics is to put *all* the words on overheads and then to just read them. If all the words are there to be read, who needs a speaker?

◗ *Refer to your visuals—do not stare at them.* Deliver your talk to your audience, not to your visuals; just refer to the visuals in passing.

Visuals need to *add to* your talk, not take away from it. If setting up the technology takes too long and you end up doing it in front of your audience, it's not worth it. Better to keep your visuals simple (keeping in mind that what is "simple" for a college student may be very different from what is "simple" for a vice president of General Motors) and foolproof. If the technology is dazzling but your talk is forgettable, the audience will remember the wrong thing (unless you're selling the technology). If tinkering with your visuals and props interrupts your presentation (the Web page won't download, the markers for the dry-erase board won't mark), you would have been better off without any visuals at all.

● ● ● **PRACTICING**

The more important your talk is, or the more nervous you feel, the more you need to practice. Try to practice as close to "game conditions" as you can—in the same kind of room, in the same voice, and at the same pace you'll be using with your visuals, and, if it's at all possible, in front of a live audience.

As you practice, pay attention to whether you are audible and clear, and try to show some enthusiasm for your talk. You do not need to be a cheerleader, but audiences take their cues in large ways from the speaker's own attitude—a speaker who seems bored will usually get a bored response, and a speaker who seems genuinely interested in the topic will usually get an interested response. And if you practice in a flat monotone, that's probably how you'll perform.

If possible, tape-record your practice sessions; even better, video-tape them. However you conduct your practice sessions, do be sure to get feedback from some listeners. Take this opportunity to ask for their suggestions, both concerning your content and concerning your delivery.

DELIVERING THE TALK

When it's time to deliver your talk, here are six key points to remember:

- Check the room.
- Speak up.
- Slow down.
- Make eye contact.
- Avoid staring at your visuals.
- Respect the time limit.

The day of your talk, you need to arrive at the site early. Unless you have specifically requested such arrangements in advance, you cannot count on anyone else to make sure the projector is in the room, or that it works, or that the flip chart has markers, or that the microphones actually work. You yourself need to assume responsibility, and the only way to do that is to get to the room early and to check on all those things. If you have a chance to go over your talk one more time before the empty room, all the better.

It's a rare speaking event that does not present at least one surprise—there's no flip chart, or the Internet server is down, or a maintenance crew is drilling holes in the wall next door, or a dance recital is taking place in the ballroom one floor above. If you arrive early, you'll be able to deal with such problems somehow. If you arrive just in time to speak, there may well be nothing you can do.

You will need to speak loudly enough to be heard. One room might have a loud fan going; in another, noise might be coming through from adjoining rooms; a third might be absolutely still and quiet. Your right volume will vary from room to room, and you need to adjust your delivery to conditions. You might ask someone sitting in the back of the room to let you know if you can't be heard. And if you talk slowly, it will be easier for people to hear what you say.

As you speak, remember to *slow way down.* Talking too fast is the most common mistake speakers make. However slowly you normally speak in conversation, you need to speak even more slowly when giving a talk. And you need to be careful to pause—at the ends of sentences, and especially at the ends of paragraphs. One way to do this is to write <PAUSE> in your notes at the right places. Audiences generally hear much more slowly than they read—about 100 words a minute is a good ballpark figure. Respect that limitation, and slow way down. Get to the end of a thought, then look up, make some eye contact, breathe, and continue.

Be careful also about any distracting gestures you might make during your talk—you should not be twisting a paper clip while you talk, nor do you need to be tapping the lectern with a pencil. Distracting speech patterns can be a problem too—the speaker who has to end every sentence with "y'know," or who repeatedly says "uuhhhh" between statements, tries the audience's patience. The distracting gesture or speech pattern gets the attention instead.

Eye contact is an important element of successful public speaking. Whether you are speaking to a large group or a small one, making some eye contact with members of the audience will help the entire audience feel a connection with you. Usually you can tell when you've achieved that contact with someone: people will nod, or smile a little bit at you (or even look down).

And remember *not* to stare at your visuals. We've all seen speakers who turn to look at each slide and actually seem to be talking to the slides rather than to the audience. You may need to glance at your slides, especially when you refer in your talk to something on them, but it will unnerve your audience if you turn your face away from them too often.

Finally, pay close attention to whatever time limits you have been given. If someone asks you to give a five- to ten-minute talk, you will annoy everyone if you go on for fifteen minutes. Even worse, you may find yourself cut off midstream. Find out in advance whether the questions and answers are included in the quoted time limit. Usually if someone asks you for a ten-minute talk, it means that you talk for ten minutes and then there are perhaps ten more minutes for Q&A. But once in a while someone says ten minutes and means that to include both the talk and the Q&A; if that's the case, you'd better stop talking after five minutes.

It is smart to have some kind of timepiece right in front of you. It's an old practice, one in which there is still no shame, to take off your wristwatch and put it right on the lectern. Remember, too, that being a minute or two too short is never a problem, but being a minute or two or three too long might well be. You've got to leave the audience time to ask questions.

ANSWERING QUESTIONS CAREFULLY

The question-and-answer period often turns out to be as important to your audience as the presentation itself. You need to leave plenty of time for that part of the program, and to approach it thoughtfully. As you plan your talk, try to anticipate what questions you are likely to be asked, and prepare (and rehearse) some good answers.

Here are three pointers to follow during the question-and-answer session:

> ○ Listen to each question in its entirety—avoid the temptation to cut the questioner off midstream and guess the rest of the question. Make eye contact with the person asking the question and keep your own mouth shut. (The only exception is for a question that rambles on and on; such questions you need to cut off with something like, "So as I understand it you're asking . . .")

> ○ Once you've heard the entire question, you can go ahead and answer. But if the question is at all complicated, or if you feel it might even be a little bit challenging, it is a good idea to first paraphrase the question: "Let me see if I understand your question: you want to know whether . . ." In addition to confirming that you and the questioner are on the same line of thought, this also gives you a little

time to think about your answer, keeping you from making the kind of snap answer you may regret later.

◖ If someone asks you a question you cannot answer, do not try to fake it. You'll do much better to say something like, "I just am not sure what the answer to that is—if you'll stop by the lectern after this session is finished and give me your name and email address, I'll see if I can find out the answer and then let you know as soon as I do." Sometimes you can also pass that kind of question on to members of the audience: "Maybe someone else in the room today knows . . ."

● ● ● **GETTING FEEDBACK**

After every presentation, you should always get feedback about how it went. If you have a friend or two in the audience, be sure to quiz them afterward. Try to ask specific questions: "Was I loud enough?" "Did I go too fast?" "Were the visuals okay?" Finally, take the opportunity to ask, "What one thing could I improve on the next time I give a talk?" Thus, each presentation you give offers you a chance to become a better speaker for the next.

Q *I'm not paralyzed by fear at the thought of standing up in front of people and giving a talk—I can make myself do it—but I'm so uncomfortable that people know it, and I start thinking I'll never be good at it. What can I do?*

A Lots of people have gone on from where you are now to be effective, even entertaining speakers—have actually grown into enjoying the opportunity to stand up in front of others and talk. But there's no magical transformation that makes it happen. What it takes, for most of us, is practice and experience—and more practice and experience. If you present only once a year (or every two years, or three), you'll never be comfortable. So this is one of those situations where you have to reach toward that which makes you uncomfortable—get to know it, learn how to handle it. That means, in most cases, taking a speaking class. Chances are you can take a basic speech class at your university pass-fail, or just audit one, so that you can maximize your gain from the instruction and the speaking opportunities without worrying much about the grade. That's the way to get past this uncomfortable place you're in. You've got to do more of it to get better at it.

FOR PRACTICE

Choose one of the paper topics you have written about in your composition class this semester, and do all the advance planning (as laid out in this chapter) for giving a seven-minute informal talk on the subject to your instructor and your classmates. Write out your plan, including, for example, a brief analysis of the room and the audience, a brief statement of purpose, a rough draft of the talk, note cards, and whatever visuals you would plan to use.

FOR WRITING

After you have gotten feedback on the planning package you prepared in the previous exercise, revise your talk and give the speech.

MODEL DOCUMENTS

Eleanor Hennessy

Professor Adams

Humanities 252

10 May 2002

Artemisia Gentileschi: Artist against the Grain

Artemisia Gentileschi, a talented painter in
seventeenth-century Italy, defied every norm of her
time--artistic, social, economic, and sexual--to emerge
as one of the most successful artists of her era. To
women art historians in the twenty-first century, she is
a hero whose work disproves the
allegation that there have been no great women artists.
But Gentileschi's story also appeals to today's women in
ways that go well beyond the specialized world
of art history. She has become a feminist icon
because of her courage, her self-confidence, her determination, and her proud defiance in refusing to bow to the
censure of a hostile and judgmental society. She would
have been an amazing woman in any time and place; for
her to have triumphed as she did in the sexist, repressive culture of seventeenth-century Italy seems no less
than a miracle.

In seventeenth-century Italy, women had almost no
rights. Except for a few wealthy women from noble families, they could not own property. Indeed, they were
considered property themselves. Anything they

1. THE FIRST PAGE OF A PRINT ACADEMIC PAPER

This model shows the first page of a straightforward academic paper formatted according to MLA guidelines, which do not require a separate cover sheet. The title forecasts the content of the paper, and the first sentence acts as a thesis sentence. The first paragraph helps readers anticipate the main points the paper will make. The font is conventional serif type; an illustration could be incorporated into this first page if appropriate.

● SOME SUGGESTIONS

◖ Put a running head with your last name and the page number in the upper right-hand corner of every page, including the first.

◖ Place your name, the instructor's name (with appropriate title), the name of the course, and the date on the upper left side of the first page, double-spaced.

◖ Center the title one double space under the date, capitalizing all words except for articles, prepositions, and conjunctions. Don't underline, italicize, boldface, or put quotations around the title.

◖ Begin the body of the essay one double space below the title, and double-space the entire essay, including any quotations.

◖ Leave one-inch margins at the sides and top and bottom of this page and every page.

◖ Ask your instructor if he or she wants you to follow MLA, APA, or some other style. If not, you may format your paper less formally, but be sure it is neat and includes all important information.

Elaine Coles
Communications 314
Professor Marilyn Adams
October 6, 2002

WHO'S USING THE INTERNET?

In its 1995 year-end issue, *Newsweek* magazine proclaimed 1995 as "The Year of the Internet," saying it "could be the greatest medium ever for linking the world together." That sounds rather like media hype, but certainly new users have joined the Net at record rates every year since then. Two demographic firms estimate there were between 30 and 34 million users by the end of 2001.

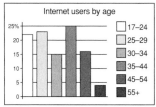

Figure 1

One firm, O'Reilly Associates, breaks down the age range of those users like this. Predictably, they're young but perhaps not as young as one might have expected. This chart shows that almost half, or 44 percent, are over 35.

So some people in the executive suites must be learning about computers although perhaps they're using the Net only for e-mail. Increasingly, e-mail dominates interoffice communication at many companies.

Here is how users break down by income. Most of them—almost two-thirds—cluster in the 25 to 75 thousand dollar range. But among the very affluent—over 150 thousand dollars—few are using the Net. Many believe that number will soon grow, however, as top executives realize that

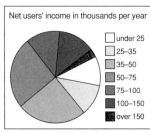

Figure 2

 MODEL DOCUMENTS

2. AN ACADEMIC PAPER WITH GRAPHS

When statistical information plays an important part in something you're writing, strengthen your work by adding charts or graphs. They add a visual element and make the data easier to read. Almost all word processing programs enable you to create graphs or charts, and you may also use PowerPoint, ClarisImpact, or another presentation program. It's worth your time to learn to use these programs.

● SOME SUGGESTIONS

○ Keep charts and graphs simple. Don't pack them with too much information.

○ Use pie charts to show relationships of part to whole, bar charts to show comparisons, and line graphs to show changes over time.

○ Add captions that identify all components clearly.

○ Use color if you can. Color works well for computer presentations and slide presentations, and the cost is minimal if you have access to a color printer.

○ Put only one or two charts on a single page.

Joachim Gonzalez
English 316
Professor N. Wang
October 18, 1996

ROSA PARKS: NO ORDINARY WOMAN

Rosa Louise Parks was a middle-aged African American woman working as a seamstress and a domestic when, in 1955, she served as the spark that ignited the celebrated bus boycott in Montgomery, Alabama. That boycott of the Montgomery bus system by black workers, and the federal lawsuit that followed in 1956, brought about the end of historically segregated transportation in the southern United States. As a result, one woman's firm refusal to go to the back of a segregated bus has become one of the landmarks in the post World War II Civil Rights movement in the United States.

Rosa Parks's role in that Civil Rights movement did not begin with the

Montgomery bus incident in 1955. Contrary to the legend that has grown up around her, she was not just a simple housekeeper who one evening decided she was too weary to obey the bus driver's order to give up her seat to a white rider. Parks had been active in the Montgomery Voters League and the NAACP Youth Council for years before she

challenged the bus ordinances of Montgomery. In 1943 she was even elected secretary of the local NAACP.

So her rebellion was no casual decision. Rather there is good reason to think that Rosa Parks knew what she was doing and perhaps intended to

3. AN ACADEMIC PAPER WITH HEADINGS AND VISUALS

If your instructor allows you to vary the form of your papers from the norms established by MLA or APA, you can choose different fonts for the title and the headings. The model here uses Helvetica, a sans serif font that is frequently used for titles and headings in textbooks and magazines. Additional headings later in the paper would also be in the Helvetica font. Note too that the caption under the picture is set in italic.

● SOME SUGGESTIONS

❍ Ask your instructor ahead of time whether it is acceptable to vary the fonts you use. If not, carefully follow the conventions of the form your instructor prefers.

❍ If you have the freedom to do so, think about how you can use fonts, pictures, graphics, and charts effectively. Keep your audience and purpose in mind as you decide what will be appropriate and effective.

❍ Traditional serif fonts—Courier, Times, Bookman, and so on—are usually best for the body of your paper because they are easy to read. Then you could put the title and headings in a sans serif display font such as Helvetica or Futura.

A	C
B	D

A ART	C TEXT
B TEXT	D ART

4. A PLAN FOR A TWO-PAGE SPREAD IN A REPORT

In many reports, especially in professional settings, you'll want or need to present information in two-page spreads. In some cases, both pages are all text. Other times, both pages are all art. Sometimes you'll have text and art on both pages, as shown in the bottom example on the facing page.

It helps to think of the spread as four quadrants to balance your use of text and art pleasingly. You may occasionally have a whole report of two-page spreads, but generally you'll want to have some variety within the overall design. Although readers never actually see the dotted lines dividing the quadrants, that underlying grid controls the final appearance of each two-page spread, and thus unifies the look of the entire document.

● SOME SUGGESTIONS

◐ Try to balance the facing pages so as to avoid having a lopsided spread—as would happen if A and C were text and B and D were art, or vice versa.

◐ A report done as two-page spreads needs to be bound, such as with plastic comb binding or a three-ring binder. When binding the report, leave the inside margins at 1.5 inches instead of 1 inch. With print on both sides of the paper, you might want to use a little bit heavier stock so that the print from one side of the page cannot "bleed through" to the other.

◐ Make sure you number the pages properly (this will keep the two-page spreads together): left-hand pages are even-numbered pages; right-hand pages are odd-numbered pages.

◐ Make sure your artwork is not crowded by the text, or vice versa. A good rule of thumb is that there always should be at least one inch of white space between art and text.

◐ Provide a caption for each piece of art or each graphic so the reader who is just flipping through the pages of the report still has an idea what the visuals are saying.

page title goes here

navigation
bar down
left side
linking to
paper's
headings

Gentileschi
self-portrait
(www.slam.org/
gentil.html)

¶ text ....
....
....
....
....
....
....
....

....
....
....
....

¶ ....
....
....
....
....
....

Rest on the Flight
into Egypt
(tigtail.org/M_View/
TVM/X1/f.Baroque/
b.Italian/gentil
eschi/M/gentileschi_
rest_on_flight_into_
egypt.1628.jpg)

Judith Slaying Holofernes
(tigtail.org/M_View/TVM/
X1/f.Baroque/b.Italian/
gentileschi/M/
gentileschi_judith_s
laying_holofernes.163
5.jpg)

5. A PLAN FOR AN ACADEMIC PAPER ON THE WEB

If you are asked to compose an essay for the Web, you have two options: to create a Web page using HTML, or to post a paper on the Web using Adobe Acrobat PDF files, often yielding a look that is much more like a traditional report (these options are illustrated in Chapter 11). Remember that all the principles of good design still apply (see Chapter 11), but in addition you need to worry over those that are particular to Web pages (see "Designing for the Web" in Chapter 11).

● SOME SUGGESTIONS

◯ Make sure that you leave enough space on the screen—readers turn away quickly from overcrowded pages.

◯ Double check the navigational elements of your pages to be sure they work. In the model, the various subheadings of the paper are planned to run down the left side of the page. Make sure to include a "back" button and a "next" button at the end of each page to make it easy for readers to travel through the document.

◯ You will probably want to use "thumbnails" for any art—that way you can get two or three pieces on each page, and people who want to see bigger versions can just click on the thumbnails to see them. This technique also decreases page-loading time, always a critical element, especially in art-heavy pages.

◯ Check your writing to be sure it's Web-friendly. Are the paragraphs and sentences short enough to hold the attention of "browsing" readers? Does each paragraph start with a clear and distinct topic sentence?

Artemisia Gentileschi, a woman painter in seventeenth-century Italy, overcame formidable obstacles to become one of the foremost artists of her day. In a time when women had almost no rights and were excluded from the professions, she served as an apprentice in her father's painting studio and developed her talent. When she was seventeen, another artist raped her, and she endured a public trial when her father sued the man for damages and won. Refusing to withdraw from life in humiliation, Gentileschi found in her ordeal the stimulus for painting several portraits of heroic women from myth and history, including the remarkable Judith Slaying Holofernes, which shows Judith and her maidservant slitting the general Holofernes's throat as he struggles. In recent years, the work of women art historians has reestablished Gentileschi's reputation and rescued her work from near oblivion. One of art historians' important tools has been the Internet; they have used it to publicize her career and show examples of the work that secured her place in the art world of early modern Italy.

6. A SUMMARY

• •

A good summary captures the essence of a longer work in a brief, informative statement that can be read and digested quickly. The summary should state the main assertion or idea of the original, give the key supporting points and the principal conclusions, and be able to stand alone as a self-contained message. The summary is what readers will read *first*. Thus it's worth taking the time to do a good job. Length is critical: one page is good; one paragraph is even better. A really good summary will also reflect the style and tone of the original.

● SOME SUGGESTIONS

◐ Read the original carefully, underlining key points.

◐ Outline the main ideas and crucial supporting evidence.

◐ Write a draft, including everything that seems important. Be sure to state the main idea clearly, to support it with the most important examples, and to end with a strong conclusion.

◐ Reread the draft, condensing it where you can.

◐ Polish the last draft, with an eye toward giving it some of the style and tone of the original.

ARE YOU AN ADDICTED SHOPPER?

1. When you're depressed, do you shop to feel better?

2. Does your shopping cause family conflicts?

3. After you shop, do you feel anxious?

4. Are many of your purchases never used?

5. Do you lie about what you spend?

6. Do you have trouble paying off your credit cards?

● ●

Presentation slides are valuable components of any oral presentation. The single most crucial element in any presentation slide is *visibility*. Be sure to use large, easy-to-read type; use only a few lines per slide; and leave plenty of space between lines. In slides such as the one on the facing page, the title forecasts the content of the whole presentation. The subpoints then give the audience an overview of the presentation and help focus their attention. The subpoints act as prompts for the speaker. Most important: the slide should serve as *reinforcement* for what the speaker is saying, not as a *text* that the speaker will read aloud.

● SOME SUGGESTIONS

◖ When you have multiple sentences, keep each to six or eight words, all on one line if possible. But be sure the font size is large enough to be easily visible.

◖ Leave plenty of space around and between lines.

◖ Number your slides clearly in the order that you will use them.

◖ Resist the temptation to decorate the slide with too many graphics.

◖ Have a pointer to work with, and stand to the side as you indicate points. Be careful not to stand in front of your slides.

June 2, 2002

Ms. Judy Conover
Whole Hearted Breads Corporation
1616 Red River
Austin, TX 78705

Dear Judy,

As manager of your midtown bakery and coffee shop for the past two years, I believe I understand what your goals are for your company. You have often spoken of your desire to expand our business if we could find additional space and if we could be sure of getting good people to staff a larger operation. We may now have the opportunity you've been wanting.

The owners of the Good Morning, Texas! cafe that adjoins our building on the south have told me they're going to retire in August, leaving their place empty after September 1. As far as I know, no one else is looking at that property.

I believe Whole Hearted Breads could take over the space of 1,100 square feet and add a delicatessen that would feature a lunch menu featuring sandwiches, salads, and oversized cookies. We have done very well with our specialty breads—Viennese rye, 9 grain health bread, bran-barley loaf, and oatmeal walnut. With a selection of such sandwiches and some simple salads to accompany them, I think we could attract substantial lunch crowds, especially from the staff of nearby St. David's hospital and from the students on the University of Texas campus. We could also attract take-out business.

I believe we could hire Esther Chang, who now runs the deli counter at the Texas Union, as manager for the deli. She has told me she's less than happy with the new management at the Union and is ready to move on.

We'd have to get estimates about cost, but my brother-in-law, who is a subcontractor for Calcasieu Lumber, thinks it could be done for around $200,000. Does that sound reasonable?

If you like this proposal, let me know and I'll be glad to get more information, especially details about costs. Thanks for your attention.

Sincerely,

Marcus Tijerino

Marcus Tijerino

8. A SIMPLE PROPOSAL

Aproposal needs to make clear the problem or opportunity it is responding to, suggest a plan clearly and succinctly, explain why it is a good and doable plan, and show how it can be put into effect. In a proposal to people outside your own organization (called an *external* proposal), make sure you do not take for granted knowledge that your readers may not in fact have (familiarity with technical vocabulary, for example). In an *internal* proposal you are likely to know the people you want to persuade, and you may need to consider whether it's appropriate to state your ideas a little less formally. Be aware, however, that if your proposal involves spending money or making a major change—and most proposals do—you should also think about any outsiders who may read what you write. In any proposal, you need to include all pertinent facts readers will need in order to make decisions, and enough specific details to show you have done your homework and speak with authority. And of course your tone should always be positive and confident.

● SOME SUGGESTIONS

◐ Identify the specific problem, need, or opportunity the proposal is responding to.

◐ Give a brief overview of your plan.

◐ Explain how your plan would address the problem or need.

◐ Identify personnel who would be required and where to get them.

◐ Estimate costs involved.

◐ Offer to provide additional information, if necessary.

1622 Exposition Blvd., Apt. 29D
Austin, TX 78703

May 16, 2002

Ms. Susanna Griffith, Senior Editor
Houghton Mifflin College Division
222 Berkeley St.
Boston, MA 02116-0764

Dear Ms. Griffith:

I would like to be considered for the position of editorial assistant in your college publishing division that was advertised in last week's Sunday edition of the *New York Times*. Specifically, I would like to work in the area of college publishing that is developing software for writing programs and working in visual literacy.

I have degrees in English and rhetorical studies from the University of Texas at Austin and from Texas Christian University. I worked as an editor on the college newspaper, the *Daily Texan*, while I attended the university in Austin. As editor at the *Texan*, I oversaw the work of columnists and contributors and acted as liaison person with the faculty sponsor. In my senior year at the University of Texas, I was a research assistant for the editor of the journal *Rhetorical Studies*.

I spent the summer of 1999 as an intern in the college publishing department of W. W. Norton in New York. In that job, I assisted editors Bruce Boxer and Martha Esquivel as they worked on manuscript development, and I did general errands within the college department.

In my two years as a graduate student at Texas Christian University, I worked in the English Department's lab designated for research in computers and writing and became proficient in navigating electronic sources. I trained instructors to teach writing in the university's networked computer classrooms, and I helped publish the newsletter put out by the Computers and Writing Lab.

Because of my editorial experience and my competence with computers, I believe I would be a useful entry-level employee in your college division. In particular, I believe I could work in tandem with the college and the computer technologies divisions, furthering the integration of online instruction and traditional textbook materials. If you believe I might fit into your company, I will be available for an interview any time after June 1.

I look forward to hearing from you.

Sincerely,

Eleanor Hennessy
Eleanor Hennessy

9. AN APPLICATION LETTER (PRINTED)

Application letters need to get to the point immediately; specify in the first paragraph the job for which you are applying. Then move on to say what qualifies you for that job. You want to sound confident and positive without seeming to exaggerate your accomplishments. Thus your focus should be strictly on facts; try to leave out adjectives that might seem boastful. Somewhere in the letter, you need to say something about the company that speaks to why *you* wish to work *there*. What is it about the company that matches something special about you?

Some Suggestions

These suggestions cover the format of the letter. For general suggestions concerning content, see Model 10.

- Begin with a full salutation, using a specific name and title if possible and the name and address of the company or organization. If you're writing to a woman, use *Ms.* rather than *Miss* or *Mrs.*

- Keep the letter to one page, leaving one-inch margins all around and double-spacing between paragraphs.

- Close with a formal *Sincerely* or *Yours truly* and sign your letter with your full name written over your typed name. Proofread the letter carefully and get someone else to check it for you. A perfectly done application letter may not get you an interview, but a sloppy one will almost certainly keep you from getting one.

- Enclose your résumé with the letter.

Date Sent: May 15, 2002
From: Bob Smith <bsmith35@statetech.edu>
To: Susan Jones, Acme Media Company
Subject: Application for Summer Internship

Dear Susan Jones,
I would like to be considered for the summer publications internship that your firm has advertised in the English Department at State Tech. I am finishing my junior year at State Tech as an English major in the Writing and Editing option, and I have prior publications experience working for the student newspaper here.

In the Writing and Editing option, I have taken three of the five core courses: Professional Writing, Basic Editing, and Desktop Publishing. In my work for the student paper, I have written stories about the various committees associated with the Office of Student Life and have contributed an occasional column ("Media Hits & Misses") to the student opinion pages. I would be happy to send you a portfolio of my work if you would like, and I have included a brief résumé below as an attachment.

I look forward to talking with you about ways I might contribute to your company's success. You can reach me via email or in the evening at 555-1234.

Sincerely,
Bob Smith
FAX 865-555-9876
5219 Wilson Lane
Collegetown, PA 37831

● ●

The model shows basic form for an email letter—here, a student's letter applying for an internship. Notice the very specific subject line, the use of a formal salutation, and the gets-right-to-the-point tone that allows the letter to be short. Notice also the full contact information included as part of the signature block. (See Model 9 for comparison with a printed job application letter.)

● SOME SUGGESTIONS

◐ In a short, three-paragraph letter, you should get right to the point. Both the subject line and the first line of the letter need to make it clear not just that this is a letter of application, but also exactly what position you are applying for.

◐ The second sentence of the first paragraph should state your biggest claim on the job—usually, that's either your education or your previous work experience. In this example, the student has both, as that sentence makes clear.

◐ The second paragraph should tell your reader more about that biggest claim. Here, since Bob has both education and work experience, his second paragraph elaborates on both.

◐ The third paragraph should make clear what you think the next step needs to be. In this case, Bob hopes Susan Jones will call him. As an alternative, he could have said, "I will call to arrange an appointment during the week of . . ." That would have been a bit more aggressive an approach.

◐ If you're going to attach a résumé, the email utility will usually show that on the letter screen as well.

Eleanor Hennessy
1622 Exposition Blvd., Apt. 29D
Austin, TX 78703
512-472-8832
ehennessy@austin.rr.com

OBJECTIVE	Beginning position as editorial assistant for college publishing firm. Special interest in working on textbooks for electronic media.
EDUCATION	M.A. in Rhetorical Studies, Texas Christian University, 2002 B.A., *magna cum laude*, double major in English and Rhetoric, University of Texas at Austin, 1998. Writers' workshop at University of Iowa, summer, 1998 Seminar in rhetorical studies at Yale, summer, 1997
AWARDS	Best Master's Thesis in Rhetoric, Texas Christian University, 2002 Member, Sigma Delta Rho, honorary liberal arts fraternity, 2001-02 Regents' Prize for Outstanding Woman Graduate, University of Texas at Austin, 1998 Presidential Scholar, University of Texas at Austin, 1998 Second prize, *Alcalde* essay competition, 1998 Richard Weaver Scholarship in rhetorical studies, 1997-98
EXPERIENCE	Part-time aide, TCU Computer Facility, 2001-02 Graduate student resident hall manager, Texas Christian University, 1998-99 Summer intern, W. W. Norton College Department, 1999 Research assistant to editor of *Rhetorical Studies*, 1997-98 Assistant editor, *Daily Texan*, University of Texas at Austin, 1996-97
ACTIVITIES	President, Youth Group, First Unitarian Church of Austin, 1997 Big Brothers and Big Sisters, Austin, Texas, 1994-96
COMPUTER SKILLS	Word, PowerPoint, PageMaker, QuarkXpress, HTML

References available on request

• •

Lots of work goes into creating an effective résumé. First, research the design you want to use. You might go to your college's placement service, look at various models of résumés, and ask about which ones would best serve your purposes. Second, find out as much as you can about any organization to which you are sending a résumé. The more you know about your audience, the more likely you are to create a résumé that will get favorable attention.

● SOME SUGGESTIONS

◐ Keep a print résumé to one page. Follow the suggestions in Chapter 11 for use of fonts, spacing, and "chunking" of information.

◐ Include information about your education, achievements, awards, and related extracurricular activities, but be sure every item you include makes an important point about you.

◐ List your employment history in reverse chronological order, starting with your most recent job, and account for all significant periods of time.

◐ Include personal information only if it is relevant to the job. (For example, the fact that you were on the staff of your high school yearbook is going to matter only if you are going into publications work.) You do not need to mention your age, sex, race, or marital status, and you should not send a photograph.

◐ Focus your résumé for a specific job, if possible, and emphasize the qualifications related to that job.

◐ Be sure to indicate how readers can reach any references or obtain additional information. (Remember, you need to ask people's permission before listing them as references.)

Bob Smith
5219 Wilson Lane
Collegetown, PA 37831
bsmith35@statetech.edu
Phone 555-555-1234

Professional Objective: To begin a career in publications work, focusing mainly on Web-based communication.

Education: English major, Writing and Editing Option, State Tech. Expected graduation, May 2003
*Major Courses: Professional Writing, Basic Editing, Desktop Publishing; in addition to 15 hours of lower-division English core requirements (freshman composition I & II, survey of world literature, survey of American literature, etc.).
*Other Important Courses: Interpersonal Communication I & II, Principles of Design, Newswriting I & II.

Foreign Language: Proficient in Spanish, reading, writing, and conversation.

Experience:_Daily Collegian_—Newswriter Fall 2001, Newswriter and Columnist Spring 2002.

References: Letters of reference are available upon request from Professor Judy Thomas (adviser), Professor Larry Kilgore (Head of the Writing and Editing Option), and Anne Owens, newspaper adviser.

This sample résumé is set up typographically to be used in email (or in a situation when someone wants a scannable résumé—both situations in which extra formatting is not going to translate well). Such a résumé should have no italics, no boldface, no other typographic variation to confuse the computers. The page layout is also simple; everything is aligned at the left margin. (See Model 11 for comparison with a print résumé.)

● **SOME SUGGESTIONS**

◗ *If you're sending your résumé out to be read on email,* it needs to be short—one or two screens at most.

◗ *If you're sending your résumé out to be scanned* ("read" into a computer database), length should not be a major concern. Be sure to use the right keywords, though, because that's what computers that search the databases containing scanned-in résumés look for. Thus if the jobs you're applying for generally involve knowledge, say, of PageMaker, you need to make sure that word appears in your résumé. Other typical terms that a personnel director at a publishing house might look for: *technical writer, merit scholar,* or *JavaScript.* Though such terms vary according to the company and job, be sure your résumé prominently includes the key terms that describe your special skills or achievements.

◗ *If you're sending your résumé out to be read as an attachment to email,* you can use pretty much the same form you would use on a paper version—similar typography, page layout, etc. Length is also the same as on paper.

◗ More and more companies are consulting Web sites when they look for job candidates. If you want to post a version of your résumé on the World Wide Web, there are many good free sites that offer this service, so there is no reason to pay anyone for it. Look on the Web under "Yahoo! Jobs" for a good list of sites.

The Hyde Park Volunteer

Volume 6 Issue 4   October, 2002

RECYCLING

Hyde Park Leads the City Again

Last month Hyde Park's citizens showed their commitment to the enviroment by recycling more newspapers and plastic containers than any other area in the city. July figures showed an increase of 14% over the same period for 2001. Members of the neighborhood Task Force for Recycling continue their push to have glass bottles and styrofoam added to the categories that can be salvaged. We urge you to attend the City Council meeting on November 1 at 7:30 to add your voice to this effort.

❖❖❖❖❖❖❖❖❖❖❖❖❖❖❖❖❖

CAN YOU BE A HOST?
JoEllen Cates, director of the HOSTS program at Pierce Elementary School, is calling for volunteers who can work one-on-one with students to improve their reading skills. HOSTS— Help One Student To Succeed—has been proven to work, but it depends on volunteers—lots of them. If you can spare one hour a week, call Mrs. Cates at 472-6000.

Champion Rosita Lopez

Texas All-Star tennis player Rosita Lopez will play an exhibition match under the lights on the River City Courts on October 15 at 7:30 pm. A graduate of Hyde Park schools, Lopez turned professional three years ago and has since become one of the state's top women players. She won the Lone Star tournament in El Paso last year.

Look for your neighbors at this benefit performance that Lopez is dedicating to her sister. Tickets for the match will be $10 at the gate. All proceeds will go to the Muscular Dystrophy Association of Texas.

❖❖❖❖❖❖❖❖❖❖❖❖❖❖❖❖❖

VOTER DRIVE

Take a Friend to Vote

The Hyde Park branch of the League of Women Voters is starting its campaign to turn out 90% of our neighborhood at the polls on November 5. Holly Johns, chair of the local branch, says the League, which has traditionally been nonpartisan, is particularly concerned this year with getting women to the polls. Chair Johns points to several national issues that she believes especially concern women.

Clean air standards
Early child care
Health care
Educational funding
Family planning bills

If you can help with the phone bank, distributing voter guides, or by driving voters to the polls, call

Carrie Jordan 346-1210
or
Richard Mann 478-2020

❖❖❖❖❖❖❖❖❖❖❖❖❖❖❖❖❖

DATES TO REMEMBER
October 30
Halloween Party
November 5
Election Day!

13. A NEWSLETTER

When you're planning a newsletter, consider first the audience and the purpose. Those two elements should help you answer many of the remaining questions. For most newsletters, there are also strong conventions that will govern your design—people expect headlines, columns, and photos to be handled in familiar ways, as Model 13 shows. In addition, newsletters usually have regular features (think, for example, of alumni newsletters that always have a "Marriages and Births" column). Those regular features usually have to vie with whatever you as editor think is the most important story for space on the first page.

Then consider what elements you want to include. What stories do you want to run, and how long do they need to be? What stories do you want on the front page? Which is the most important and where should it go? What headlines will you use? If you want to use pictures, where will you get them, and where should they go?

Once you make tentative decisions about content, decide whether it will work best in a two- or three-column format. Remember that articles will need to be shorter for a three-column format. Then do a pencil sketch or two to experiment with different layouts.

How will the newsletter be reproduced? Most newsletters are sent out as print documents, so the costs of printing and postage control much of what you do. But more and more newsletters are sent out as email, which means that you can do much more with color, graphics, and so on, and that the costs of postage and printing are nonexistent.

● SOME SUGGESTIONS

◖ A newsletter needs to have a name, at the top of the page, in a type font and style that reflect the spirit and purpose of the newsletter.

◖ Put the most important story in the upper right-hand corner.

◖ Short paragraphs are usually best—newsletter articles aren't essays.

◖ Consider separating items with borders, boxes, or screens.

◖ Position graphics or photographs near the top of the page.

◖ Leave plenty of space around elements; try not to crowd things.

Wizardspace

Student run ~ student owned

Whether you've just arrived on campus with your new computer or you've recently upgraded to a super machine and it's intimidating you, we can help. At Wizardspace, everyone speaks plain English, not cybertalk. All our consultants are computer teachers, not programmers. We'll get you started, then be on call when you need us.

● ●

**CLASSES FOR MAC
AND WINDOWS**

Introductory: Sept. 2 to Oct. 3
 Introduction to Macintosh
 Introduction to Windows
 Microsoft Word
 ClarisWorks

● ●

DESKTOP PUBLISHING

Classes begin October 10
 QuarkXPress
 PageMaker
 Adobe Illustrator
 Photoshop
 PowerPoint
Call Horace McNally, our document design consultant, for more information on advanced classes.

● ●

FOR SMALL BUSINESSES

Classes begin September 14
 FileMaker Pro
 Quicken
 Adobe PageMill
 Claris Organizer

● ●

☎ For additional information, schedules and fees, call
 Carrie 473-3367
 Mark 343-6859

SPECIAL SERVICES

Introduction to the Internet
 Research Online
 Choosing a Search Engine
 Designing a Home Page

Advice on Selecting Software
 Analysis of your needs
 Comparative pricing
 Program demonstration

On-Site Troubleshooting
 House Calls
 Information Retrieval

● ●

Partners in Wizardspace
 Mayling Tso
 Raymondo Garcia
 Roosevelt Curtis
 Horace McNally

Visit us at ·
 1505 College Drive
 Boulder, Colorado
 303-477-6868
or at
 www.wizardspace.com

Brochures require careful planning. Once again, start with careful consideration of audience and purpose. Where will the brochure be distributed? Will it need to catch readers' attention, or is it only informational (and if so, how *much* information does it need to give)? Don't try to cover too much information. A brochure should give just an overview—say, of an agency's main services, or the theme of a museum exhibit. Then the brochure should let readers know where they can get more information.

Once you've made some decisions about audience, purpose, and content, start thinking in more detail about design. For a three-panel brochure, you could begin by folding a piece of paper of the size you propose to use into three equal sections and then decide what content is going to go on the inside and what on the outside. Looking at the panels will also help you see how much information you can get on each one. Decide what your main headings will be and whether you will use a photograph or some clip art. Then make some sketches to try out possible arrangements. When you start working on the computer, divide your screen into three columns and use the landscape page setup. Insert open boxes where you want to put pictures or clip art and wrap your copy around them. Decide how you're going to break the information up into units and how you will separate them. Then you're ready to compose your copy and fit it in.

● SOME SUGGESTIONS

◗ The cover of a brochure should be simple but attractive, with a title and design that make potential readers want to pick it up.

◗ Keep it simple. Readers expect only basic information but want to know how to learn more if they wish.

◗ Break the information into chunks with lines, boxes, and white space.

◗ Make each panel a self-contained unit.

◗ Use simple graphics or symbols to catch the reader's eye.

◗ Leave plenty of white space at the edges and between elements.

The Austin Sierra Club
presents

Dr. Joan Gardner Lewis

speaking on

SUFFER THE CHILDREN
The environmental disaster in Eastern Europe
and its effects on children's health

 Dr. Gardner, a pediatrician at Northwestern Clinic
in Seattle, recently returned from spending six months
in the industrial regions of Albania and Hungary.
She will talk about her work there with children
suffering from asthma and other respiratory diseases.

7:30 pm, Tuesday, October 15
Jessen Auditorium
University of Texas at Austin

15. A POSTER

● ●

Your first goal with any poster is to get your readers' attention. Make sure yours is eye-catching and easy to read. Often posters on colored paper stand out more. Give all the information your readers need, but no more. Be sure your poster answers the basic questions: Who? What? When? Where? Why?

● SOME SUGGESTIONS

◐ Put the most important information in the largest print, and position it close to the top of the poster.

◐ Use a font that conveys a mood and tone appropriate to the subject.

◐ Separate information on the poster into chunks that are easily read.

◐ Leave plenty of white space.

You are invited to the Grand Opening of

The Family Place

A NEW COMMUNITY CENTER FOR CENTERVILLE

opening on
October 18

FEATURING
- An activity center for young adults
- Parenting classes for new families
- A well-child clinic
- Programs on healthy eating and shopping
- Flu shots and immunizations for everyone
- Adult literacy courses

SOUTHWESTERN VILLAGE PLAZA

SOUTHWESTERN BLVD. AT 19TH STREET ☎ PHONE 346-7733

16. A FLYER

Whereas posters are made to be mounted on a wall somewhere and have some durability, flyers are made to be passed out, read, and thrown away. You might print posters to put up a month in advance of a campus event; flyers would be distributed in the two or three days just before the event. Flyers can also include more information than posters because readers will pick them up and read them rather than view them from a distance. Keep the text and the design of your flyer simple, but be sure you answer the important questions: Who? What? Where? When? Why? (or For what purpose?).

● SOME SUGGESTIONS

◗ Make sure to have some kind of heading at the top that tells readers what the flyer is about.

◗ Consider putting the most important information in the largest print.

◗ Position the main announcement close to the top of the page.

◗ Present information in chunks or lists. Avoid paragraphs of text just as you would when writing for the Web; you're writing for readers who will browse and scan.

◗ Leave plenty of white space; don't crowd your text.

◗ Include necessary contact information (phone numbers, email or Web site addresses) so people who want more information can find it easily.

The Haydn-Mozart Ensemble
presents
AN EVENING OF BAROQUE MUSIC

Marilyn Szcyki   *First Violin*
Joanna Stiles   *Second Violin*
Hai-li Nguyen   *Cello*
Claude Childs   *Viola*
Ida Kashikurian   *Guest Violist*

∿∿∿∿∿∿∿

Wolfgang Amadeus Mozart (1756 –1791)

Quintet in C, K. 515
  Allegro
  Andante
  Menuetto: Allegretto: Trio
  Allegro

Wolfgang Amadeus Mozart (1756 –1791)

Sonata for Violin and Viola, K. 423
  Allegro
  Adagio
  Rondeau: Allegro

Intermission

Luigi Boccherini (1743–1805)

Quartet in B Minor, Op. 58, No. 4
  Allegro Molto
  Andantino lento
  Rondo

Johann Sebastian Bach (1685–1750)

Suite No. 6 for Cello in D Major, BWV 1012
  Prelude
  Allemande
  Courante
  Sarabande
  Gavottes 1 & 2
  Gigue

∿∿∿∿∿∿∿

The Haydn-Mozart Ensemble thanks Christopher Brothers Music Company and the Anastasia Pottery Shop for their generous support of this concert.

• •

The purpose of a program is to list the order of events in a performance, whether it's a school production of "Rip Van Winkle" or the philharmonic orchestra's spring concert featuring Mendelssohn's *Elijah*. When you create a program, your main concern should be to organize the information on the page in an attractive and accessible format so readers can immediately see what to anticipate and can easily follow the program as it proceeds. You accomplish that goal by chunking your information in various ways—with borders, with lists, and with information put into blocks. Choose fonts that help to set the mood you want to create. For a jazz concert, you would choose fonts quite different from the ones for a choral concert or a children's Christmas play. The font used for the title in the model is Harrington, an elegant, rather formal font that meshes with the eighteenth-century classical music featured in the concert. If you have access to clip art, you will find a wealth of symbols and graphics for almost any occasion. You could also choose bells and snowflakes from your dingbat or symbols menu to decorate a Christmas program, a cross on a church program, or a Star of David on a Hanukkah program. But use symbols and graphics sparingly—you don't want them to overwhelm the content of the program.

● **SOME SUGGESTIONS**

◐ Organize the information in the program in order of presentation, and break it into separate, easy-to-follow elements.

◐ Leave plenty of space around the sections of the program.

◐ Put the heading in larger type.

◐ If your program is more than one page, try to lay the information out on two facing pages so the complete program can be seen at one time.

◐ Give credits or acknowledgments at the bottom of the program in slightly smaller type.

Saint Stephen's Episcopal Church

OAK RIDGE, TENNESSEE 37993

AGENDA
Executive Committee Meeting

Wednesday, April 10, 2002
7:00 p.m.
Emerson Room

1. Call to Order

2. Approval of Agenda*

3. Approval of Minutes*
   March 11, 2002 meeting

4. Report from Finance Committee on proposed budget
   Matt Barnes, Finance Chair

5. Report from Stewardship Committee; pledge total to date
   Mary Ann Lewis, Chair

6. Report from Stewardship Committee; for new director of
   religious education
   Louise Tanaka and John Abbott, Co-chairs

7. Items for discussion
   Possible relocation of minister's office
   Secretary's request for new copy machine
   Tentative date for annual meeting

8. Old Business

9. New Business

10. Adjournment

*Action item

18. AN AGENDA

The purpose of an agenda is to let participants in a meeting know what business is going to be discussed and in what order. It often indicates who will be at the meeting and shows which items require action. Usually it's important for the agenda to be distributed ahead of time. An agenda also stands as an official record for an organization, and any discussion of an item can be challenged if it was not included on the agenda. Thus it's important that the agenda be complete and specific. If you write the agenda for a meeting, confer with the person running the meeting to be sure you include the important items and in the right order. You may be asked also to include a suggested time limit for discussing each item.

● SOME SUGGESTIONS

◗ In the heading, include the official name of the organization and the day, date, and time of the meeting. (Notice that in the model the heading from the organization's official stationery is used.)

◗ Set forth the order of business, starting with the call to order, approval of the agenda, and approval of minutes from the previous meeting. Number the items.

◗ List any committee reports next, followed by items for discussion. This order is flexible, however, depending on participants' schedules and needs.

◗ Conclude with a call for follow-up on old business, and any new business, and finish with adjournment.

◗ Put items in the list in parallel form. Indent subtopics.

◗ Leave space between items; keep the format readable.

CHILDREN'S ORTHOPEDIC CENTER OF DALLAS
1123 Harry Hines Boulevard
Dallas, TX 75321

FOR IMMEDIATE RELEASE   Contact: Melinda Nguyen
                                                         Public Relations
                                                         214-655-7200

CHILDREN'S ORTHOPEDIC CENTER SELECTS NEW HEAD

The trustees of Children's Orthopedic Center of Dallas announced yesterday, October 3, that Dr. Lucy Brigham Johnstone will become its Chief Executive Officer on January 1, 2002. Dr. Johnstone comes to Dallas from Memphis, Tennessee, where she has served as Executive Director of Shriner's Children's Hospital since 1996.

Dr. Johnstone received her M.D. from the University of Texas Southwestern Medical Center at Dallas in 1984 and did her residency in orthopedic medicine at Parkland Hospital in Dallas. She was on the faculty of Fisk Medical College in Nashville, Tennessee, from 1984 to 1995, and supervised the residency program in pediatric orthopedics there from 1993 to 1995. She held the Christine Holt Endowed Chair of Pediatric Medicine at Fisk during those two years.

Dr. Johnstone's specialty is pediatric hip and knee malformations; she received an award for her work in this area while she was at Fisk Medical School and hopes to continue her research at the Children's Center. She says she was especially drawn to Children's Orthopedic because of its outstanding staff of physicians working on children's hip problems.

Dr. Johnstone is married to Dr. Claude DuBois, who will also move to Dallas and join the surgical staff of Baylor Medical Center. Drs. Johnstone and DuBois have two sons, ages 12 and 14.

--30--

When you write a press release, you're putting out information about an organization or program and hoping that the newspaper, radio and TV stations, or newsletters to which you send the information will publish it or write a news story based on it. In a sense, you're looking for free advertising. Put the most important information at the beginning, and arrange the paragraphs in descending order of importance so only the least significant information is lost if the release is cut from the bottom. Press releases usually follow the typical format of a news story, answering the questions who, what, where, when, and why. You need to make your press release accurate, clear, and succinct so the editor who reads it can use the information as efficiently as possible to produce a story.

● SOME SUGGESTIONS

◖ Print the press release on the organization's letterhead stationery, or put the organization's name and address at the top of the sheet.

◖ Give your press release an informative heading that announces the topic clearly. Think of it as a headline.

◖ At the top of the page, put the name and phone number of the person to contact for more information.

◖ Focus on facts and avoid adjectives or adverbs that might be viewed as self-promoting.

◖ Be sure your press release supports the image you want to project of the organization. The formal, neutral tone of the model release, for example, reflects the dignified image a hospital would want to project. A press release for a different occasion—for example, the opening of a children's library—would call for a more informal, friendlier tone.

◖ Double-space the press release so it can be easily edited if necessary.

◖ Close with a centered "30" preceded and followed by dashes. If it runs more than one page, write "—more—" at the end of a page that is to be followed by another, and put the "—30—" at the end of the last page.

Mastering the Conventions of Documentation

I f you have ever used the endnotes or bibliographies provided in books and articles to augment your own search for information, you already know how helpful clear documentation can be. There are three reasons for documenting the sources you use in your own writing:

- ❍ To let readers know where you found the material that you include in your paper
- ❍ To make it possible for readers to locate and use that material themselves if they choose to follow up on your research
- ❍ To show your instructor you have mastered the careful science of documentation, an essential component in all academic fields

Many of the basics of using borrowed material correctly were covered in the section on managing sources and quotations in Chapter 12. The purpose of this chapter is to look in greater depth at two especially important sides to documentation and then to present the basics of citing sources according to the *MLA Handbook,* Fifth Edition, and the *Publication Manual of the American Psychological Association,* Fifth Edition.

Documenting sources correctly involves more than using the correct form of footnotes and bibliography entries. Whatever form your documentation takes, your readers still need to be able to tell exactly which materials are your own, and which come from someone else's words or ideas.

And however you choose to cue your reader that a particular idea or fact is one you have taken from someone else, those materials still will need to be smoothly integrated into your writing.

This double task—letting your readers know you're borrowing words, facts, or ideas from some other source, while at the same time integrating that material smoothly into your own writing—places a particular burden on the writing you do *around* such borrowings. In the case of direct quotations, the task is only *partly* accomplished by using quotation marks (for quoted material that is four lines or fewer) or block indentation (for quoted material that is five lines or longer). You also need to introduce that borrowed material. For material that you paraphrase or summarize, such introductory comments are especially necessary, both to indicate the act of borrowing and to make a smooth connection with your own ideas. The following paragraph, part of an essay on capital punishment, illustrates a number of problems in the ways it uses borrowed material:

> Capital punishment is one of the features of American society today that most distinguish us from the rest of the world. No country anywhere—not Russia, not China—executes its citizens at anything like the rate we do ours. Other than brute revenge, perhaps the only possible justification for such activities on the part of the State would be the argument that the existence and frequent, well-publicized use of capital punishment discourages other potential criminals and prevents other crimes. In support of that claim, a recent study concludes that capital punishment has a strong deterrent effect. "An increase in any of the three probabilities—arrest, sentencing, or execution—tends to reduce the crime rate. In particular, each execution results, on average, in 18 fewer murders—with a margin of error of plus and minus 10." As Iain Murray concludes, "On the final day of 1999 (the last day for which we have accurate figures), there were 3,527 prisoners under sentence of death in American prisons. This study suggests that if all those sentences were carried out 63,000 lives would be saved." One is left agreeing with noted philosopher John Stuart Mill, who in a speech before the English Parliament on April 21, 1868, aptly concluded that "I confess it appears to me that to deprive the criminal of the life of which he has proved himself to be unworthy . . . is the most appropriate as it is certainly the most impressive, mode in which society can attach to so great a crime the penal consequences which for the security of life it is indispensable to annex to it."

You could point to many faults in this writer's handling of source material:

○ The writer has failed to provide any documentation at all showing the sources she used.

○ If the second sentence ("No country anywhere . . .") reflects a fact the writer discovered somewhere, a source must be cited; if not, it probably cannot be supported and should be omitted.

○ Most of the paragraph—three sentences—is direct quotation, none so memorable that it needs to be quoted. Paraphrase or summary would suffice. All of those direct quotes overpower the writer's own language. If the whole essay were to go on like that, the result would be a patched together assemblage of various people's words and ideas instead of an essay by one writer.

○ In the first quote, the writer has in fact appropriated quoted words as her own. ("Capital punishment has a strong deterrent effect" should be part of the quote.)

○ Readers cannot tell if the first quote comes from the same source (Iain Murray) as the second quote. In fact, it does not.

○ The third quote, taken out of context from the words of a famous philosopher nearly 150 years ago, in another country, does not really support the point at hand.

The following revision eliminates the unnecessary use of direct quotes and shortens the remaining quotes to just the key phrases needed. Where others' ideas are being used, the language around those ideas clearly indicates the fact, and there is internal documentation (here in MLA form) that will lead readers to the right items in the Works Cited or References at the end of the essay. Finally, the superfluous John Stuart Mill quote has been eliminated entirely.

> Capital punishment is one of the features of American society today that most distinguish us from the rest of the world. Other than brute revenge, perhaps the only possible justification for such activities on the part of the State would be the argument that the existence and frequent, well-publicized use of capital punishment discourages other potential criminals

and prevents other crimes. In support of that claim, a recent study by Emory University researchers Hashem Dezhbakhsh, Paul H. Rubin, and Joanna Mehlhop Shepherd concludes that "capital punishment has a strong deterrent effect" (2). The researchers discovered that increases in either arrests, or sentencings, or executions in fact reduce the crime rate. For each execution performed, they claim 18 fewer murders will take place. As Iain Murray concludes, writing in *American Outlook Magazine* online, "On the final day of 1999 [. . .] there were 3,527 prisoners under sentence of death in American prisons. This study suggests that if all those sentences were carried out 63,000 lives would be saved" (par. 17). If these researchers are right, then it may just be the case that capital punishment, barbaric and morally repugnant as it may seem to many in America and to perhaps most of the rest of the world, in fact makes sense for society.

Of course the internal documentation in the paragraph would lead to full citations at the end of the paper.

STYLES OF DOCUMENTATION

Styles of documentation vary considerably across disciplines, so you will need to find out which style is preferred in the field for which you are writing. Your professor will probably indicate which type of documentation you should use and which style manual you should consult if you have questions. Another way to find out this kind of information, particularly if you do not have an instructor's guidance, is to check the form of notes and bibliography entries of articles used in the scholarly journals of your field. Most journals publish a page of guidelines for submitting manuscripts at least once a year that includes this information.

The most common styles of documentation currently used in academic writing are those endorsed by the MLA (Modern Language Association), the APA (American Psychological Association), and the CSE (Council of Science Editors, formerly known as CBE, Council of Biology Editors), and those published by the University of Chicago Press (both in the *Chicago Manual of Style* and in Turabian's *A Manual for Writers of Term Papers, Theses, and Dissertations*). Each of these organizations publishes its own style manual, which explains the basic principles of its documentation style and illustrates note and bibliography entries for a wide variety of sources.

◐ **Humanities:** *MLA Handbook for Writers of Research Papers,* Fifth Edition, 1999

◐ **Social sciences:** *Publication Manual of the American Psychological Association,* Fifth Edition, 2001

◐ **Life sciences:** *Scientific Style and Format: The CBE Manual for Authors, Editors, and Publishers,* Sixth Edition, 1994

◐ **Business and technical communication:** *The Chicago Manual of Style,* Fourteenth Edition, 1993

◐ **Engineering:** *Information for IEEE Transactions, Journals, and Letters Authors,* available online at www.ieee.org/organizations/pubs/ transactions/information.htm (click on "Information for Authors")

◐ **Chemistry:** *The ACS Style Guide,* 1997 (American Chemical Society)

◐ **Physics:** *The AIP Style Manual,* 1990 (American Institute of Physics)

◐ **Medical fields:** *American Medical Association Manual of Style,* Ninth Edition, 1998

◐ **Journalism:** *AP Stylebook,* 2000 (Associated Press)

◐ **Geology:** *Suggestions to Authors of the Reports of the United States Geological Survey,* Seventh Edition, 1991

◐ **Law:** *The Bluebook: A Uniform System of Citation,* Seventeenth Edition, 2000 (see "Practitioners' Notes," pp. 11–19)

Most college libraries have copies of these style manuals and many more. In the remainder of this chapter, you will find sample documentation entries in MLA and APA style for commonly cited types of sources, including electronic sources.

● FINDING INFORMATION ABOUT DOCUMENTATION STYLES ON THE WEB

Many Web pages are available to show you how to document in MLA or APA style. Unfortunately, the vast majority of them that we have checked are not up-to-date. Within the last few years, both the MLA and the APA have brought out new editions of their style manuals, each with small but significant changes, especially in the ways they cite Internet pages and other electronic materials. If you want to see the MLA's own home page for its style manual, check out www.mla.org/www_mla_org/style/; there's a great list of frequently asked questions (FAQs), covering such sticky subjects as underlining versus italics, what to do if the Web page you're citing has no page numbers, and so on. Similarly, if you want to see the APA's home page for its style manual, that is at www.apastyle.org.

IN-TEXT CITATION

APA and MLA are the most widely used documentation styles for research writing in the social sciences and the humanities. For acknowledging sources within the body of your writing, both styles advocate the use of *parenthetical documentation,* with an accompanying References (APA) or Works Cited list (MLA). Thus brief citations appear in parentheses in the text immediately after the cited material. These parenthetical citations contain enough information to enable the reader to identify the cited sources from the Works Cited or References list, where full bibliographic information is given for all of the sources the writer has consulted in order to write the paper. Thus footnotes or endnotes are used only to give explanatory material that is somehow tangential to the text.

The major differences between APA and MLA in-text citation styles involve page numbers (APA often does not use them; MLA always uses them) and publication years (APA always uses them; MLA usually does not). The following examples demonstrate the basic way the same source would be cited in papers using MLA style and APA style:

MLA IN-TEXT CITATION

This approach corresponds to the frequently cited theory that scientific revolutions come about through paradigm shifts (Kuhn 79).

APA IN-TEXT CITATION

This approach corresponds to the frequently cited theory that scientific revolutions come about through paradigm shifts (Kuhn, 1970).

The basic *MLA in-text citation* uses the author's last name and the page number (notice there is no "p." and no punctuation between the two). For electronic sources, you can cite the paragraph number if that is possible (preceded by "par." or "pars." with no comma after the author's name), or the screen number if available, or the heading for that part of the document. If the electronic source has no page numbers, screen numbers, headings, or any other way to designate where you found your information, you must cite the source in its entirety. In such a situation, MLA recommends including the name of the source's author in your text rather than in a parenthetical reference, then letting the corresponding entry in the Works Cited list provide the longer information (thus there would in effect be no parenthetical citation at all).

With an *APA in-text citation,* what you include depends on whether the source was in print or electronic form. The basic citation in text uses the author's name and the year of the publication, separated by a comma. If the author's name has already appeared in the text, only the year appears in the parentheses. If you are using a direct quotation, or if for some other reason you need to cite a specific part of a source, the page number (or, in the case of electronic sources, the paragraph number or the heading for that section of the document) can be added to the citation. Thus the citation in the preceding example would become (Kuhn, 1970, p. 79). Of course, this material is only enough to allow the reader to find the more complete bibliographical information. Notice that the APA system includes the date of publication in the parenthetical citation, whereas MLA style usually does not.

● ● ● **BIBLIOGRAPHIC DOCUMENTATION**

A bibliography is a list of all the sources that helped you formulate the content of your paper, whether or not you have cited them specifically in your text. In APA format, this is called the References; in MLA, Works Cited. Bibliographical entries for both MLA and APA systems are arranged alphabetically according to the first word of the entry, usually but not necessarily the last name of the author. The following bibliography entries for Kuhn's book illustrate the major difference between the MLA and APA styles:

MLA WORKS CITED

Kuhn, Thomas S. <u>The Structure of Scientific Revolutions</u>. Chicago: U of Chicago P, 1970.

Kuhn, T. (1970). *The structure of scientific revolutions.* Chicago: University of Chicago Press.

Notice that in APA style only the first letter of a book title is capitalized, and the date comes immediately after the author's name. In MLA, the date comes last. For detailed information on compiling these Works Cited and References pages for your research paper, see the appropriate manual. The examples from here to the end cover only some of the most common kinds of citations.

● ● ●   **MLA DOCUMENTATION**

The sample Works Cited entries here illustrate the current MLA style. For more information about documenting other kinds of sources, consult the *MLA Handbook for Writers of Research Papers,* Fifth Edition (New York: MLA, 1999).

BOOK WITH A SINGLE AUTHOR

Hellman, Lillian. <u>Scoundrel Time</u>. Boston: Little, 1976.
King, Martin Luther, Jr. <u>The Trumpet of Conscience</u>. New York: Harper, 1968.

BOOK WITH A SUBTITLE

Kaplan, Robert D. <u>Eastward to Tartary: Travels in the Balkans, the Middle East, and the Caucasus</u>. New York: Random, 2000.

BOOK WITH NO AUTHOR

<u>The New English Bible</u>. London, UK: Oxford UP, 1970.

SAME AUTHOR OR EDITOR FOR TWO OR MORE BOOKS

Kaplan, Robert D. <u>The Coming Anarchy: Shattering the Dreams of the Post Cold War</u>. New York: Random, 2000.
---. <u>Eastward to Tartary: Travels in the Balkans, the Middle East, and the Caucasus</u>. New York: Random, 2000.

BOOK BY TWO OR THREE AUTHORS

Nasta, Marie, and Marilyn Abildskov. <u>Stranger Than Fiction: The Literary Development of the Nonfiction Essay</u>. New York: Simmons, 1996.

Lunsford, Andrea A., Helene Moglen, and James Slevin. <u>The Right to Literacy</u>. New York: MLA, 1990.

BOOK BY FOUR OR MORE AUTHORS

Sobel, Robert, et al. <u>The Challenge of Freedom</u>. Mission Hills: Glencoe, 1990.

ANTHOLOGY OR COLLECTION OF WORKS BY VARIOUS AUTHORS

Hunt, Douglas, ed. <u>The Riverside Anthology of Literature</u>. Boston: Houghton, 1988.

PART OF A BOOK OTHER THAN THE MAIN TEXT

Tanner, Tony. Introduction. <u>Pride and Prejudice</u>. By Jane Austen. London: Penguin, 1972. 7-46.

ARTICLE IN A SCHOLARLY JOURNAL

If the pagination is continuous:

Walters, Samuel K. "Survival Tips for Third World Travelers." <u>Journal of the American Travel Association</u> 12 (1995): 32-40.

If the journal pages each issue separately ("50.2" signifies volume 50, issue number 2):

Zhao, Yuezhi. "From Commercialization to Conglomeration: The Transformation of the Chinese Press within the Orbit of the Party State." <u>Journal of Communication</u> 50.2 (2000): 3-26.

ARTICLE IN A MAGAZINE

Cloud, John. "Should SATs Matter?" <u>Time</u> 12 Mar. 2001: 62+.

UNSIGNED MAGAZINE ARTICLE

"Reporter." <u>Texas Monthly</u> Feb. 1997: 20.

INTERVIEW IN A PERIODICAL

"No Exit." Interview of Israeli soldiers by Uri Blau.
    Trans. Tal Haran. <u>Harper's</u> Apr. 2002: 24-27.

ARTICLE IN A NEWSPAPER

Margulies, David L. "Smarter Call Centers: At Your Ser-
    vice?" <u>New York Times</u> 14 Mar. 2002, late ed.: G1+.

WORK IN AN ANTHOLOGY

Adorno, Theodor. "On the Concept of Ugliness." <u>Contem-
    porary Critical Theory</u>. Ed. Dan R. Latimer. New
    York: Harcourt, 1989. 350-54.
Poe, Edgar Allan. "The Raven." <u>The Oxford Book of Chil-
    dren's Verse in America</u>. Ed. Donald Hall. New
    York: Oxford UP, 1985. 74-77.
Synge, John M. <u>Riders to the Sea. The Complete Plays
    of John M. Synge</u>. Ed. M. W. Steinberg. New York:
    Holt, 1960. 447-55.

ARTICLE OR ENTRY IN A REFERENCE BOOK

"Geologic Time." <u>Merriam-Webster's Collegiate Dictio-
    nary</u>. 10th ed. 1996.

TRANSLATION

Dostoevsky, Fyodor. <u>Crime and Punishment</u>. Trans. Rich-
    ard Pevear and Larissa Bolokhonsky. New York: Vin-
    tage, 1992.
Lueth, Elmar. <u>Niemandsland</u>. Trans. Rebecca Soglin and
    Ellen Fagg. Lincoln: U of Nebraska P, 1995.

PAMPHLET

<u>John Brown's Entrance into Hell</u>. Baltimore: C.T.A.,
    1863.

GOVERNMENT DOCUMENT

New York City. Dept. of Health. HIV/AIDS Surveillance Program. <u>AIDS Surveillance Update</u>. June 2001.

United States. Cong. Joint Committee on the Investigation of Alternative Energy Resources. <u>Hearings</u>. 104th Cong., 1st sess. 11 vols. Washington: GPO, 1983.

ORGANIZATION AS AUTHOR

American Psychological Association. <u>Publication Manual of the American Psychological Association</u>. 5th ed. Washington: Amer. Psychological Assn., 2001.

LEGAL CASE, LAW, OR HISTORICAL DOCUMENT

Brown v. Board of Ed. of Topeka. 347 United States Reports 483. U.S. Supr. Ct. 1954. United States. 97th Cong. 1st sess. H. Res. 16. Washington: GPO, 1981. US Const. Art. 1, sec. 8.

INTERVIEW BY WRITER OF RESEARCH PAPER

Berra, Yogi. Personal interview. 17 June 1974.
Brayton, Abigail. Telephone interview. 2 Oct. 1996.
Pinsky, Robert. Telephone interview. 1 Aug. 2000.

LETTER TO THE EDITOR

Taylor, Annette. Letter. <u>Mount Vernon Sun</u> 57 (1996): 11-12.

TELEVISION PROGRAM

"Buddy Holly: Rave On." <u>Biography</u>. Host Harry Smith. Arts and Entertainment Network. 19 Apr. 2002.

"Ludwig von Beethoven: A Musical Biography and a Salute to Genius." Narr. Nancy Ratner and Charlotte Bonavia. Writ. and prod. Patricia Vivian. <u>Famous Figures in the Arts</u>. NBC. KCRG, Portland, OR. 27 May 1995.

MATERIAL FROM A PERIODICALLY PUBLISHED CD-ROM, DISKETTE, OR MAGNETIC TAPE

Hwang, S. L. "Marketscan: While Many Competitors See Sales Melt, Ben and Jerry's Scoops Out Solid Growth." <u>Wall Street Journal</u> 5 May 1993: B1. CD-ROM. Proquest. June 1993.

MATERIAL ON A SINGLE-ISSUE CD-ROM

<u>Othello</u>. By William Shakespeare. CD-ROM. Princeton: Films for the Humanities and Sciences, 1997.

MATERIAL FROM AN ONLINE PROJECT, DATABASE, OR PERSONAL OR PROFESSIONAL SITE

<u>bartleby.com: Great Books Online</u>. 1999. bartleby.com. 7 Apr. 2002 <http://www.bartleby.com/sv/welcome.html>.

Cohen, Robert. Home page. 8 Apr. 2002 <http://drama.arts.uci.edu/cohen>.

"Compaq Computer Corporation: Company Capsule." <u>Hoover's Online</u>. 2001. Hoover's Company Information. 14 Sept. 2001 <http://www.hoover.com/capsules/1/0,2163,10381,00.html>.

ONLINE BOOK OR PART OF PROJECT, DATABASE, OR PERSONAL OR PROFESSIONAL SITE

Anderson, Sherwood. "The Philosopher." <u>Winesburg, Ohio</u>. 1919. <u>bartleby.com: Great Books Online</u>. 1999. bartleby.com. 7 Apr. 2002 <http://www.bartleby.com/156/5.html>.

ARTICLE IN AN ONLINE PERIODICAL

From a popular online magazine:

Cave, Damien. Rev. of <u>Stud</u>, by Kevin Conley. <u>Salon</u> 4 Apr. 2002. 7 Apr. 2002 <http://www.salon.com/books/review/2002/04/04/conley/index.html>.

From a scholarly journal:

Reiff, Mary Jo. "Rereading 'Invoked' and 'Addressed' Readers through a Social Lens: Toward a Recognition of Multiple Audiences." Journal of Advanced Composition 16.3 (1996). 15 Aug. 2001 <http://jac.gsu.edu/jac/12.2/Articles/8.html>.

From a newspaper or newswire:

Walsh, Mary Williams. "At 8:48, Two 'Normal Guys' Are Transformed." New York Times on the Web 16 Sept. 2001. 17 Sept. 2001 <http://www.nytimes.com/2001/09/16/nyregion/16HERO.html>.

APA DOCUMENTATION

The sample References entries here illustrate the current APA style. For information about documenting other kinds of sources, consult the *Publication Manual of the American Psychological Association*, Fifth Edition (Washington: APA, 2001).

BOOK WITH A SINGLE AUTHOR

King, M. L. (1968). *The trumpet of conscience.* New York: Harper.
Sacks, O. (1997). *The island of the colorblind.* New York: Knopf.

BOOK BY TWO OR MORE AUTHORS

Nasta, M., & Abildskov, M. (1996). *Stranger than fiction: The literary development of the nonfiction essay.* New York: Simmons.
Wolfe, D., & Antinarella, J. (1997). *Deciding to lead: The English teacher as reformer.* Portsmouth, NH: Heinemann.

BOOK WITH A SINGLE EDITOR

Dickens, J. (Ed.). (1995). *Family outing: A guide for parents of gays, lesbians and bisexuals.* London: Peter Owen.

BOOK WITH NO AUTHOR, EDITOR, OR OTHER CONTRIBUTOR

Roget's II: The new thesaurus (Expanded ed.). (1988). Boston: Houghton.

ARTICLE OR CHAPTER IN A LONGER WORK

Doder, D., & Branson, L. (1999). The end of the caravan of dreams. In *Milosevic: Portrait of a tyrant* (pp. 279-299). New York: Free Press.

Harris, I. M. (1999). Types of peace education. In A. Raviv, L. Oppenheimer, & D. Bar-Tal (Eds.), *How children understand war and peace: A call for international peace education* (pp. 299-317). San Francisco: Jossey-Bass.

PART OF A BOOK OTHER THAN THE MAIN TEXT

Tanner, T. (1972). Introduction. In J. Austen, *Pride and prejudice* (pp. 7-46). London: Penguin. (Original Austen work published 1813)

SIGNED PERIODICAL ARTICLE

If the pagination is continuous:

Walters, Samuel K. (1995). Survival tips for third world travelers. *Journal of the American Travel Association, 12,* 32-40.

If the journal pages each issue separately ("*50*(2)" signifies volume 50, issue number 2):

Zhao, Y. (2000). From commercialization to conglomeration: The transformation of the Chinese press within the orbit of the party state. *Journal of Communication, 50*(2), 3-26.

REVIEW IN A PERIODICAL

Scull, A. (2002, April 18). Last words of a medical historian [Review of the book *Madness: A brief history*]. *Nature, 416,* 681.

INTERVIEW IN A PERIODICAL

Blau, U. (2002, April). No exit [Interview of Israeli soldiers] (T. Haran, Trans.). *Harper's*, 24-27.

ARTICLE IN A MAGAZINE

Webster, D. (2002, May). Drawn from prehistory. *Smithsonian, 33,* 100-107.

Wegner, R., & Schiermeier, Q. (2002, April 18). Conservationists under fire in the Philippines. *Nature, 416,* 669.

UNSIGNED MAGAZINE ARTICLE

Reporter. (1997, February). *Texas Monthly,* 20.

WORK IN AN ANTHOLOGY

Adorno, Theodor. (1989). On the concept of ugliness. In Dan R. Latimer (Ed.), *Contemporary critical theory* (pp. 350-354). New York: Harcourt.

WORK IN A NEWSPAPER

Barringer, F. (2002, May 7). Some big papers buck trend of circulation drops. *The New York Times,* p. C9.

TRANSLATION

Lueth, E. (1995). *Niemandsland* (R. Soglin, Trans.). Lincoln: University of Nebraska Press.

PAMPHLET

John Brown's entrance into hell. (1863) [Pamphlet]. Baltimore: C.T.A.

GOVERNMENT OR ORGANIZATION DOCUMENT

U.S. Bureau of the Census. (2001). *Statistical abstract of the United States* (121st ed.). Washington, D.C.: U.S. Government Printing Office.

National Assessment of Educational Progress. (1990). *The civics report card.* Princeton, NJ: Educational Testing Service.

LEGAL CASE

Brown v. Board of Ed. of Topeka, 347 United States Reports 483 (U.S. Supr. Ct. 1954).

LETTER TO THE EDITOR

Taylor, A. (1996, October 15). Fund seeks equity-building investments [Letter to the editor]. *Mount Vernon Sun,* pp. 11-12.

TELEVISION PROGRAM

Vivian, P. (Writer/Producer). (1995, May 27). Ludwig von Beethoven: A Musical Biography and a Salute to Genius [Television series episode]. In KCRG (Producer), *Famous figures in the arts.* New York: National Broadcasting Company.

INTERVIEW

APA specifies that "personal communications," a category which includes personal interviews, should not be cited in the References, but in text only.

(A. Brayton, personal communication, October 2, 1996)

MATERIAL FROM AN ELECTRONIC DATABASE

Compaq computer corporation: Company capsule. (2001). Retrieved September 14, 2001, from Hoover's Online database http://www.hoover.com/capsules/1/0,2163,10381,00.html

ARTICLE IN AN ONLINE PERIODICAL

From a scholarly journal:

Dayal, S. (2002). Inhuman love: Jane Campion's *The Piano. Postmodern Culture, 12*(2), 86 paras. Re-

trieved April 26, 2002, from http://jefferson
.village.virginia.edu/pmc/12.2dayal.htm

Reiff, M. J. (1996). Rereading "invoked" and "addressed" readers through a social lens: Toward a
recognition of multiple audiences. *Journal of Advanced Composition, 16*(3), 407-424. Retrieved August 15, 2001, from http://jac.gsu.edu/jac/
12.2/Articles/8.html

From a newspaper or newswire:

Walsh, M. W. (2001, September 16). At 8:48, two "normal
guys" are transformed. *New York Times on the Web*
[Electronic version]. Retrieved September 17,
2001, from http://www.nytimes.com/2001/09/16/nyre-
gion/
16HERO.html

Index